The Internet
FOURTH EDITION ILLUSTRATED

INTRODUCTORY

The Internet
FOURTH EDITION ILLUSTRATED

INTRODUCTORY

Gary P. Schneider
Jessica Evans
Katherine T. Pinard

THOMSON
COURSE TECHNOLOGY™

Australia • Canada • Mexico • Singapore • Spain • United Kingdom • United States

THOMSON

TM

COURSE TECHNOLOGY

The Internet, Fourth Edition - Illustrated Introductory

Gary P. Schneider, Jessica Evans, and Katherine T. Pinard

Managing Editor:
Marjorie Hunt

Production Editors:
Danielle Slade, Jennifer Goguen

QA Manuscript Reviewers:
John Freitas, Jeff Schwartz,
Shawn Day

Product Manager:
Kim T. M. Crowley

Developmental Editor:
Kim T. M. Crowley

Text Designer:
Joseph Lee, Black Fish Design

Associate Product Manager:
Shana Rosenthal

Proofreader:
Harry Johnson

Indexer:
Liz Cunningham

Composition House:
GEX Publishing Services

ISBN-13: 978-1-4188-3950-5
ISBN-10: 1-4188-3950-7

The Illustrated Series Vision

Teaching and writing about computer applications and information literacy can be extremely challenging but rewarding. How do we engage students and keep their interest? How do we teach them skills that they can easily apply on the job? As we set out to write this book, our goals were to develop a textbook that:

- works for a beginning student
- provides varied, flexible, and meaningful exercises and projects to reinforce the skills
- serves as a reference tool
- makes your job as an educator easier, by providing a variety of supplementary resources to help you teach your course

Our popular, streamlined format is based on feedback we've received over the years from instructional designers and customers. This flexible design presents each lesson on a two-page spread, with step-by-step instructions on the left, and screen illustrations on the right. This signature style, coupled with high-caliber content, provides a comprehensive introduction to the crucial skills for using the Internet effectively and a rich learning experience for the student.

Acknowledgments

Thanks to Majorie Hunt, Karen Stevens, and the team at Course Technology for giving me the opportunity to work on this book and to Danielle Slade for keeping track of the many details. Thank you to Jessica Evans and Gary Schneider for providing such wonderful material and for being so easy to work with. Special thanks go to Kim Crowley for her superb editing skills and for helping me to conquer many a "sticky wicket." Finally, thank you to my husband, Andrew, and my children Shelagh, Maura, and Helen, who endured far too many nights of take-out dinners as I worked on this book.
Katherine T. Pinard, Adapting Author

We want to thank the outstanding team of professionals at Thomson Course Technology for making this book possible. The editorial, development, and production staff members have done their usual outstanding job. We are grateful for the continuous support and encouragement of our spouses, Cathy Cosby and Richard Evans. We also thank our children for tolerating our absences while we were busy writing.
Gary P. Schneider and Jessica Evans, New Perspectives Series Authors

Preface

Welcome to *The Internet, Fourth Edition–Illustrated Introductory*. Each lesson in the book contains elements pictured to the right in the sample two-page spread.

How is the book organized?

The book is organized into nine units. Students first learn basic Internet concepts. The book features coverage on how to access, navigate, browse, and search the Internet using Internet Explorer and Firefox. Students also learn how to use Outlook Express and Hotmail to compose, send, receive and manage e-mail. Other communication tools such as mailing lists, newsgroups, instant messaging, chat, and virtual communities are also covered. Students learn how to research, locate, and download files and programs from the Internet. Finally the book contains coverage on browser extensions and security issues and countermeasures.

What kinds of assignments are included in the book? At what level of difficulty?

Each unit includes a different realistic case study, developed specifically to suit the concepts and skills covered in that unit. The assignments are found on the light purple pages at the end of each unit and they progressively increase in difficulty. Assignments include:

- **Concepts Reviews** to test your knowledge with multiple choice, matching, and screen identification questions.

- **Skills Reviews** to provide additional hands-on, step-by-step reinforcement.

- **Independent Challenges** that are case projects requiring critical thinking and application of the skills learned in the unit. The Independent Challenges increase in difficulty, with the first Independent Challenge in each unit being the easiest (with the most step-by-step, detailed instructions).

Each 2-page spread focuses on a single skill.

Concise text that introduces the basic principles in a real-world case study.

UNIT B
Internet

Saving and Opening a Web Page in a Browser

If you travel with a laptop, want to decrease the time you are connected to the Internet, or are concerned that a Web page might change and you want to show it to someone in its current state, you can save the Web page to a disk. Sometimes when you save a Web page and open it later, you find that not all of the images were saved. This happens when the file that contains the image is not actually stored on the Web server that holds the files for the Web site you are viewing. When images on a page are stored on another Web server, the image will not be saved when you save the complete Web page. If you want to save the image that is missing, you can save the image in its own file on a disk. You will learn more about saving images in the lesson titled "Copying Text and Graphics from a Web Page" later in this unit. You decide to save the home page of Midland Pet Adoption Agency so Trinity can view it in its current form whenever she wishes.

STEPS

1. If the home page of Midland Pet Adoption Agency is not open in your browser window, type www.midlandpet.com in the Address or Location bar of your browser, then press [Enter]

2. Click File on the menu bar, then click Save As or Save Page As
   A dialog box similar to the standard Save As dialog box opens. This dialog box is usually titled Save Web Page or Save As.

3. Click the Save in list arrow, navigate to the drive and folder where your Solution Files are stored, select the text in the File name text box, then type MidlandHomePage
   Note in the Save as type text box that the file will be saved as a complete Web page. This means the file will be saved as an HTML file with the graphics and other components that are built into the page.

   TROUBLE
   If a dialog box titled Downloads or something similar opens, click the Close button in its title bar.

4. Click Save
   The Save As dialog box closes and the Web page is saved in its current state. You decide to try opening it to make sure it saved as you expected.

5. Click the Home button on the toolbar
   The home page for your browser appears in the browser window.

6. Click File on the menu bar, then click Open or Open File
   If you are using Internet Explorer, the Open dialog box appears, as shown in Figure B-18. If you are using most other browsers, including Firefox, the Open File dialog box appears.

   TROUBLE
   If you are not using Internet Explorer, skip Step 7.

7. If you are using Internet Explorer, click Browse in the Open dialog box
   A dialog box similar to the standard Open dialog box opens. The Internet Explorer Open dialog box is shown in Figure B-19. The Firefox Open File dialog box is shown in Figure B-20.

8. If necessary, click the Look in list arrow and navigate to the drive and folder where your Solution Files are stored, click MidlandHomePage, then click Open
   If you are using Internet Explorer, the dialog box closes and the path and file name of the file you selected appears in the Open text box in the Open dialog box.

   TROUBLE
   If you are using Firefox, skip Step 9.

9. If you are using Internet Explorer, click OK in the Open dialog box
   The Midland Pet Adoption Agency home page appears in the browser window. Notice that the path and file name of the saved Web page appears in the Address or Location bar instead of the URL of the page on the Web.

38 UNIT B: UNDERSTANDING BROWSER BASICS

Hints as well as troubleshooting advice, right where you need it — next to the step itself.

Every lesson features large, full-color representations of what the screen should look like as students complete the numbered steps.

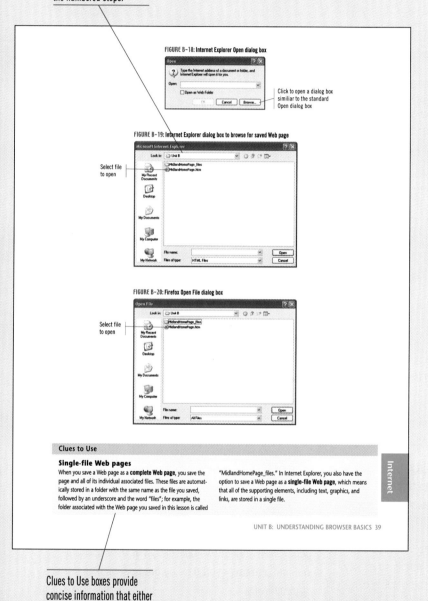

FIGURE B-18: Internet Explorer Open dialog box

Click to open a dialog box similiar to the standard Open dialog box

FIGURE B-19: Internet Explorer dialog box to browse for saved Web page

Select file to open

FIGURE B-20: Firefox Open File dialog box

Select file to open

Clues to Use

Single-file Web pages

When you save a Web page as a **complete Web page**, you save the page and all of its individual associated files. These files are automatically stored in a folder with the same name as the file you saved, followed by an underscore and the word "files"; for example, the folder associated with the Web page you saved in this lesson is called "MidlandHomePage_files." In Internet Explorer, you also have the option to save a Web page as a **single-file Web page**, which means that all of the supporting elements, including text, graphics, and links, are stored in a single file.

Internet

UNIT B: UNDERSTANDING BROWSER BASICS 39

Clues to Use boxes provide concise information that either expands on the major lesson skill or describes an independent task that in some way relates to the major lesson skill.

Subsequent Independent Challenges become increasingly open-ended, requiring more independent thinking and problem solving.

- **Advanced Challenge Exercises** set within the Independent Challenges provide optional tasks for more advanced students.

- **Visual Workshops** are practical, self-graded capstone projects that require independent problem solving.

What Web resources supplement the book?

The Internet, Fourth Edition–Illustrated Introductory features a Student Online Companion (SOC) Web site. Use the SOC to access all the links referenced in the book. Because the Internet and its content changes frequently, the SOC will also contain any updates or clarifications to the text after its publication.

Instructor Resources

The Instructor Resources CD puts the resources and information needed to teach and learn effectively directly into your hands. This integrated array of teaching and learning tools offers you and your students a broad range of technology-based instructional options, and we believe this CD represents the highest quality, most cutting edge resources available to instructors today. Many of the components are available at www.course.com. The resources available with this book are:

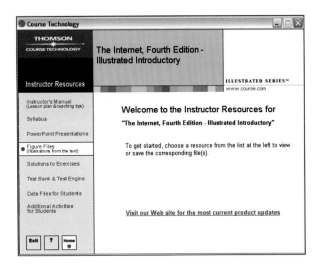

Instructor's Manual-Available as an electronic file, the Instructor's Manual is quality-assurance tested and includes unit overviews and detailed lecture topics with teaching tips for each unit.

Sample Syllabus-Prepare and customize our course easily using this sample course outline.

PowerPoint Presentations-Each unit has a corresponding PowerPoint Presentation that you can use in lecture, distribute to your students, or customize to suit your course.

Figure Files-The figures in the text are provided on the Instructor Resources CD to help you illustrate key topics or concepts. You can create traditional overhead transparencies by printing the figure files. Or you can create electronic slide shows by using the figures in a presentation program such as PowerPoint.

Solutions to Exercises-Solutions to Exercises contain every file students are asked to create or modify in the lessons and End-of-Unit material. A Help file on the Instructor Resources CD includes information for

using the Solution Files. There is also a document outlining the solutions for the End-of-Unit Concepts Review, Skills Review, and Independent Challenges.

ExamView Test Bank and Test Engine-ExamView is a powerful testing software package that allows you to create and administer printer, computer (LAN-based), and Internet exams. ExamView includes hundreds of questions that correspond to the topics covered in this text, enabling students to generate detailed study guides that include page references for further review. The computer-based and Internet testing components allow students to take exams at their computers, and also saves you time by grading each exam automatically.

Data Files for Students-To complete some of the units in this book, your students will need **Data Files**. Put them on a file server for students to copy. The Data Files are available on the Instructor Resources CD-ROM, the Review Pack, and can also be downloaded from www.course.com

Brief Contents

Contents

UNIT G

Downloading Programs and Sharing Files   163

UNIT H

Extending Browser Capabilities   191

Read This Before You Begin

Are there any prerequisites for this book?

The steps in this book assume you are familiar with Microsoft Windows XP and that you know how to perform basic operations with that operating system, including starting and exiting programs, working with windows and dialog boxes, and managing files.

What software do I need in order to use this book?

You will need an Internet connection, a Web browser, an e-mail program and account or an account on a Webmail service, and the text editing program WordPad (which is included with the installation of Windows XP) in order to complete the lessons and exercises in this book. This book was written and tested using a typical installation of Microsoft Windows XP SP2; two popular Web browsers, Internet Explorer 6.0 and Firefox 1.0; the e-mail program Outlook Express 6; and the Webmail service Hotmail. In most cases the steps can be performed using either browser or e-mail program. When necessary, steps and lessons specific to Internet Explorer, Firefox, Outlook Express, or Hotmail have been included. For students using other programs, there is an Appendix that includes alternative instructions for Netscape 7.2, Opera 7.2, iRider 2.21, Netscape 7.2 Mail, Eudora 6.2, Thunderbird 1.0, and Gmail.

What are Data Files and how do I use them?

To complete some of the units in this book, you need to use Data Files. Your instructor will either provide you with copies of the Data Files or ask you to make your own copies. Your instructor can also give you instructions on how to organize your files, as well as a complete file listing, or you can find the list and instructions for organizing your files in the Review Pack.

What is the Student Online Companion and how do I use it?

You use the Student Online Companion (SOC), located at *www.course.com/illustrated/internet4*, to access all the links used in the book. Because the Internet changes frequently, the SOC will provide updates to the text as necessary. If you notice a link on the SOC that is not working properly, use the Report Broken Links link to report the problem so it can be corrected. To access the SOC quickly, add the SOC URL to your Favorites or Bookmarks, or set it as your home page. (If you are working in a lab, please ask your instructor before doing this.) The URL is provided throughout the book in steps and tips for easy reference as well.

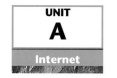

UNIT
A
Internet

Understanding Internet Basics

OBJECTIVES

Explore uses for the Internet
Understand networks
Understand network connectors
Learn the origins of the Internet
Understand the growth of the Internet
Understand how the World Wide Web works
Connect to the Internet
Evaluate Internet service options

The Internet offers many communication tools and information resources. To use the Internet effectively, you need to know what it is, what tools and information are available on it, and how you can connect to it. ▰▰▰ As the sales manager for the Tropical Exotic Produce Company (TEPCo), you are responsible for finding new and innovative ways to market the company's line of organically grown, exotic fruits and vegetables from South America, Africa, and Asia in the United States. You know that many businesses are using the Internet as a marketing tool. The president of TEPCo has asked you to research the Internet to determine its potential for TEPCo.

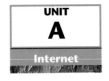

Exploring Uses for the Internet

The **Internet** is a collection of computers all over the world that are connected to one another. You can use the Internet to communicate with people throughout the world; read newspapers; join discussion groups; play games; and sell and purchase goods and services. Figure A-1 shows some of the tools and resources available on the Internet. 🖐️ The president of TEPCo has asked you to prepare a report on the use of the Internet for commercial purposes. You start by learning a few of the common uses for the Internet.

DETAILS

The following are common uses for the Internet:

- **Obtaining Information**

  The **World Wide Web** (or simply the **Web**) is a subset of the computers on the Internet. The Web organizes resources on the Internet to make them easily accessible to users. Documents formatted to be viewed on the Web are called **Web pages**, and a **Web site** is a collection of related Web pages stored on a computer. Millions of Web sites offer information on almost any imaginable topic. Some sites are like encyclopedias and offer a wide range of information on many topics. Other sites specialize in specific types of information; for example, you can find Web sites that offer DVD player reviews, recipes for Mexican food, or instructions for growing house plants.

- **Communicating**

  You can use e-mail and instant messages to communicate electronically with people all over the world. Electronic messages are transferred between two or more computers via **e-mail** (short for **electronic mail**). You can use **instant messages (IM)** to chat with others in real time over the Internet.

- **Talking to Others with Shared Interests**

  Almost any topic you can imagine is being discussed on the Internet in electronic discussion groups.

  - A **mailing list** is a list of names and e-mail addresses for a group of people who subscribe to the list. You send messages to a mailing list by **posting** (or sending) an e-mail message; posted messages are automatically forwarded to every person who subscribes to the list.
  - A **newsgroup** (also called a **forum** or **Internet discussion group**) is similar to a mailing list, but messages are stored in a location on the Internet. Users can access some newsgroups on a Web site; other newsgroups require users to use software called a **newsreader** to access messages.
  - A **blog** (short for **Web log**) is an online journal in which the blog owner (the **blogger**) posts entries for public viewing. Most blogs include an interface that lets readers comment on the blogger's postings.

- **Buying and Selling Goods and Services**

  All kinds of businesses provide information about their products and services on the Internet. Figure A-2 shows an example of a commercial business marketing its goods on the Internet.

- **Downloading Software**

  Many Web sites offer software to download and install. Some software is free; other software is a **trial** or **demo version** (a version you can use for a limited amount of time or without all the features of the full version).

- **Accessing Multimedia**

  You can access a wide variety of images, sounds, music, and videos on the Internet. For example, you can subscribe to a music downloading service and download songs that you can then burn to a CD or transfer to an MP3 player. You can also watch movie previews, news clips, or animated videos.

- **Playing Online Multiuser Games**

  Several types of online adventure games allow hundreds, and even thousands, of users to assume character roles and interact with each other. These games are known by a variety of names, such as **MUDs** (multiuser dungeons), **MOOs** (MUD object-oriented), and **MMOGs** (massively multiuser online games).

QUICK TIP

Newsgroups grew out of **Usenet**, an acronym for User's News Network, which was started in 1979 by a group of students and programmers at Duke University and the University of North Carolina.

QUICK TIP

An **avatar** is an online character that a game player uses to represent him or herself.

FIGURE A-1: Communication tools and information resources on the Internet

Information Resources

The Internet contains information resources on almost any imaginable topic. Online versions of newspapers, magazines, government documents, research reports, and books offer a wealth of information greater than the holdings of libraries.

Electronic Mail (E-Mail) and Instant Messages (IM)

You can use the Internet to exchange messages inexpensively and efficiently with people around the world.

Software Programs

Hundreds of thousands of programs are available to you on the Internet. These programs, many of which you can download free or for a small fee, include utilities, word processors, various kinds of graphics programs, and games.

Business-to-Business Communication

Many business firms that have multiple locations throughout the world use the Internet to transmit data internally. These firms also use the Internet to conduct business with each other.

Discussions

Thousands of different topics are avidly debated and discussed every day in electronic discussion groups.

Entertainment Activities

The Internet offers reviews of restaurants, movies, theater, musical events, and books. You even can play interactive games with people around the world using the Internet.

Retail Business

Many businesses place information about their products and services on the Internet. Every day, more firms are opening online stores on the Internet that you can visit to make purchases.

FIGURE A-2: Example of a commercial business on the Internet

Internet

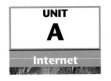

UNIT A
Internet

Understanding Networks

You will often hear the Internet referred to as a collection of networks. A **network** is created when two or more computers are connected to each other. A computer can become part of a network by connecting to a nearby computer or to the Internet. A network allows computers to share resources, such as printers or programs. As you continue your research, you encounter the concept of computer networks. You know that TEPCo does not have its computers networked, that is, connected to each other or to the Internet. You decide to learn more about what computer networks are and how to connect computers to form a network.

DETAILS

The following terms are associated with networking:

- **Server**

  A **server** is any computer that accepts requests from other computers that are connected to it and shares some or all of its resources, such as printers, files, or programs, with those connected computers. A server can be a powerful personal computer (PC) or a larger computer, such as a minicomputer or a mainframe computer.

- **Client**

  Each computer connected to a server is called a **client**.

- **Network Operating System**

  The software that runs on the server is called a **network operating system**. This software coordinates how information flows among its various clients.

- **Network Interface Card**

  A **network interface card (NIC)**, or **network card**, is a removable circuit board that is used to connect a computer to a network. After inserting a NIC into a computer, you can connect it to a network by running a cable from the NIC to the server or to another client.

- **Client/Server Network**

  A **client/server network** is a network consisting of one server that shares its resources with multiple clients. Client/server networks commonly are used to connect computers that are located close together (for example, in the same room or building) so that each computer can share resources, such as a printer or a scanner.

- **Local Area Network (LAN)**

  A **local area network (LAN)** consists of a group of computers connected through NICs. This network is described as local because the direct connection from one computer to another through NICs works only over relatively short distances (no more than a few thousand feet). Figure A-3 shows how a typical client/server LAN could be set up in an office environment.

- **Wide Area Network (WAN)**

  Several LANs connected together form a **wide area network (WAN)**. For example, a typical college has several computer labs scattered throughout its many buildings. Each computer lab is a client/server LAN. The LANs in the college are interconnected to form the WAN.

Clues to Use

What is the difference between an internet and the Internet?

The word "internet" (lowercase "i") is short for interconnected network. For example, computer lab LANs are networks, whereas a college's WAN is a network of networks, or an internet. In fact, any network of networks is an internet. The college's WAN is also connected to an internet called the Internet (capital "I"). The Internet is a specific worldwide collection of interconnected networks whose owners have voluntarily agreed to share resources and network connections with one another.

FIGURE A-3: A client/server LAN

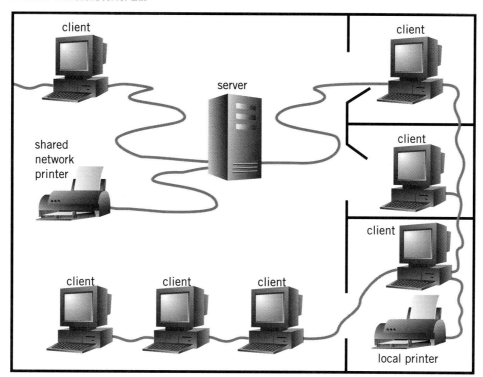

Understanding Network Connectors

Networks are connected in a variety of ways, depending on the available technology. Network connections create **communications circuits** through which data can travel. You can connect computers using old-fashioned twisted-pair cables, more powerful coaxial cables, or modern fiber-optic cables. Figure A-4 shows these three types of cables. Alternatively, you could dispense with cables altogether and use a wireless network. 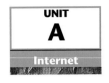 After researching networks, you decide to include in your report the suggestion that TEPCo create a LAN, which will be connected to the Internet. To be better informed, you decide to further investigate the different types of network connectors.

DETAILS

The following terms describe network connectors and connections:

- **Twisted-Pair Cable**

  The oldest cable type is **twisted-pair cable**, which consists of two or more insulated copper wires twisted around each other and enclosed in a layer of plastic insulation. The wires are twisted to reduce interference from any current-carrying wires located nearby. Twisted-pair cable is much less expensive than other cable types. Telephone companies have used one type of twisted-pair cable, called **Category 1 cable**, for years to wire residences and businesses. Category 1 cable transmits information more slowly than other cable types. Newer types of twisted-pair cables, called **Category 5 cable** and **Category 5e cable**, are used in computer networks.

- **Coaxial Cable**

  Coaxial cable is an insulated copper wire encased in a metal shield that is enclosed with plastic insulation. The signal-carrying wire is completely shielded, so it resists electrical interference better than twisted-pair cable. Coaxial cable carries signals about 20 times faster than Category 1 cable, but Category 5 cable transmits information 10 to 100 times faster than coaxial cable, and Category 5e cable transmits data even faster—up to 10 times faster—than Category 5 cable. Additionally, coaxial cable is considerably more expensive than Category 1, 5, or 5e cable. Most cable television connections use coaxial cable.

- **Fiber-Optic Cable**

  Fiber-optic cable transmits information by pulsing beams of light through very thin strands of glass. It does not use an electrical signal. Fiber-optic cable transmits signals much faster than coaxial cable and, because it does not use electricity, it is completely immune to electrical interference. Fiber-optic cable is lighter and more durable than coaxial cable, but it's more difficult to work with and much more expensive. However, the price of fiber-optic cable and the laser sending and receiving equipment needed at each end of the cable has dropped dramatically in the past few years. Thus, companies are using fiber-optic cable in more and more networks as the cost becomes more affordable.

- **Wireless Connections**

  Wireless networks use technologies such as radio frequency (RF) and infrared (IR) to link computers. Wireless networks are becoming more common as the cost of the wireless transmitters and receivers that plug into NICs continues to drop. Wireless LANs (**WLANs**) are well suited to organizations and households in which cables are difficult to install. **Wireless fidelity (Wi-Fi)** is the term used to describe a short-range wireless network that connects a wireless access point to wireless devices located within a distance of approximately 200 feet. Figure A-5 depicts a wireless home network that includes two desktop PCs, two laptop PCs, and a shared printer. **WiMAX** (Worldwide Interoperability for Microwave Access), is a technology being developed for use in metropolitan areas. Although still in development by Intel and approximately 140 other companies, WiMAX will have a range of up to 31 miles, creating a way to make wireless broadband network access available in metropolitan areas.

FIGURE A-4: Twisted-pair, coaxial, and fiber-optic cables

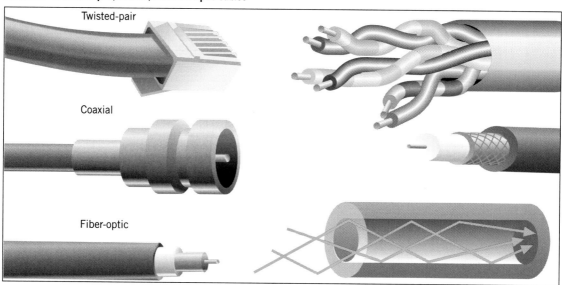

Twisted-pair

Coaxial

Fiber-optic

FIGURE A-5: A wireless home network

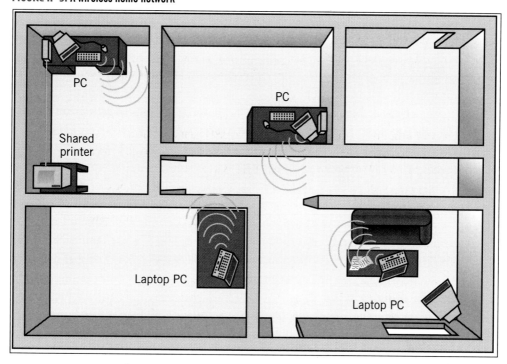

PC

PC

Shared printer

Laptop PC

Laptop PC

Clues to Use

Transporting data

Bandwidth is a measure of the amount of data that can be transmitted simultaneously through a communications circuit. Bandwidth is commonly used to compare the maximum possible transmission speed through different connectors and to evaluate transmission speed through a given circuit. The circuit's bandwidth is limited to the narrowest bandwidth in the network, so the amount of data transmitted through any connector, known as **throughput**, is much lower than each connector's maximum value. Bandwidth is measured in multiples of **bits per second (bps)**. A bandwidth of 28,800 bps means that 28,800 bits of data are transferred each second. The following terms are often used when discussing Internet bandwidth: **kilobits per second (Kbps)**, which is 1,024 bps; **megabits per second (Mbps)**, which is 1,048,576 bps; and **gigabits per second (Gbps)**, which is 1,073,741,824 bps.

Learning the Origins of the Internet

In the early 1960s, the U.S. Department of Defense (DOD) became concerned about the possible effects of nuclear attack on its computing facilities. The DOD created the **Defense Advanced Research Projects Agency (DARPA)**, which began to examine ways to connect its computers to one another and to weapons installations distributed all over the world.  You decide to find out how the Internet developed from the activities of DARPA into the vast network of computers now available to anyone.

DETAILS

Here is how the Internet began:

- **ARPANET**

  The **Advanced Research Projects Agency Network (ARPANET)** was four computers networked together by DARPA researchers in 1969. These first four computers were located at the University of California at Los Angeles, SRI International, the University of California at Santa Barbara, and the University of Utah.

- **Packet Switching and Routers**

  The **circuit switching** method for data transmission (once commonly used by telephone companies) could not be easily secured. DARPA researchers needed to find a more secure method for sending information. DARPA developed the **packet switching** method, which breaks down files and messages into **data packets** (small chunks of data). Each data packet is labeled electronically with codes that describe its origin and destination. The destination computer collects the data packets and reassembles the original data. Each computer that an individual data packet encounters while traveling through the network determines the best way to move the data packet forward to its destination. These computers are often called **routers**, and the programs they use to determine the best path for data packets are called **routing algorithms**.

- **Protocols**

  The **Network Control Protocol (NCP)** was developed as the first collection of rules for formatting, ordering, and error-checking data sent across a network. Vincent Cerf, who is often referred to as the Father of the Internet, along with his colleague Robert Kahn, developed the Transmission Control Protocol and the Internet Protocol (referred to by their combined acronym **TCP/IP**). The **Transmission Control Protocol (TCP)** includes rules that computers on a network use to establish and break connections. The **Internet Protocol (IP)** includes rules for routing individual data packets.

- **TCP/IP Tools**

  The TCP/IP suite of protocols includes a tool to facilitate file transfer, and another to access computers that aren't part of a user's immediate network over the Internet. **File Transfer Protocol (FTP)** enables users to transfer files between computers. **Telnet** enables users to log on to a remote server.

- **Open Architecture Philosophy**

  Open architecture philosophy ensured that each network connected to the ARPANET could continue using its own protocols and data-transmission methods internally. Four key points characterize this philosophy:

  - Independent networks should not require internal changes to have a connection to the Internet.
  - Data packets that do not arrive at their destinations must be retransmitted from their source network.
  - Computers that route data packets do not retain information about the data packets they handle.
  - No global control exists over the network.

- **Interconnecting Networks**

  The Internet is a network of networks. Table A-1 describes some of the most well-known networks that eventually became the Internet (see Figure A-6). These networks are connected via a **network backbone**, the long-distance lines and supporting technology that transport large amounts of data between the **network access points (NAPs)**, physical locations where networks connect to the Internet.

FIGURE A-6: Networks that became the Internet

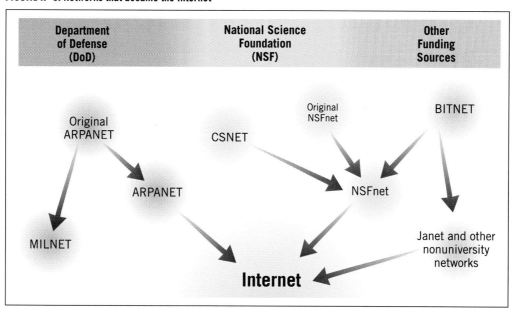

TABLE A-1: Interconnecting networks

Network	Descriptions
ARPANET (Advanced Research Projects Agency Network)	Specialized network used for advanced research studies that originated in 1984 when the DOD split the original ARPANET into ARPANET and MILNET
BITNET (Because It's Time Network)	Developed by City University of New York to link IBM mainframes at universities
CSNET (Computer Science Network)	Funded by the National Science Foundation (NSF) for educational and research institutions that did not have access to the ARPANET
Janet (Joint Academic Network)	Developed in the United Kingdom to link universities
MILNET (Military Network)	Specialized network reserved for high-security military uses that originated in 1984 when the DOD split the original ARPANET into ARPANET and MILNET
NSFnet (National Science Foundation Network)	Developed as an addition to CSNET

Clues to Use

Understanding transfer protocol

The transfer protocol is the set of rules that computers use to move files from one computer to another on an internet. The most common transfer protocol used on the Internet is the Hypertext Transfer Protocol (HTTP). People do use other protocols to transfer files on the Internet, but most of these protocols were used more frequently before the Web became part of the Internet. Two protocols that you still might see on the Internet are the file transfer protocol (FTP) and the Telnet protocol.

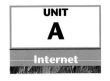

Understanding the Growth of the Internet

As PCs became more powerful, affordable, and available during the 1980s, firms increasingly used them to construct intranets. **Intranets** are LANs or WANs that use the TCP/IP protocol but do not connect to sites outside the firm. Prior to 1989, most universities and businesses could not communicate with people outside their intranet. Because the National Science Foundation (NSF) prohibited commercial network traffic on the networks it funded, businesses that wanted to communicate outside their intranets turned to commercial e-mail services. Larger firms built their own TCP/IP-based WANs that used leased telephone lines to connect field offices to corporate headquarters. ▓▓▓▓ As you continue your research about the Internet, you learn more about how the Internet evolved from a resource used primarily by the academic community to one that became accessible to commercial services.

DETAILS

The growth of the Internet can be attributed to:

- **Commercial E-Mail Services**

  In 1989, the NSF permitted two commercial e-mail services, MCI Mail and CompuServe, to establish limited connections to the Internet. These commercial providers allowed their subscribers to exchange e-mail messages with members of the academic and research communities who were connected to the Internet. These connections allowed commercial enterprises to send e-mail directly to Internet addresses and allowed members of the research and education communities on the Internet to send e-mail directly to MCI Mail and CompuServe addresses. The NSF justified this limited commercial use of the Internet by describing it as a service that would primarily benefit the Internet's noncommercial users.

- **Internet Engineering Task Force**

  People from all walks of life, not just scientists or academic researchers, started thinking of these networks as a global resource that we now know as the Internet. Information systems professionals began to form volunteer groups, such as the **Internet Engineering Task Force (IETF)**, which first met in 1986. The IETF is a self-organized group that makes technical contributions to the engineering of the Internet and its technologies; it is also the main body that develops new Internet standards.

- **Federal Networking Council**

  The National Science and Technology Council's Committee on Computing, Information, and Communications (CCIC) set up the **Federal Networking Council (FNC)** to meet the CCIC's research and education goals. The FNC also coordinates the use of its agencies' technologies by the commercial sector. In 1995, the FNC adopted the formal definition of Internet shown in Figure A-7. Many people find it interesting that a formal definition of the term did not appear until 1995. The Internet was a phenomenon that surprised the world.

- **Commercialization of the Internet**

  In 1991, the NSF eased its restrictions on Internet commercial activity and began implementing plans to eventually privatize much of the Internet via **Internet hosts**, computers that connect a LAN or a WAN to the Internet. Businesses and individuals began to connect to the Internet in ever-increasing numbers. Figure A-8 shows the dramatic growth of Internet host computers during the years 1991 through 2005.

FIGURE A-7: The Federal Networking Council's October 1995 resolution to define the term "Internet"

RESOLUTION: The Federal Networking Council (FNC) agrees that the following language reflects our definition of the term Internet. Internet refers to the global information system that

(i) is logically linked together by a globally unique address space based on the Internet Protocol (IP) or its subsequent extensions/follow-ons;

(ii) is able to support communications using the Transmission Control Protocol/Internet Protocol (TCP/IP) suite or its subsequent extensions/follow-ons, and/or other IP-compatible protocols; and

(iii) provides, uses or makes accessible, either publicly or privately, high level services layered on the communications and related infrastructure described herein.

Source: http//www.fnc.gov/internet_res.html

FIGURE A-8: Growth of the number of Internet hosts

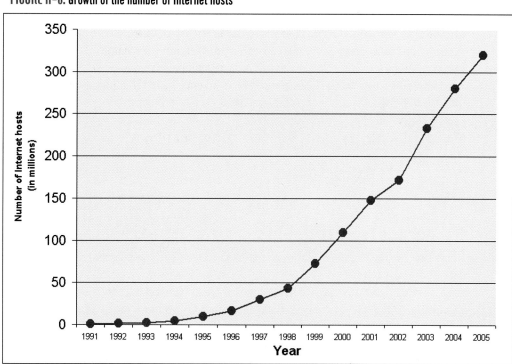

Source: Adapted from Internet Systems Consortium (http://www.isc.org/) and other sources

Clues to Use

How many Internet users are there?

Many people are surprised to learn that no one knows how many users are on the Internet. The Internet has no central management or coordination, and the routing computers do not maintain records of the data packets they handle. Therefore, no one has the capability of finding out how many individual e-mail messages or files travel on the Internet. Researchers estimate that at least 300 million host computers are connected to the Internet and that more than 700 million people worldwide use it.

Internet

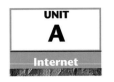

Understanding How the World Wide Web Works

The development of the World Wide Web worked hand in hand with the commercialization of the Internet to spur its growth. In a short amount of time, the number of Web sites has rapidly increased. Figure A-9 shows the fast growth of the Web during its short lifetime. Many people use "the Web" and "the Internet" interchangeably, but they are not the same thing. The Internet is the entire system of networked computers, and the World Wide Web is a method used to access information contained on a subset of those networked computers. Think of the difference this way: You connect to the Internet, and then use the World Wide Web to access information. The Web's success is due to links that enable you to connect to any document on the Web, and user-friendly Web tools that enable users to view and search for Web pages with ease. As you continue your research about the Internet, you decide to learn more about how the Web works.

DETAILS

The World Wide Web can be described using the following terms:

- **Hypertext Markup Language**

  Hypertext Markup Language (HTML) is a computer language that marks text with a set of **tags**, or codes, that define the structure and behavior of a Web page. For example, HTML includes a tag to create a header, a numbered list, or the placement of a graphic. Every Web page is created using HTML tags. When you view a Web page on the Internet, however, you don't see the HTML tags—you see just the resulting formatted Web page.

- **Web Server**

  A **Web server** is a computer that stores files written in HTML and lets other computers connect to it and read those files.

- **Web Browser**

  A **Web browser** is software that reads HTML documents. Web browsers let you read (or browse) HTML documents and move from one HTML document to another. You can use a Web browser to view any HTML document that resides on a computer connected to the Internet. Currently, the most widely used Web browser is Microsoft Internet Explorer. A browser that is rapidly rising in popularity is Mozilla's Firefox. Figure A-10 shows a Web page from the Course Technology Web site accessed using Internet Explorer. Web browsers use a **graphical user interface** (**GUI**, pronounced "gooey"), which uses text, pictures, icons, and other graphical elements to present information and allow users to perform a variety of tasks. For example, you could click the Print button, which looks like a picture of a printer, to print the Web page.

- **Links**

  Links (also called **hypertext links**, or **hyperlinks**) are text, graphics, or other Web page elements that connect to additional data on the Web. On a Web page, a text link is usually underlined, and the mouse pointer typically appears as a pointing hand when positioned over a link. When you click a link, a new HTML document, such as a page of text and graphics, or an audio or video file, appears. This HTML document could be part of the Web site you are currently exploring or part of a Web site halfway around the world.

FIGURE A-9: Growth of the World Wide Web

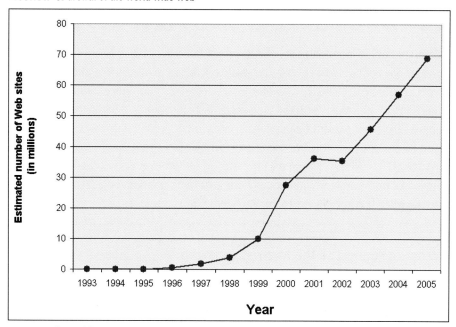

Source: Adapted from Netcraft Web Survey (http://www.netcraft.com/survey/Reports)

FIGURE A-10: Example of a Web page

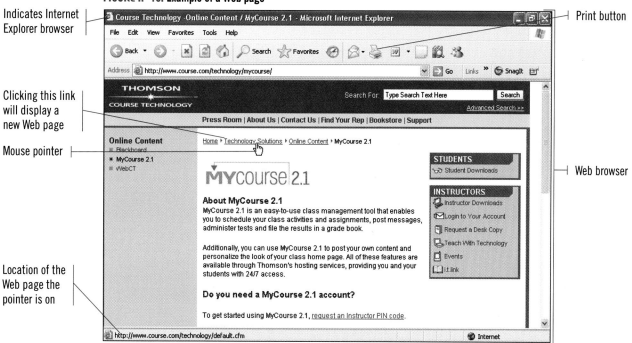

Indicates Internet Explorer browser

Clicking this link will display a new Web page

Mouse pointer

Location of the Web page the pointer is on

Print button

Web browser

What is XML?

Another markup language that you might hear about is **XML**, which stands for **Extensible Markup Language**. XML was originally developed to meet the needs of large-scale electronic publishers, but today XML is becoming popular as a way of exchanging data between applications and organizations. While HTML uses predefined tags to describe how to format and display data, XML uses customized tags to describe data and its structure. The developer defines and uses the customized tags to describe the data in an XML document. For example, an XML document might define a product's ID number, style, name, and price using customized tags such as <product_id> and </product_id>, <style> and </style>, <name> and </name>, and <cost> and </cost>. These tags only describe the data contained within them, they do not describe how the data will look. XML also lets the developer define validation rules for data and hierarchical relationships of data.

Internet

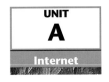

Connecting to the Internet

Remember that the Internet is a set of interconnected networks. To become a part of the Internet, you need to be part of a communications network. Network access points (NAPs) maintain the core operations of the Internet and the backbone used to transmit data over long distances. NAPs do not, however, offer direct connections to individuals or small businesses. Instead, they offer connections to large organizations and businesses that, in turn, provide Internet access to other organizations and individuals. In order for individuals and businesses to connect to the Internet, they need to set up an account with an **Internet Service Provider (ISP)**. Your research has provided you with a good background on the history of the Internet and the Web. Next, you research the nature of Internet connections. You can use this information to decide what TEPCo needs to access the Internet.

DETAILS

In order to connect to the Internet you need:

- **ISPs**

  At minimum, ISPs provide access to a NAP so individuals and businesses can connect to the Internet. Usually, the ISP provides you with the software you need to connect to the Internet. Some ISPs also provide Web browser software, software to send and receive e-mail messages, and software you can use to transfer files. ISPs also often provide advice and help in setting up networks, and some even help their customers design Web pages. Many larger ISPs not only sell Internet access to users, but also sell Internet access to other ISPs, which then sell access and service to their own customers. This hierarchy of Internet access is illustrated in Figure A-11.

- **Types of Connections**

  To connect to the Internet, data must be able to travel between your computer and the Internet. Common connections include the following: telephone service connection (sometimes referred to as **POTS**, or **plain old telephone service**); **T1** and **T3** line connections; **Digital Subscriber Line (DSL)**; **cable**; **satellite**; and **wireless**. Table A-2 summarizes the most popular types of connections currently used on the Internet.

- **Modem**

  To connect to the Internet, you usually need a **modem**, which is a device that converts signals between a computer and the transmission line. The term modem is short for **modulator-demodulator**. When you connect your computer, which communicates using digital signals, to another computer through a twisted-pair or coaxial cable, which uses analog signals, the signal must be converted. Converting a digital signal to an analog signal is called **modulation**; converting that analog signal back into digital form is called **demodulation**. A modem performs both functions; that is, it acts as a modulator-demodulator. The general term "modem" usually refers to a device used with a telephone line; most computers sold today include this variety of modem. Other methods of connecting to the Internet require different types of modems. For example, a cable connection through a cable television company requires a **cable modem**, and a DSL connection requires a **DSL modem**.

- **WLAN Card**

  To connect a device to the Internet without cables, you need a **wireless network interface card (WLAN card)** or a Wi-Fi compatible device, and you must be within range of a wireless access point that is connected to the Internet. Some public locations, such as airports, restaurants, and hotels, include wireless access points for people to use for free or for a small daily fee.

Clues to use

Public-access Internet service

Although many options exist for setting up Internet service in your home, some people find that they can meet their Internet access needs for free using public facilities. Many public libraries offer free Internet access to library card holders or to the general public. You might find it unnecessary to maintain Internet service at home if you have minimal Internet access requirements and such public access is available in a convenient location.

FIGURE A-11: The hierarchy of Internet service options

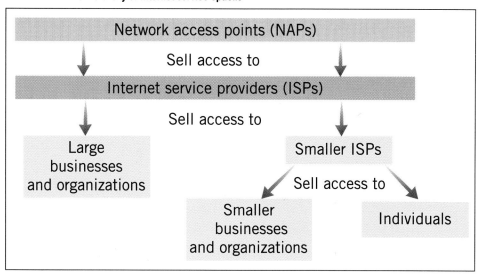

TABLE A-2: Types of Internet connections

Type of service	Description	Speed
Telephone service	Available through regular phone lines; used by individuals and small businesses to connect to an ISP	28.8 Kbps to 56 Kbps
T1 line	Offers a higher grade of service for connecting to the Internet than telephone service does; used by large companies and organizations that must link hundreds or thousands of individual users to the Internet; more expensive than telephone service connections	1.544 Mbps
T3 line	Same as T1 line	44.7 Mbps
Digital Subscriber Line (DSL)	Creates a high-speed connection using the customer's telephone wiring; used by individuals and businesses	100 Kbps to 9.0 Mbps
Cable	Uses the customer's television cable to connect to the Internet; used by individuals and businesses	300 Kbps to 10.0 Mbps
Satellite	Uses a satellite dish receiver; particularly useful for people in remote areas	125 Kbps to to 500 Mbps
Wireless	Uses high frequency radio waves to connect to a network access point	722 Kbps to 54 Mbps

Internet

Evaluating Internet Service Options

To connect to the Internet, individuals or small businesses must use an ISP. Users can choose one of five ways to link to an ISP. The first way, which is available only to individuals, is a connection through your school or employer. The second option is a connection over standard telephone lines. The third option is to connect through a cable television company. The fourth option is to use a satellite, and the fifth option is a wireless connection. 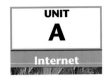 As your research continues, you evaluate the various connection options to determine which option you will recommend for TEPCo.

DETAILS

The ways you can connect to an ISP are listed below:

- **School or Employer Connection**

  One of the easiest ways to connect to the Internet is through your school or employer, if it already has an Internet connection. Such a connection is generally free or very reasonably priced. Most schools and employers have an **acceptable use policy (AUP)** that specifies the conditions under which you can use their Internet connection. For example, many AUPs expressly prohibit you from engaging in commercial activities. In such cases, you could not use your Internet account to start a small business on the Web. An important concern when using your school's or employer's Internet connection is that the school or employer generally retains the right to examine any files or e-mail messages you transmit. You need to consider carefully whether the limitations placed on your use of the Internet are greater than the benefits of the low cost of this access option.

- **Telephone Line Connection**

  Depending on where you live, you might find that a telephone line service (using either standard dial-in service or DSL) is the best way to connect to the Internet. In major metropolitan areas, many ISPs offering these services compete for customers and, therefore, connection fees are often very reasonable. Additionally, some companies offer free Internet access in exchange for displaying advertising on your computer screen each time you connect. Smaller towns and rural areas have fewer ISPs offering these connection options and therefore might be less competitively priced. Figure A-12 lists some of the information you need to learn about such an ISP before signing on. Figure A-13 shows a Web page on an ISP's Web site.

- **Cable Connection**

  A cable modem allows you to connect to the Internet through your cable television company. A cable connection can provide very fast downloads to your computer from the Internet (as much as 170 times faster than a telephone line connection). Although the cost of a cable connection is usually higher than the cost of a telephone line connection, you save the cost of a second telephone line. The greatest disadvantage for most people is that the cable connection might not be available yet in their area.

- **Satellite Connection**

  Many rural areas in the United States do not have cable television service and never will because their low population density makes it too expensive. A cable company simply cannot afford to run miles of cable to reach one or two isolated customers. People in these areas often buy satellite receivers to obtain television signals and Internet connections. The major advantage of a satellite connection is speed. Although the speeds are not as high as those offered by cable modems, they are approximately 5 to 10 times higher than those achieved with telephone connections. For users in remote areas, this technology often offers the best connection solution.

- **Hot Spots**

  A **hot spot** is a wireless access point to a LAN that offers Internet access to the public. Some hot spot locations charge a fee, but many do not. Your computer or other device must have the necessary hardware to be compatible with the access point and to connect to a hot spot.

What is the monthly base fee and how many hours of Internet service are included?
What is the hourly rate for time used over the monthly base amount?
Is the telephone access number local or long distance?
Which specific Internet services are included?
What software is included?
What user-support services are available?

FIGURE A-13: Web site of an Internet service provider

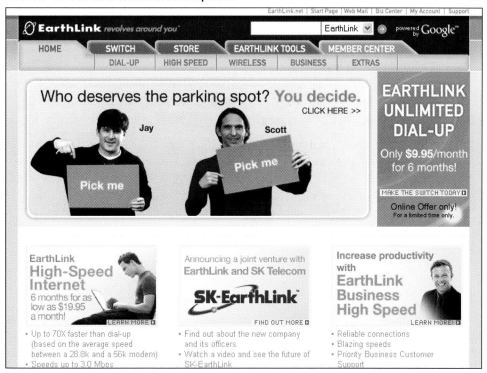

Clues to Use

Connecting to the Internet with a wireless device

Wireless devices such as cell phones and personal digital assistants (PDAs) can upload and download e-mail, transfer files, and access the Web. Some wireless devices, such as cell phones, connect to the wireless provider's network and these services automatically when they are within range of the cellular network. Other wireless devices, such as personal digital assistants (PDAs), might access the wireless provider's network using a connection to the cellular network or by being within range of a hot spot.

Practice

▼ CONCEPTS REVIEW

Match each term with the statement that best describes it.

1. Internet
2. Server
3. ARPANET
4. IETF
5. LAN
6. TCP/IP
7. ISP
8. FTP
9. Links
10. HTML

a. An organization responsible for developing new Internet standards
b. A computer that accepts requests from computers connected to it and shares resources with those computers
c. A method used to transfer files over the Internet
d. A business that offers an Internet connection to your home or office
e. Clickable text, graphics, or other Web page elements that connect to other HTML documents
f. Four computers networked together by DARPA in 1969
g. A network of computers located close together
h. A worldwide collection of interconnected networks
i. The language used to create a Web page
j. Protocols used by all computers connected to the Internet

Select the best answer from the list of choices.

11. Which of the following is a way to chat with friends in real time over the Internet?
    a. E-mail
    b. Newsgroups
    c. Instant messages
    d. Blogs

12. The type of cable used in telephone connections is called:
    a. twisted-pair cable.
    b. TCP/IP cable.
    c. coaxial cable.
    d. fiber-optic cable.

13. Which of the following methods is the switching method used by the Internet?
    a. Cable switching
    b. Circuit switching
    c. Packet switching
    d. Transmission switching

14. Which of the following is the term for the collection of rules that computers follow when formatting, ordering, and error-checking data sent across a network?
    a. Router
    b. ARPANET
    c. Open architecture
    d. Protocol

15. **Which of the following terms is used to describe computer networks that use the TCP/IP protocol but do not connect to sites outside the firm?**
    a. Internet
    b. ARPANET
    c. World Wide Web
    d. Intranet

16. **Which of the following is a requirement for all home and business Internet connections?**
    a. A T1 line
    b. Cable television service
    c. DSL service
    d. An ISP

17. **The device that converts signals between a computer and the transmission line is a:**
    a. satellite connection.
    b. WLAN.
    c. hot spot.
    d. modem.

18. **A wireless access point to a LAN that offers Internet access to the public is a(n):**
    a. WLAN.
    b. hot spot.
    c. satellite connection.
    d. ISP.

▼ INDEPENDENT CHALLENGE 1

As you learned in this unit, the Internet includes many resources. If you are new to the Internet, you might be wondering how you can use the Internet in your life.

   a. List several topics that you are interested in exploring on the Internet. Think of your own hobbies and interests. Would you like to find travel information about Alaska? Gather information for a research paper on Mars? Learn new yoga techniques? Explore nuclear physics databases? Identify at least five topics that interest you, and then list the Internet tools you would use to find more information about the topics.
   b. Describe three specific activities you want to engage in on the Internet. For example, you might want to send your resume to an employer across the country, write messages to a distant pen pal, view a clip of your favorite movie, chat in real time with friends, or listen to music performed by your favorite band. Briefly describe how you will perform these activities.

▼ INDEPENDENT CHALLENGE 2

Most companies and public institutions that offer Internet access require users to sign, or at least be aware of, an acceptable use policy (AUP).

   a. Obtain a copy of your school's or employer's AUP.
   b. Outline the main restrictions that the AUP places on student (or employee) activities.
   c. Compare those restrictions with the limits that it places on faculty (or employer) activities.
   d. Analyze and evaluate any differences in treatment; if there are no differences, discuss whether the policy should be rewritten to include differences.
   e. If your school or employer has no policy, outline the key elements that you believe should be included in such a policy.

Internet

▼ INDEPENDENT CHALLENGE 3

Your school probably has a number of computer networks. At most schools, you can find information about computing facilities from the Department of Academic Computing, the school library, or the network administrator.

    a. What LANs, WLANs, and WANs do you have on your campus?

    b. Which of these networks are interconnected?

    c. Are there any hot spots on campus?

    d. Determine if the file server is a PC or a larger computer.

    e. Which network operating system is used?

▼ INDEPENDENT CHALLENGE 4

You purchased a new computer and want to connect to the Internet. You need to determine which Internet service provider you should choose.

    a. Find out the names of three ISPs in your area. If possible, include one ISP that provides Internet access via cable connection. Your local cable television company is a good place to start. (*Hint*: If you have Internet access and know how to use a search engine, open your browser, then use a search engine to do your research.)

    b. Create a table in a new word processing document and list the following information about each of the three ISPs you have chosen:

        1. What is the monthly base fee?

        2. How many hours of Internet service are included in the base fee?

        3. What is the hourly rate for time used over the monthly base amount?

        4. Is the telephone access number local or long distance?

        5. Which specific Internet services are included?

        6. What software is included?

        7. What user-support services are available?

        8. What is the best feature of the services provided by the ISP?

        9. What is the worst feature of the services provided by the ISP?

    c. Identify which ISP you would choose based on your answers to the preceding questions.

Understanding Browser Basics

OBJECTIVES

Understand Web browsing
Understand Hypertext Markup Language (HTML)
Understand Web site addresses
Start a Web browser
Find a Web site
Navigate through a Web site
Create and manage favorites in Internet Explorer
Create and manage bookmarks in Firefox
Save and open a Web page in a browser
Print a Web page
Copy text and graphics from a Web page

The Web consists of millions of Web sites, which are made up of millions of Web pages. To use the Web as an effective tool for both research and entertainment purposes, it's helpful to understand how the Web is structured and how to use a Web browser to find and view information. Trinity Andrews, director of the Danville Animal Shelter, places ads on television and in newspapers to let the public know about specific pets available for adoption. However, the pets available for adoption change from day to day, and often, by the time an ad runs, the pet highlighted in the ad has already been adopted. You volunteer at the shelter, and you offer to help Trinity identify ways that the shelter can use the Internet to let the community know about the shelter and about specific pets available for adoption.

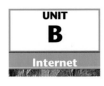
Understanding Web Browsing

The Web consists of a collection of files that reside on computers located all over the world. These computers are connected to one another through the Internet. **Browsing** is the term that describes using your computer and Internet connection to view these files. As you investigate how to use the Web for the Danville Animal Shelter, you decide to begin your exploration of the World Wide Web by learning some common terms related to Web browsing.

DETAILS

The following terms are associated with Web browsing:

- **Worldwide Client/Server Network**

  When you use your Internet connection to become part of the Web, your computer becomes part of a worldwide client/server network. As a Web client, your computer makes requests of Web servers on the Internet. Figure B-1 shows how this client/server structure uses the Web to provide multiple interconnections among the various kinds of client and server computers.

- **Home Page**

  The term **home page** is commonly used when talking about the Web. It has three common meanings:

  - A home page is the main Web page that all the Web pages on a Web site are organized around and link back to; it is typically the first Web page that opens when you visit a Web site. Figure B-2 shows the home page of PetFinder.com. Many of the links on this home page link to Web pages on the PetFinder.com Web site.

  - A home page is also the first Web page that opens when you start your Web browser. This type of home page might be an HTML document stored on your own computer or the main Web page of a favorite Web site. If you are using a computer on your school's or employer's network, the Web browser might be configured to display the main Web page for the school or firm.

  - A home page is also a Web page that a Web browser displays the first time you use it. This Web page is typically the main Web page of the firm or other organization that installed or created the Web browser software.

- **Start Page**

  A home page (in the sense of the second and third definitions listed above) is sometimes called a **start page**. For example, at some colleges and businesses, the Web page that opens when a browser on the network is first started might be related to the college or business; in other words, the Web page is the Web browser's start page as well as the home page of the college's or business's Web site.

FIGURE B-1: Client/server structure of the World Wide Web

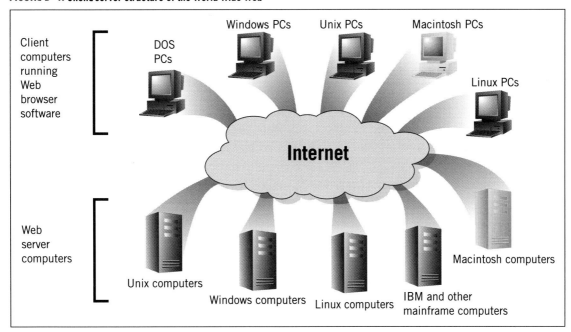

FIGURE B-2: Home page of PetFinder.com

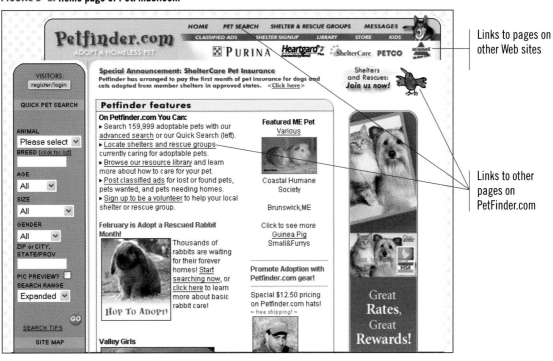

Understanding Hypertext Markup Language (HTML)

The public files on Web servers are ordinary text files that contain text and codes. The text and codes must follow a generally accepted standard so that Web browser software can read these files. As explained in Unit A, the standard used for formatting files viewed on the Web is Hypertext Markup Language (HTML). An **HTML document** is a text file that contains the Web page content and the instructions in HTML tags for formatting that content. A Web page is the result of a browser reading the tags in an HTML document and displaying the content by evaluating the tags. ▓▓▓▓ As you watch a Web-savvy friend use a Web browser to display various Web sites devoted to pet adoption, you are intrigued by how clicking the text on one Web page links to another Web page. You decide to research how text and graphics can be linkable.

DETAILS

The following terms are associated with formatting documents as Web pages:

QUICK TIP

To view the HTML document for a Web page, click View on the menu bar of your Web browser, then click Source or Page Source.

- **Hypertext Markup Language (HTML)**

  HTML uses tags to tell Web browser software how to display text and other elements contained in a document. Every Web page is created using HTML tags. When you view a Web page on the Internet, however, you don't see the HTML tags—you see just the resulting formatted Web page. Here is an example of a line of text that includes HTML tags:

  <b>Welcome to the <i>Danville Animal Shelter</i></b>

  When the Web browser reads this line of HTML, it recognizes the <b> and </b> tags as instructions to display the enclosed text in bold and the <i> and </i> tags as instructions to display the enclosed text in italics. In a Web browser, the line of text would appear as follows:

  Welcome to the *Danville Animal Shelter*

- **HTML Anchor Tag**

  An **HTML anchor tag** links multiple HTML documents together. Of all the HTML tags used to create a Web page, the HTML anchor tag is perhaps the most important because it enables you to easily open other Web pages that are relevant to the one you're viewing.

- **Links**

  When Web page authors use an anchor tag to reference another HTML document, they create a link that points to other Web pages containing related information. As shown in Figure B-3, a Web page can link to other Web pages inside or outside a Web site. Links often appear as underlined text with a color different from the other text on the Web page so that they are easily distinguishable. An image, such as a picture or company logo, can also contain a link to another Web page. Figure B-4 shows a Web page that contains several links. When you move the mouse pointer over a link in a Web browser, the mouse pointer changes to 🖑 and usually the address of the linked Web page appears in the status bar.

FIGURE B-3: Linked Web pages

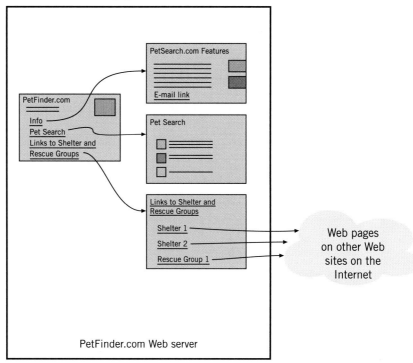

PetFinder.com Web server

FIGURE B-4: Web page with links

Example of text link

Example of image link

Mouse pointer changes to a pointing finger when moved over a link

Understanding Web Site Addresses

The Internet contains many servers answering requests for Web documents from many clients. To facilitate these interactions, each computer, whether client or server, is identified by a unique number called an **Internet Protocol address (IP address)**. Many servers and the individual Web sites on the servers can also be referenced by their **domain name**, which is the equivalent of an IP address that uses words and abbreviations. ▓▓▓▓ You decide to research terms that will help you understand the unique identification associated with each computer and each Web page.

DETAILS

The elements of Web site addresses are described below:

- **IP Addressing**

  An IP address consists of a four-part number. Each part is a number ranging from 0 to 255. For example, one possible IP address is 106.29.242.17.

- **Domain Name Addressing**

  IP addresses can be difficult to remember, so most people use a domain name to identify a Web site. Domain names are identifiers made up of words and abbreviations that are associated with specific IP addresses. For example, the domain name gsb.uchicago.edu is an Internet server at the Graduate School of Business (gsb), which is an academic unit of the University of Chicago (uchicago), which is an educational institution (edu). No other computer on the Internet has the same domain name.

- **Top-Level Domain**

  The last part of a domain name is called its **top-level domain**. In the example gsb.uchicago.edu, the top-level domain is "edu." Internet host computers outside the United States often use two-letter country domain names. Table B-1 shows the original seven top-level domains, some of the more popular country top-level domains, and newer top-level domains that were approved in 2000.

- **Uniform Resource Locators (URLs)**

  IP addresses and domain names identify particular computers on the Internet, but they do not identify where a Web page's HTML document resides on that computer. To find a specific Web page, you need to enter a **Uniform Resource Locator (URL)**, which tells the Web browser the following information:

  - The transfer protocol to use when transporting the file (HTTP is the most common)
  - The domain name of the computer on which the file resides
  - The pathname of the folder or directory on the computer on which the file resides
  - The name of the file

  Figure B-5 shows an example of a URL. This URL is for a pet rescue organization in Great Britain. It uses HTTP as the protocol and points to a computer at the Scottish Council for Voluntary Organisations (scvo), which is a non-profit organization (org) in the United Kingdom (uk). The path name refers to the subfolder in which the files that contain the listings for voluntary organizations is stored. The file name (a.htm) is the file that contains the listings that start with the letter *a*.

FIGURE B-5: Structure of a URL and its Web page in Internet Explorer

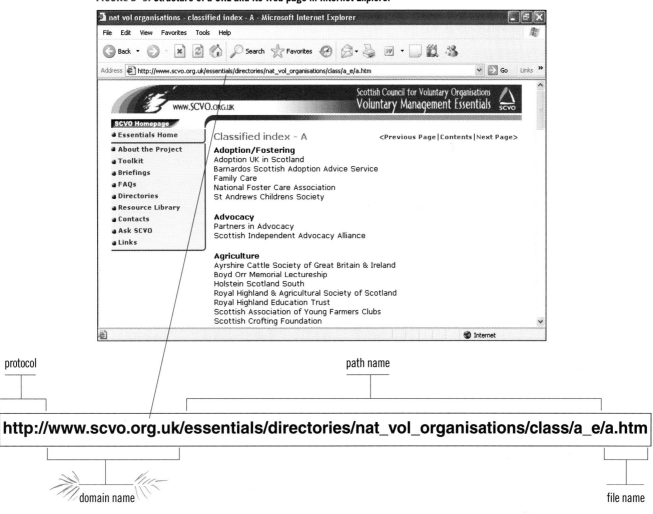

TABLE B-1: Common top-level domains (TLDs)

Original General TLDs		Country TLDs		General TLDs Approved in 2000	
TLD	**Use**	**TLD**	**Country**	**TLD**	**Use**
.com	U.S commerical	**.au**	Australia	**.aero**	Air-transport industry
.edu	U.S. four-year educational institution	**.ca**	Canada	**.biz**	Businesses
.gov	U.S. federal government	**.de**	Germany	**.coop**	Cooperative organizations
.mil	U.S. military	**.fi**	Finland	**.info**	General use
.net	U.S. general use	**.fr**	France	**.museum**	Museums
.org	U.S. not-for-profit organization	**.jp**	Japan	**.name**	Individual persons
.us	U.S. general use	**.se**	Sweden	**.pro**	Professionals (accountants, lawyers, physicians)
		.uk	United Kingdom		

Internet

Starting a Web Browser

You use a Web browser to access the millions of Web pages on the Web. The most popular Web browser is Internet Explorer. Firefox is growing in popularity as people discover it. You want to research Web sites devoted to pet adoptions. You begin by starting a Web browser.

STEPS

Use the browser installed on your computer to complete the steps and exercises in this unit. The steps in the book and in the unit are written for Internet Explorer and Firefox. If you use Netscape, Opera, or iRider, refer to Appendix A.

QUICK TIP
You may need to point to a folder on the All Programs menu before you can click the name of your browser.

1. **To start your Web browser, click** Start **on the taskbar, point to** All Programs, **then click the name of the browser you are using**

2. **If the Web browser window is not maximized, click the** Maximize button **in the browser window**

   Figure B-6 shows the Internet Explorer Web browser window. If you are using Firefox, continue with the next step.

TROUBLE
If you are using Internet Explorer, skip Step 3.

3. **If you are using Firefox, click** File **on the menu bar, click** New Tab, **and then click the** Mozilla Firefox Start Page tab

   Figure B-7 shows the Firefox browser window.

4. **Find the following components in your Web browser window, then read the description of each component:**

   - **Title bar**: Shows the name of the open Web page and the Web browser's name and contains the Minimize, Restore Down/Maximize, and Close buttons.
   - **Menu bar**: Contains the File, Edit, View, and Help menus and other specialized menus that allow you to navigate the Web.
   - **Address bar** or **Location Bar**: Indicates the URL of the current Web page; you can type a new URL in this bar and press [Enter] or click the Go button next to the bar to go to another Web page.
   - **Page tab**: Allows you to switch between multiple Web pages in the same Web browser window. The name of the Web page appears in the page tab. Firefox has page tabs. Currently Internet Explorer does not offer tabbed windows, but some industry observers expect Microsoft to include this feature in that browser in its next version.
   - **Scroll bar**: Allows you to move a Web page up, down, right, and left if the Web page is longer or wider than the window. The scroll bar does not appear if the page completely fits in the window.
   - **Status bar**: Indicates the name of the Web page that is loading, the load status (partial or complete), and important messages such as "Transferring data" or "Downloading images." When you point to a link, its URL appears in the status bar.

5. **Find the following buttons in your Web browser window, then read the description of each button:**

   - **Back button**: Allows you to go back to a previously viewed Web page. If you have just opened your Web browser, the Back button will be dimmed, or inactive.
   - **Refresh button** or **Reload button**: Allows you to load again the Web page that currently appears in your Web browser so that you can view the latest information (such as news headlines).
   - **Home button**: Allows you to return to the home page (or start page) for your Web browser.
   - **Stop button**: Allows you to stop loading the contents of a Web page. In Firefox, the Stop button will be dimmed if you just started the program.

FIGURE B-6: Internet Explorer Web browser window

Title bar —
Menu bar —
Back button —
Stop button —
Refresh button —
Home button —

— Address bar

— Scroll bar

— Status bar

FIGURE B-7: Firefox Web browser window

Title bar —
Menu bar —
Back button —
Reload button —
Stop button —
Home button —

— Location Bar

— Page tabs

V-1P

Clues to Use

Using the History feature

In addition to using the Back and Forward buttons to move to and from previously visited Web pages, most browsers include a History feature. The **History feature** is a list of Web sites you've visited over the past days or weeks, and it can help you locate Web sites you've visited in previous sessions on the Web. To access the History list in Internet Explorer, click the History button on the toolbar. To access the History list in Firefox, click Go on the menu bar, then click History. A window opens to the left of the browser window or in its own window, and the list of Web sites recently visited appears sorted by date. You can click a Web site to see the list of pages visited at that site, or click a Web page to jump to that page.

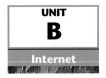

Finding a Web Site

After you start your Web browser, you can begin learning how to use it to find information on the Web. The fastest way to go to a specific Web site on the Web is to enter its URL in the Address bar in Internet Explorer or the Location Bar in Firefox. In your research of Web sites featuring information on pet adoptions, you discovered Midland Pet Adoption Agency. You will examine their home page to learn more about their services.

STEPS

QUICK TIP
You can quickly select a URL by clicking once in the Address and Location bars.

1. **Select the URL in the Address or Location bar in the browser window**

   The selected URL in the Internet Explorer Address bar is shown in Figure B-8, and the selected URL in the Firefox Location Bar is shown in Figure B-9.

2. **Type www.midlandpet.com**

   As soon as you start to type the new URL, the selected URL disappears. Even though a complete URL contains the protocol (such as http), followed by a colon and two slashes, most browsers add this prefix automatically, making it unnecessary to type it.

3. **Press [Enter]**

   The home page of the Midland Pet Adoption Agency **loads**, or appears, in your Web browser window. Figure B-10 shows the Midland Pet Adoption Agency home page.

Clues to Use

Understanding error messages

Sometimes an error message appears in the browser window when you click a link. Common messages are "Server busy," "DNS entry not found," "File not found," and "Page cannot be displayed." These messages indicate that your Web browser cannot communicate with the Web server that stores the Web page you requested or cannot find the Web page because the server is busy, the Web page's location has changed permanently, or the Web page no longer exists on the Web. In Firefox, some of these errors result in a dialog box opening telling you that the connection was refused or the server timed out. Click OK in these dialog boxes to close them.

FIGURE B-8: Selected address in the Internet Explorer Address bar

Address bar

FIGURE B-9: Selected address in the Firefox Location Bar

Location Bar

FIGURE B-10: Midland Pet Adoption Agency home page

Navigating Through a Web Site

You can move from one Web page to a related one by clicking links. Links allow you to browse through a Web site in Paris, France one minute and then look at a Web site in Tokyo, Japan the next minute, simply by clicking links. Most well-designed Web sites have a link to the Web site's home page on each of the other pages in the site. This is different from clicking the Home button on the browser toolbar, which opens the browser's defined start page. ▓▓▓▓ You continue exploring the Midland Pet Adoption Agency Web site by clicking several of the links on the home page.

STEPS

1. Click the Home button on the toolbar

The Home button looks like a house in most browsers. Your browser's home page appears.

2. Select the URL in the Address or Location bar

You will start to type the URL of the Midland Pet Adoption Agency again.

3. Type www.mid

Because you typed this domain name previously, a list box appears below the Address or Location bar before you finish typing. The list box contains all URLs that you previously typed that start with "www.mid." Figure B-11 shows the list box in Internet Explorer and in Firefox. You can click the URL in the list box instead of typing the full URL.

4. Click the URL for Midland Pet Adoption Agency in the list box

The Midland Pet Adoption Agency home page appears again.

QUICK TIP

Note that the pointer does not always change to 🖑 when positioned on a link.

5. Point to the Training Programs link near the top of the window

Notice that your mouse pointer changes to 🖑 and the URL of the link appears in the status bar in the browser window. Figure B-12 shows the pointer on a link in Internet Explorer; Figure B-13 shows the pointer on a link in Firefox.

6. Click the Training Programs link

The Training Programs Web page appears. When a new page appears in the browser window as a result of clicking a link, it is referred to as **jumping** to that page. This Web page contains information about the pet training programs offered by Midland Pet Adoption Agency.

TROUBLE

Be sure to click the Home *link* in the Web page and not the Home button on the toolbar (which will display the start page for your Web browser). If you clicked the Home button, repeat Steps 3 through 6.

7. Click the Home link near the top of the window

You return to the home page for Midland Pet Adoption Agency.

8. Click the Pets link in the last sentence of the paragraph in the middle of the page

The Web page that lists the pets currently available for adoption appears. Next you will use the Back button to go back one page. The Back button looks slightly different in each browser, but it always is an arrow pointing to the left.

9. Click the Back button on the toolbar

The Midland Pet Adoption Agency home page reappears. Next you will use the Forward button to move forward one page. The Forward button is an arrow pointing to the right.

10. Click the Forward button on the toolbar

The page listing available pets reappears.

FIGURE B-11: Choosing a URL from a list box in a browser

List box in
Internet Explorer

List box in Firefox

FIGURE B-12: Pointing to a link in Internet Explorer

Mouse pointer
positioned over link

URL of hyperlink that
the mouse pointer is
pointing to

FIGURE B-13: Pointing to a link in Firefox

Mouse pointer
positioned over link

URL of hyperlink that
the mouse pointer is
pointing to

Creating and Managing Favorites in Internet Explorer

In Internet Explorer, you can create a customized menu containing shortcuts to Web sites you specify. These shortcuts are called **favorites** in Internet Explorer. You use favorites to store and organize the URLs of Web pages that you have visited so you can return to them easily. If you think you won't be visiting the page again, you can delete favorites you've added so that you don't have to weed through a long list searching for the one you want. ░░░░░ You decide to save the home page of Midland Pet Adoption Agency as a favorite so that you can easily find it later.

STEPS

TROUBLE

If you are using Firefox, skip to the next lesson.

1. **Click the** Home link **near the top of the page**
   The home page of the Midland Pet Adoption Agency Web site appears in the browser window.

2. **Click** Favorites **on the menu bar, click** Add to Favorites **to open the Add Favorite dialog box, then, if necessary, click** Create in >> **to expand the dialog box**
   See Figure B-14. It can be helpful to organize favorites in folders.

QUICK TIP

You can change the name of the favorite by selecting the text in the Name text box, then typing the new name.

3. **Click** Favorites **in the Create in list box to select the folder in which the new folder will be stored, then click** New Folder
   The Create New Folder dialog box opens.

4. **Type** Pet Adoption Agencies **in the Folder name text box, then click** OK
   The Create New Folder dialog box closes, and the Pet Adoption Agencies folder appears in the Create in list box in the Add Favorite dialog box.

5. **Click** Pet Adoption Agencies **in the Create in list box to select it, if necessary, then click** OK
   The favorite is saved in the selected folder.

QUICK TIP

You can click the Favorites button on the toolbar to open the Favorites bar on the left side of the browser window to make all the favorites visible at all times.

6. **Click the** Home button **on the toolbar, click** Favorites **on the menu bar, then point to** Pet Adoption Agencies
   The favorite you added—the Midland Pet Adoption Agency home page—appears in the Favorites list. See Figure B-15.

7. **Click** Midland Pet Adoption Agency
   The home page of Midland Pet Adoption Agency appears in the browser window again. Sometimes you will want to delete a favorite.

8. **Click** Favorites **on the menu bar, then click** Organize Favorites
   The Organize Favorites dialog box opens.

QUICK TIP

You can also right-click the item you want to delete on the Favorites menu, then click Delete on the shortcut menu.

9. **Click** Pet Adoption Agencies **in the list on the right, click** Delete, **then, if a dialog box opens asking if you are sure you want to delete the folder, click** Yes
   The Pet Adoption Agencies folder and its contents are deleted.

10. **Click** Close
    The Organize Favorites dialog box closes.

FIGURE B-14: Add Favorite dialog box

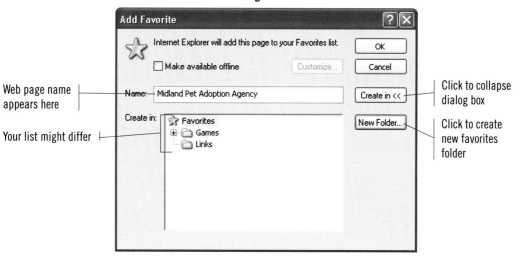

Web page name appears here

Your list might differ

Click to collapse dialog box

Click to create new favorites folder

FIGURE B-15: Selecting a favorite from the Favorites menu

Your list might differ

Folder you created

Added favorite

Clues to Use

Moving a favorite into another folder

To move a favorite into another folder:
- Click Favorites on the menu bar, then click Organize Favorites.
- If necessary, click the folder containing the favorite you want to move, then scroll until the favorite is visible in the list.
- If you want to create a new folder, click Create Folder in the

Organize Favorites dialog box, type the name of the new folder in the list on the right, then press [Enter].
- Drag the favorite that you want to move onto the new folder.
- Click Close.

Creating and Managing Bookmarks in Firefox

In Firefox, you can create a customized menu containing shortcuts to Web sites you specify. These shortcuts are called **bookmarks** in Firefox. You use bookmarks to store and organize the URLs of Web pages that you have visited so you can return to them easily. If you think you won't be visiting the page again, you can delete bookmarks you've added so that you don't have to weed through a long list searching for the one you want. ▰▰▰ You decide to save the home page of Midland Pet Adoption Agency as a bookmark so that you can easily find it later.

STEPS

TROUBLE
If you are using Internet Explorer, skip to the next lesson.

1. **Click the** Home link **near the top of the page**

   The home page of the Midland Pet Adoption Agency Web site appears in the browser window. You decide you want to have both the home page and the Pets page open when you click the bookmark you are about to save.

2. **Click the** (Untitled) tab, **click in the** Location Bar, **type** www.midlandpet.com, **press** [Enter], **then click the** Pets link

   The Pets page opens in the second tab. Note that the page title of the Pets page (in the title bar and in the tab name) is different than the page title of the home page.

   QUICK TIP
   You can change the name of the bookmark by selecting the text in the Name text box, then typing the new name.

3. **Click the** Midland Pet Adoption Agency tab, **click** Bookmarks **on the menu bar, click** Bookmark This Page **to open the Add Bookmark dialog box, then click** ⏷ **to expand the dialog box**

   The Add Bookmark dialog box displays the name of the Web page in the Name text box. See Figure B-16. It can be helpful to organize bookmarks in folders.

4. **Click** Bookmarks **in the Add Bookmark dialog box to select the folder in which the new folder will be stored, click** New Folder **to open the Properties for "New Folder" dialog box, type** Pet Adoption Agencies **in the Name text box, then click** OK

   The Properties for "New Folder" dialog box closes and the Pet Adoption Agencies folder appears in the list in the Add Bookmark dialog box. You want to save both open tabs at once.

5. **Select the** Bookmark all tabs in a folder check box, **click** Pet Adoption Agencies **in the list to select it, if necessary, then click** OK

   Both open tabs are saved as bookmarks in a new folder that has the same name as the first tab.

   QUICK TIP
   You can click View on the menu bar, point to Sidebar, then click Bookmarks to open the Bookmarks sidebar on the left side of the browser window to make all the bookmarks visible at all times.

6. **Click the** Home button **on the toolbar, right-click the** Midland Pet Adoption Agency — Pets tab, **click** Close Tab **on the shortcut menu, then click the** Home button **on the toolbar**

   Now there is only one open tab in the browser window.

7. **Click** Bookmarks **on the menu bar, point to** Pet Adoption Agencies, **then point to** Midland Pet Adoption Agency

   The two pages from Midland Pet Adoption Agency are listed. See Figure B-17.

8. **Click** Open in Tabs

   Both pages in the folder open in tabs in the browser window. Sometimes you will want to delete a bookmark.

   QUICK TIP
   You can also right-click the item you want to delete on the Bookmarks menu, then click Delete on the shortcut menu.

9. **Click** Bookmarks **on the menu bar, then click** Manage Bookmarks **to open the Bookmarks Manager dialog box, click** Pet Adoption Agencies **in the list on the right, then click the** Delete button **on the Bookmarks Manager toolbar**

   The Pet Adoption Agencies folder and its contents are deleted.

10. **Click the** Close button **in the Bookmarks Manager window, right click** Midland Pet Adoption Agency - Pets tab, **then click** Close Tab **on the shortcut menu**

FIGURE B-16: Add Bookmark dialog box in FireFox

Web page name appears here

Click to save all open tabs as bookmarks

Your list might differ

Click to create new bookmarks folder

Click to collapse dialog box

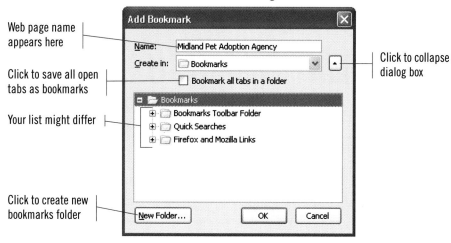

FIGURE B-17: Selecting a bookmark from the Bookmarks menu

Your list might differ

Folder you created

Bookmark folder automatically created because more than one tab was saved

Names of added bookmarks are Web page titles

Click to open all bookmarks in folder

Clues to Use

Moving a bookmark into another folder

To move a bookmark into another folder:

- Click Bookmarks on the menu bar, then click Manage Bookmarks.
- If necessary, click the plus sign next to the folder containing the bookmark you want to move, then scroll until the bookmark is visible in the list.

- If you want to create a new folder, click the New Folder button in the toolbar in the Bookmarks Manager, type the name of the folder in the Name text box in the Properties for "New Folder" dialog box, then click OK.
- Drag the bookmark that you want to move onto the new folder.
- Click the Close button in the title bar of the Bookmarks Manager.

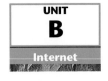
Saving and Opening a Web Page in a Browser

If you travel with a laptop, want to decrease the time you are connected to the Internet, or are concerned that a Web page might change and you want to show it to someone in its current state, you can save the Web page to a disk. Sometimes when you save a Web page and open it later, you find that not all of the images were saved. This happens when the file that contains the image is not actually stored on the Web server that holds the files for the Web site you are viewing. When images on a page are stored on another Web server, the image will not be saved when you save the complete Web page. If you want to save the image that is missing, you can save the image in its own file on a disk. You will learn more about saving images in the lesson titled "Copying Text and Graphics from a Web Page" later in this unit. ▰▰▰ You decide to save the home page of Midland Pet Adoption Agency so Trinity can view it in its current form whenever she wishes.

STEPS

1. **If the home page of Midland Pet Adoption Agency is not open in your browser window, type** www.midlandpet.com **in the Address or Location bar of your browser, then press** [Enter]

2. **Click** File **on the menu bar, then click** Save As **or** Save Page As

   A dialog box similar to the standard Save As dialog box opens. This dialog box is usually titled Save Web Page or Save As.

3. **Click the** Save in list arrow, **navigate to the drive and folder where your Solution Files are stored, select the text in the** File name text box, **then type** MidlandHomePage

   Note in the Save as type text box that the file will be saved as a complete Web page. This means the file will be saved as an HTML file with the graphics and other components that are built into the page.

   > **TROUBLE**
   > If a dialog box titled Downloads or something similar opens, click the Close button in its title bar.

4. **Click** Save

   The Save As dialog box closes and the Web page is saved in its current state. You decide to try opening it to make sure it saved as you expected.

5. **Click the** Home button **on the toolbar**

   The home page for your browser appears in the browser window.

6. **Click** File **on the menu bar, then click** Open **or** Open File

   If you are using Internet Explorer, the Open dialog box appears, as shown in Figure B-18. If you are using most other browsers, including Firefox, the Open File dialog box appears.

   > **TROUBLE**
   > If you are not using Internet Explorer, skip Step 7.

7. **If you are using Internet Explorer, click** Browse **in the Open dialog box**

   A dialog box similar to the standard Open dialog box opens. The Internet Explorer Open dialog box is shown in Figure B-19. The Firefox Open File dialog box is shown in Figure B-20.

8. **If necessary, click the** Look in list arrow **and navigate to the drive and folder where your Solution Files are stored, click** MidlandHomePage, **then click** Open

   If you are using Internet Explorer, the dialog box closes and the path and file name of the file you selected appears in the Open text box in the Open dialog box.

   > **TROUBLE**
   > If you are using Firefox, skip Step 9.

9. **If you are using Internet Explorer, click** OK **in the Open dialog box**

   The Midland Pet Adoption Agency home page appears in the browser window. Notice that the path and file name of the saved Web page appears in the Address or Location bar instead of the URL of the page on the Web.

FIGURE B-18: Internet Explorer Open dialog box

Click to open a dialog box
similiar to the standard
Open dialog box

FIGURE B-19: Internet Explorer dialog box to browse for saved Web page

Select file
to open

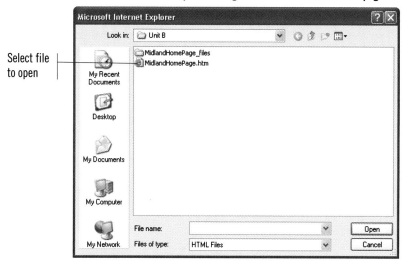

FIGURE B-20: Firefox Open File dialog box

Select file
to open

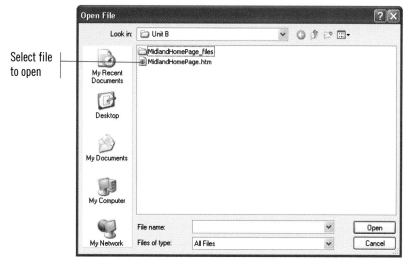

Clues to Use

Single-file Web pages

When you save a Web page as a **complete Web page**, you save the page and all of its individual associated files. These files are automatically stored in a folder with the same name as the file you saved, followed by an underscore and the word "files"; for example, the folder associated with the Web page you saved in this lesson is called "MidlandHomePage_files." In Internet Explorer, you also have the option to save a Web page as a **single-file Web page**, which means that all of the supporting elements, including text, graphics, and links, are stored in a single file.

Internet

Printing a Web Page

You can easily print the contents of a Web page so that you can view the information when you are not at your computer. When you print a Web page, the Web site source and the date on which the Web page was printed also appear. ▰▰▱▱ In addition to the saved version of the Midland Pet Adoption Agency home page, you decide to print a copy of the Web page.

STEPS

1. **Click File on the menu bar, then click Page Setup**

   The Page Setup dialog box opens. This dialog box allows you to set options for paper, headers and footers, page orientation, and margins.

2. **If the Page Setup dialog box on your screen has tabs, click them so you can see the settings on each tab**

3. **After examining the settings available in the Page Setup dialog box, click Cancel**

   You can preview the page to see how it will look when printed.

QUICK TIP
You can print directly from the Print Preview window by clicking Print on the Print Preview toolbar.

4. **Click File on the menu bar, then click Print Preview**

   The Web page appears in the Print Preview window. The Internet Explorer Print Preview window is shown in Figure B-21, and the Firefox Print Preview window is shown in Figure B-22. The current page number and the total number of pages appear on the toolbar, and you can see the headers and footers that will appear on the page.

5. **Scroll down the page to see the footers, then click Close on the Print Preview toolbar**

   Print Preview closes and you are returned to the Web page.

6. **Click File on the menu bar, then click Print**

   The Print dialog box opens. You want to print only one page.

7. **Click the Pages option button, then type 1 in the Pages text box in Internet Explorer or type 1 in both the from and to text boxes in Firefox**

8. **Click Print or OK in the Print dialog box**

   The Print dialog box closes and the Web page prints.

Clues to Use

Making Web pages printer-friendly

Sometimes a Web page is wider than a standard sheet of paper. On some Web pages, most of the space is occupied by Web site navigation elements, with the main page content occupying only a narrow column in the center of the Web page. This can cause part of the Web page to be cut off on the printout, which can result in the use of many sheets of paper for a relatively small amount of information. To make Web page printouts as practical as possible, some Web pages include a **printer-friendly link**, which opens a Web page containing the same information as on the original Web page, but it's formatted like a printed page rather than a Web browser window. You should get in the habit of looking for a printer-friendly link on Web pages you want to print to ensure that you get a practical printout.

FIGURE B-21: Internet Explorer Print Preview window

Print Preview toolbar ⊢

Total number of pages ⊢

Click to close
Print Preview

FIGURE B-22: Firefox Print Preview window

Print Preview toolbar ⊢

Total number of pages ⊢

Click to close
Print Preview

Internet

Copying Text and Graphics from a Web Page

You can save portions of Web page's text to a file, so that you can use the text in other programs. One way to save the text is to copy it into a word processing or text editor document. You can also save images from a Web page to a file. This is useful if you don't need to save the entire Web page or if you want to use the image in another document. 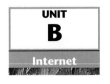 Trinity would like to visit Midland Pet Adoption Agency so that she can meet with the director and learn more about how they developed their Web site. You can copy the agency's address and telephone number from their Web site and paste it into a word processing document such as a WordPad document. You can also save the street map image, which shows the location of the agency, on their Web site to a disk so that you can give it to Trinity.

STEPS

1. **Return to the Midland Pet Adoption Agency home page if it is not already displayed in your browser, then click the Directions & Contact link**
   The page with the address, phone number, and map opens.

2. **Drag the mouse pointer over the address and telephone number to select them**
   See Figure B-23.

3. **Click Edit on the menu bar, and then click Copy**
   The selected text is copied to the Clipboard. You want to paste the text into a WordPad document.

4. **Click the Start button on the taskbar, point to All Programs, point to Accessories, then click WordPad**
   The WordPad program starts with a new document open in the WordPad window.

5. **Click Edit on the menu bar, then click Paste**
   The text you copied from the Web page is pasted into the WordPad document.

6. **Click File on the menu bar, click Save As to open the Save As dialog box, click the Save in list arrow and navigate to the drive and folder where your Solution Files are stored, select the text in the File name text box, type MidlandAddressPhone, then click Save**
   The WordPad file is saved. Now you need to save the map image to disk.

7. **Click the Close button on the WordPad title bar to exit WordPad and switch back to your browser window, then right-click the map image to open a shortcut menu**
   The image shortcut menu in Internet Explorer is shown in Figure B-24. The image shortcut menu in Firefox is shown in Figure B-25.

8. **Click Save Picture As or Save Image As on the shortcut menu**
   The Save Picture or Save Image dialog box opens.

9. **Click the Save in list arrow, navigate to the drive and folder where your Solution Files are stored, select the text in the File name text box, type MidlandMap, and then click Save**
   The image is saved in a file.

10. **Click the Close button in the browser window title bar**
    Your Web browser closes.

QUICK TIP
If you are using Internet Explorer, you can simply point to the image you want to save so that a shortcut toolbar appears in the upper-left corner of the image, then click the Save button on the shortcut toolbar to open the Save Picture dialog box.

FIGURE B-23: Selecting text on a Web page

Selected text —

FIGURE B-24: Saving the map image to a disk in Internet Explorer

Click Save button on shortcut toolbar to save image

Shortcut menu

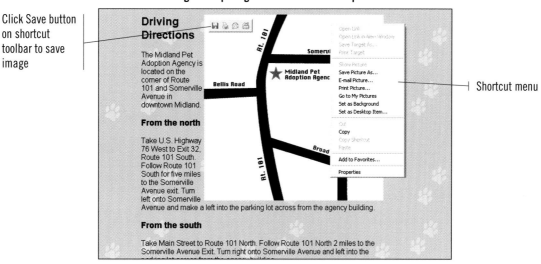

FIGURE B-25: Saving the map image to a disk in Firefox

Shortcut menu

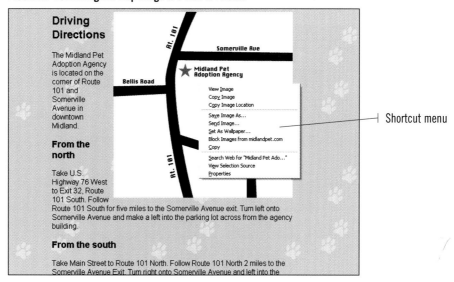

Internet

Practice

▼ CONCEPTS REVIEW

If you are using Internet Explorer, identify each element of the Internet Explorer window shown in Figure B-26. If you are using Firefox, identify each element of the Firefox window shown in Figure B-27.

FIGURE B-26

FIGURE B-27

Match each term with the statement that best describes it.

11. **Web browser**
12. **Anchor tag**
13. **Web site**
14. **Start page**
15. **URL**
16. **Domain name**

a. The first Web page that opens when a Web browser starts
b. The software that runs a computer to make it work as a Web client
c. The four-part addressing scheme that identifies the location of a Web page
d. The equivalent of an IP address
e. A collection of linked Web pages that has a common theme or focus
f. A tag that links multiple HTML documents together

Select the best answer from the list of choices.

17. **Web page authors link HTML documents using:**
    a. HTML anchor tags.
    b. Internet Explorer.
    c. Netscape.
    d. encryption.

18. **The numerical address that identifies each computer on the Internet is called the:**
    a. domain name address.
    b. hierarchical address.
    c. IP address.
    d. URL.

19. **The unique identifier composed of words or abbreviations that you can use to reference a server or Web site on a server is called the:**
    a. IP address.
    b. domain name.
    c. Web client.
    d. top-level domain.

20. **Which of the following is not a common top-level domain name?**
    a. com
    b. coop
    c. ca
    d. int

21. **If you want to view a Web page when you are not connected to the Internet, you can:**
    a. save the page as a favorite or bookmark.
    b. save the page to a disk.
    c. create a favorite or bookmark folder.
    d. use the Back button.

▼ SKILLS REVIEW

1. Start a Web browser.
   a. Start your Web browser.
   b. Wait for the home page to load.
   c. Follow links on the home page to two or three Web sites that interest you. (*Note*: If there are no links on your home page, go to *www.course.com* and follow links on that page.)
   d. Make a list of the Web sites you visited. Include the URL of each Web site and provide a brief description of each Web site.
   e. Close the Web browser.

2. Find a Web site.
   a. Start your Web browser.
   b. Wait for the home page to load.
   c. Type the URL for Course Technology www.course.com, then press the Enter key.
   d. On the Course Technology Web site, move the mouse pointer around the Web page to identify links.
   e. Consider these questions: How are the links identified on the Web page? Are there any links that surprised you because they didn't look like links until you placed the mouse pointer over them?
   f. Follow one link.
   g. Consider these questions: What link did you follow? How did you identify the link on the Web page? Did the linked content relate to the link you followed?

3. Navigate through a Web site.
   a. Go to www.course.com/illustrated/internet4, click the Unit B link, then click the American Kennel Club link under Skills Review 3.
   b. Follow links to the page about breeds. (*Note*: The pointer may not change to indicate a link in Firefox.)
   c. Click the Home button to go to your browser's home page.
   d. Click the Back button to go back to the breed page on the American Kennel Club Web site, then click the Back button again to go back to the home page on the American Kennel Club Web site.
   e. Click the Forward button to go forward to the breed page on the American Kennel Club Web site.

4. Create and manage favorites or bookmarks.
   a. Go to www.course.com/illustrated/internet4, click the Unit B link, then click the New York Times link under Skills Review 4. (*Note*: If you are using Internet Explorer and a dialog box opens explaining the Information bar alert at the top of the window, click OK.)
   b. Create a favorites or bookmarks folder called Newspapers.
   c. Add the New York Times Web site to the Newspapers folder in your list of favorites or bookmarks.
   d. If you are using a browser that offers page tabs, open a new tab.
   e. Go to www.course.com/illustrated/internet4, click the Unit B link, then click the Boston Globe link under Skills Review 4.
   f. If you are using a browser that does not offer page tabs, add the Boston Globe home page to your list of favorites or bookmarks.
   g. If you are using a browser that offers page tabs, add the two open Web pages (the New York Times home page and the Boston Globe home page) to your list of bookmarks in an automatically created folder.
   h. Go back to your Web browser's home page.
   i. Test the favorites or bookmarks you created to make sure they open to the correct Web pages.
   j. Delete the Favorites or Bookmarks Newspapers folder, then delete the other favorites or bookmarks you created.

5. **Save and open a Web page in a browser.**

   a. Go to www.course.com/illustrated/internet4, click the Unit B link, then click the American Kennel Club Breed Rescue link under Skills Review 5.

   b. Save the Breed Rescue Web page as BreedRescue to the drive and folder where your Solution Files are stored.

   c. Display your Web browser's home page.

   d. Open the BreedRescue Web page file you saved.

6. **Print a Web page.**

   a. Make sure the BreedRescue Web page is still open in your browser.

   b. View the page in Print Preview.

   c. Set the print options to print only one page.

   d. Print one page.

7. **Copy text and graphics from a Web page.**

   a. Go to www.midlandpet.com, click the Pets link, then click the Meet Maxie link.

   b. Copy the paragraph describing Maxie to a WordPad document.

   c. Save the document as MaxieDescription to the drive and folder where your Solution Files are stored.

   d. Exit WordPad.

   e. Save the picture of the cat as MaxiePicture to the drive and folder where your Solution Files are stored.

   f. Close your Web browser.

▼ INDEPENDENT CHALLENGE 1

As part of your research for the Danville Animal Shelter, you want to explore Web sites of pet rescue agencies.

   a. Start your Web browser. Go to www.course.com/illustrated/internet4, click the Unit B link, then click the link under Independent Challenge 1. Use this link as a starting point for your search.

   b. Find four pet adoption agencies in your state or neighboring states.

   c. Create a favorites or bookmark folder called Pet Rescue Agencies.

   d. Store the URLs of the four Web sites you have chosen in the Pet Rescue Agencies folder.

   e. Test each favorite or bookmark you stored.

   f. Save the home page of one of the Web sites you saved as a favorite or bookmark to the drive and folder where your solution files are stored as PetRescuePage.

   g. Print one page of the home page of another one of the sites you saved as a favorite or bookmark.

   h. Delete the Pet Rescue Agencies favorites or bookmark folder and its contents, then close your Web browser.

▼ INDEPENDENT CHALLENGE 2

You work for a small business and are learning about the Web as part of your job training. You are intrigued by the concept of "easy domain names" and think that your business would benefit from having such a domain name for its Web presence. You decide to see how many well-known organizations that you're familiar with use such domains.

a. Make a list of at least five large organizations that you would expect to have Web sites. Then list two possible easy domain names for each. For example, you might expect United Airlines to have a Web site at united.com or ual.com.

b. Start your Web browser. Enter each of your guesses in your Web browser's Address bar or Location Bar.

c. Record the correct domain name for each organization, or write "not found" if both of your guesses were unsuccessful.

d. Identify a subject in which you are interested, and then try entering an easy domain name that might lead to a Web site connected with your interests. For example, if you are interested in skiing, see whether a Web site exists at www.skiing.com. If you are interested in Beethoven, check out www.beethoven.com. You will know the domain name is invalid if your Web browser requires more than 10 or 20 seconds to find the Web site. If the Web browser takes too long, just click the Stop button and try another domain name. You might find all kinds of intriguing Web sites related to your interests just by entering a descriptive domain name.

e. Record the names of at least three subject-based domain names that produced the resources you were seeking.

f. Close your Web browser.

▼ INDEPENDENT CHALLENGE 3

Business Web sites range from simple informational Web sites to comprehensive Web sites that offer information about the firm's products or services, history, current employment openings, and financial information. An increasing number of businesses offer products or services for sale via their Web sites. You have just landed a position on the public relations staff of Value City Central, a large chain of television and appliance stores. Your first assignment is to research and report on the types of information that similar large firms offer on their Web sites.

a. Start your Web browser. Go to www.course.com/illustrated/internet4, click the Unit B link, then examine the links for Independent Challenge 3. There you will find a list of appliance retailers.

b. Choose two of the business Web sites listed that you believe would be most relevant to your assignment.

c. Add each Web site to your list of favorites or bookmarks.

Advanced Challenge Exercise

- Examine the properties for one of the bookmarks in the Organize Favorites dialog box or the Bookmarks Manager.
- Rename one of the favorites or bookmarks you created.
- Create a folder named Appliances in the Favorites or Bookmarks, then move the favorites or bookmarks you created into this folder.

d. Copy a picture of an appliance from one of the Web sites you chose and save it as Appliance Image to the drive and folder where your Solution Files are stored.

e. Spend about 10 minutes exploring each of the two Web sites you have chosen, then write a paragraph comparing the two Web sites in terms of the overall presentation of the corporate image (is it clear? easy to understand? effective? attractive?) and the description of products or services offered (are the descriptions easy to follow? engaging? non-threatening?). In your comparison, indicate which of the two Web sites you believe projects its image most effectively. Which of the two Web sites would encourage you to purchase the company's products? Why?

f. Delete the favorites or bookmarks you created, then close your Web browser.

▼ INDEPENDENT CHALLENGE 4

The Columbus Suburban Area Council is a charitable organization devoted to maintaining and improving the general welfare of people living in Columbus-area suburbs. As the director of the council, you are interested in encouraging donations and other support from area citizens and want to stay informed of grant opportunities that might benefit the council. You are especially interested in developing an informative and attractive presence on the Web.

    a. Start your Web browser. Go to **www.course.com/illustrated/internet4**, click the **Unit B link**, then examine the links for Independent Challenge 4. There you will find a list of charitable organizations.

    b. Follow the links to charitable organizations to find out more about what other organizations are doing with their Web sites.

    c. Add each Web page to a favorites or bookmark folder named **Charities**. For each Web site, record a list of its contents. Note if each Web site includes financial information and if the Web site discloses how much the organization spent on administrative or non-program activities.

Advanced Challenge Exercise

    ■ Use the History feature to select two of the Web sites you visited.

    ■ Change the sort order of the items in the History so they are sorted by site or location.

    ■ Delete one of the pages you visited today from the History list.

    d. Identify which Web site you believe would be a good model for the council's new Web site. Explain why the Web site you chose would be the best example to follow.

    e. Delete the Charities favorites or bookmark folder and its contents, then close your Web browser.

Many organizations update their Web sites on a daily basis. In this Visual Workshop, you will analyze the changes made to a Web site for a popular magazine. Go to the Student Online Companion at www.course.com/illustrated/internet4, then click the Sony Music link under Visual Workshop to go to the Sony Music Web site. Find four differences between the Sony Music home page on your screen and the Sony Music home page shown in Figure B-28. Make a list of these differences.

FIGURE B-28

Using E-Mail

OBJECTIVES

Understand e-mail
Start Outlook Express and explore the mail window
Connect to your Hotmail account and explore the mail window
Send an e-mail message
Check incoming e-mail
Attach a file to an e-mail message
Save an e-mail attachment in Outlook Express
Save an e-mail attachment in Hotmail
Reply to an e-mail message
Forward an e-mail message
Organize e-mail messages
Delete e-mail messages
Maintain an Address Book in Outlook Express
Maintain a Contacts list in Hotmail
Create a group in Outlook Express
Create a group in Hotmail

Several programs for managing e-mail are currently available. You can use any of these programs to send e-mail to people who use the same or different e-mail programs. The recipients can read your e-mail just as you can read the e-mail you receive from other people, regardless of the e-mail programs they use. ▓▓▓ Kikukawa Air is an air charter service based in Maui, Hawaii, which offers service to all of the Hawaiian Islands. Sharon Kikukawa, one of the owners, wants to use e-mail as the company's primary means of communication to save on long distance phone bills. She asked you to find out more about e-mail.

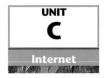

Understanding E-Mail

E-mail is one of the most prevalent forms of business communication and the most popular way individuals use the Internet. In fact, many people view the Internet as simply an electronic highway that transports e-mail messages, without realizing that the Internet provides a wide variety of other services. Whether for business or recreational use, people rely on e-mail as an indispensable way of sending messages and data to one another. You begin your research by learning some basic e-mail concepts.

DETAILS

The following are some basic e-mail concepts:

- **E-Mail Programs**

  You can send and receive e-mail messages in two ways:

  - **Mail client software** is a program that lets you send and receive e-mail and store e-mail on your computer. An advantage of being able to store e-mail on your computer is that you can read e-mail that you've received even after disconnecting from the Internet. Popular e-mail client programs are Outlook Express and Eudora; and a new e-mail client program, Thunderbird, is growing in popularity. Figure C-1 shows the opening screen in the Outlook Express program window.

  - A **Web-based e-mail service** (often called **Webmail**) allows you to send and receive e-mail by using a Web browser and the service's Web site. This service lets you read your stored e-mail messages from different computers (for example, at home, work, or school). However, you can only access your stored e-mail messages when you're connected to the Internet. Most Webmail is free, but you can upgrade to a paid version for more options. Many Webmail services cancel your account if you don't use it for a specified amount of time. Popular Web-based e-mail services include Microsoft's Hotmail, Yahoo! Mail, and Google's Gmail. Figure C-2 shows the Hotmail window.

- **E-Mail Addresses**

  E-mail addresses uniquely identify an individual or organization that is connected to the Internet. An e-mail address includes the **user name** (the name your ISP uses to identify you), the at sign (@), and the **host name** (the computer that stores the e-mail). For example, the e-mail address of a Kikukawa Air employee named Chris Breed might be chrisbreed@kikukawaair.com, where "chrisbreed" is the user name and "kikukawaair.com" is the host name.

- **Mail Server**

  Like other Internet data, e-mail travels across the Internet in small data packets, which are reassembled at the destination and delivered to the addressee. When you send an e-mail message to a particular addressee, the message is sent to a **mail server**, which is a server that runs special software for handling e-mail tasks. Based on the recipient's e-mail address, the mail server determines which of several electronic routes it will use to send your message. When you send an e-mail message, the message is routed from one computer to another and passes through several mail servers until it reaches the recipient. Each mail server determines the next route for your message until it finally arrives at the recipient's electronic mailbox.

- **Message Header**

  The **message header** in an e-mail contains all the information about the message—the recipient's e-mail address (To), the sender's e-mail address (From), and a subject line (Subject), which indicates the topic of the message. In addition, the message header can list other people who have received copies of the message and sometimes, the file name of an **attachment** (a separate file sent with an e-mail message).

- **Message Body**

  The **message body** contains the actual message. It appears in the **message body pane** in a message window. Figure C-3 shows a sample e-mail message in Outlook Express.

- **Junk E-Mail**

  Junk e-mails, also called **spam**, are unsolicited e-mails usually selling an item or service. Some e-mail programs include a **Junk E-Mail** or **Spam folder** to which messages that the program thinks might be junk e-mails are automatically filed when they are copied from the server. Other e-mail programs allow you to block mail from specific people or domains, or with certain words in the subject. Some Webmail services and ISPs block suspected junk e-mail before it ever reaches your Inbox.

FIGURE C-1: Starting screen for Outlook Express

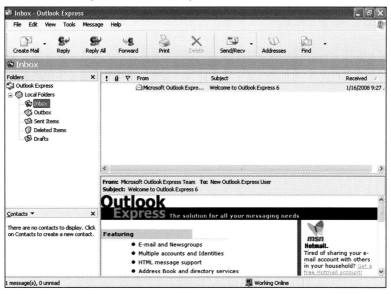

FIGURE C-2: Hotmail window

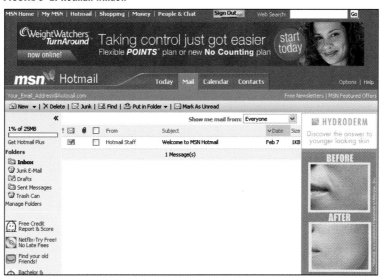

FIGURE C-3: Sample e-mail message in an Outlook Express message window

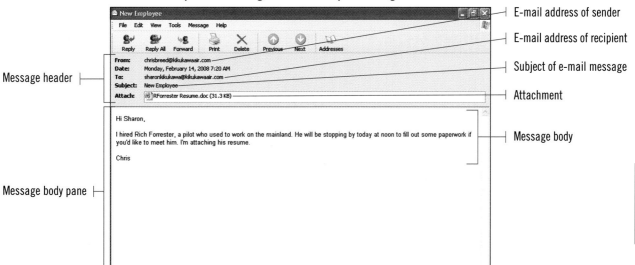

Message header

Message body pane

E-mail address of sender

E-mail address of recipient

Subject of e-mail message

Attachment

Message body

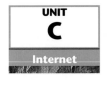

Starting Outlook Express and Exploring the Mail Window

Before you can send e-mail you need to start your e-mail program. The **mail window** is the interface in an e-mail program that allows you to compose, send, receive, and manage your e-mails. You decide to get started with e-mail.

STEPS

 Use the e-mail program installed on your computer to complete the steps and exercises in this unit. The steps in the book and in the unit are written for Outlook Express and Hotmail. If you use Netscape Mail, Eudora, Thunderbird, or Gmail, refer to Appendix A.

TROUBLE
If you are using Hotmail, skip to the next lesson.

1. **Click** Start **on the menu bar, point to** All Programs, **then click** Outlook Express
   Outlook Express starts.

TROUBLE
If you are prompted for log on information, see your instructor or technical support person for help.

2. **If a dialog box opens telling you that Outlook Express is not your default e-mail program, decide if you want it to be the default e-mail program, then click** Yes **or** No

3. **Click the** plus sign **next to Local Folders in the pane on the left, if necessary, then click** Inbox **in the list**
   If you click the plus sign next to a drive or folder, all folders within that folder are listed. If you click the minus sign next to a drive or folder, the folder list for that folder collapses. See Figure C-4.

TROUBLE
Because you can customize the Outlook Express mail window by resizing, hiding, and displaying different panes and their individual elements, your screen might look different from Figure C-4.

4. **Examine Figure C-4 to locate the following elements of the Outlook Express mail window:**
   - **Toolbar**, which contains buttons for creating, sending, and organizing e-mail messages.
   - **Folders list**, which consists of the following default folders:
     - **Inbox folder**, which stores messages that you have received.
     - **Outbox folder**, which stores messages waiting to be sent.
     - **Sent Items folder**, which contains copies of messages you sent.
     - **Deleted Items folder**, which stores messages you delete until you permanently delete them.
     - **Drafts folder**, which contains saved messages that you are not yet ready to send.
   - **Message list**, which displays the message header summaries of the messages stored in the selected folder.
   - **Contacts pane**, which lists the names of the people stored in the Address Book. The **Address Book** stores people's names and e-mail addresses, as well as other information, such as the person's postal address and telephone number.
   - **Preview pane**, which displays the contents of the selected message in the message list.

FIGURE C-4: Outlook Express mail window

Toolbar

Expanded Folders list (you might have additional folders in your list)

Contacts pane (your list might contain names)

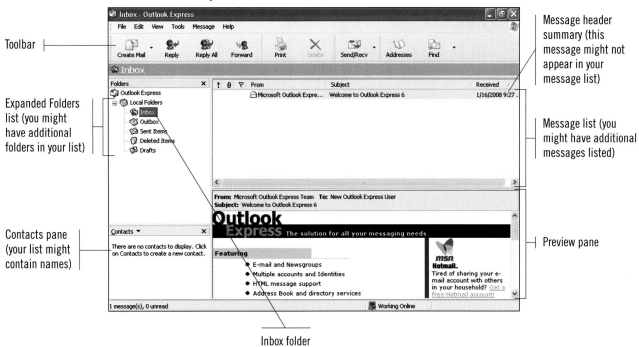

Message header summary (this message might not appear in your message list)

Message list (you might have additional messages listed)

Preview pane

Inbox folder

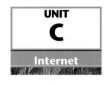

UNIT C
Internet

Connecting to Your Hotmail Account and Exploring the Mail Window

Before you can send e-mail you need to connect to your Webmail account. The **mail window** is the interface in a Webmail program that allows you to compose, send, receive, and manage your e-mails. You decide to get started with e-mail.

STEPS

Use the e-mail program installed on your computer to complete the steps and exercises in this unit. The steps in the book and in the unit are written for Outlook Express and Hotmail. If you use Netscape Mail, Eudora, Thunderbird, or GMail, refer to Appendix A.

> **TROUBLE**
> If you are using Outlook Express, skip to the next lesson.

1. **Start your browser, click in the Address or Location bar, type www.hotmail.com, then press [Enter]**
   The sign-in page for Hotmail appears.

2. **Type the e-mail address you used when you registered with Hotmail in the E-mail Address text box, press [Tab], type your password, then click Sign In**
   Your Today page in your MSN Hotmail account appears. See Figure C-5.

3. **Click the Mail tab**
   The mail window appears. See Figure C-6.

4. **Examine Figure C-6 to locate the following elements of the Hotmail mail window:**
   - **Page Tabs**, which provide access to different parts of the Hotmail service organized in the following four pages:
     - **Today page**, which appears when you first log into your Hotmail account. It displays the total number of messages in your mailbox and the percentage of your storage space on the Hotmail server that you have used.
     - **Mail page**, which contains the mail window as described above.
     - **Calendar page**, which provides you with an electronic calendar. You can use this to track appointments and to-do lists, and to write notes to yourself. You can also allow anyone with Internet access to view your calendar.
     - **Contacts page**, which lists the names of the people stored in the Contacts list. The **Contacts list** stores people's names and e-mail addresses, as well as other information, such as the person's postal address and telephone number.
   - **Toolbar**, which contains buttons for creating, sending, and organizing e-mail messages.
   - **Folders list**, which consists of the following default folders:
     - **Inbox folder**, which stores messages that you have received.
     - **Junk E-Mail folder**, to which possible junk e-mails are automatically sent when they arrive in the Inbox.
     - **Drafts folder**, which contains saved messages that you are not yet ready to send.
     - **Sent Messages folder**, which can be configured to contain copies of messages you sent.
     - **Trash Can folder**, which stores messages you delete until you permanently delete them.
   - **Message list**, which displays the message header summaries of the messages stored in the selected folder.

FIGURE C-5: Today page in Hotmail

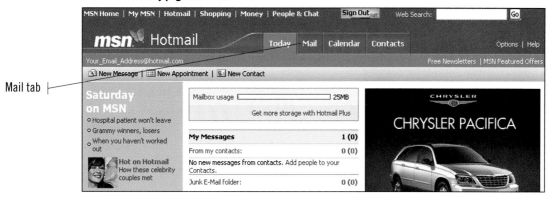

Mail tab

FIGURE C-6: Hotmail mail window

Page tabs

Toolbar

Message list (you might have additional messages listed)

Folders list (you might have additional folders in your list)

Message header summary (this message might not appear in your message list)

Inbox folder

UNIT C

Internet

Sending an E-Mail Message

After your e-mail account is set up, you can send e-mail messages. E-mail programs include fields for entering an e-mail address for each recipient. You enter the recipient's e-mail address in the **To** text box. You can use the **Cc** (carbon copy) text box to send a copy of the message to recipients. You can also use the **Bcc** (Blind carbon copy) text box to send a copy to recipients without the knowledge of the other addressee(s). You can enter multiple e-mail addresses in each of these text boxes. The **From** text box may not appear in the message window; your name, your e-mail address, or both are automatically entered in this box. The **Subject** text box is where you summarize the main topic of an e-mail message. You then enter the message content in the message body pane. When you click the Send button, the message is transferred to your mail server for delivery to the e-mail recipient(s). You decide to use e-mail to send a message to Sharon. You will also send a copy of the message to your own e-mail address so that you can verify that the message is sent correctly.

STEPS

1. **If you are using Outlook Express, click the Create Mail button on the toolbar; if you are using Hotmail, click the New button on the toolbar at the top of the mail window**
   The New Message window opens with the insertion point in the To text box.

TROUBLE
If you are using Hotmail, skip Step 2.

2. **If you are using Outlook Express, click the Maximize button in the New Message window title bar, if necessary**

QUICK TIP
Messages sent to this e-mail address are deleted without being opened or read, so do not send important messages to this address.

3. **Type sharonkikukawa@yahoo.com in the To text box**
4. **Press [Tab] to move the insertion point to the Cc text box, then type your e-mail address**
5. **Click in the Subject text box, then type Practice**
   The information in the Subject text box appears in the message header summary in the recipient's Inbox. In most e-mail programs, it also becomes part of the title of the message window in the window's title bar.

QUICK TIP
If you are using Outlook Express and want to use the Bcc option, click View on the menu bar, then click All Headers to make the Bcc text box appear.

6. **Click in the message body pane, type Sharon, press [Enter] twice, type I'm testing e-mail. Please let me know that this message arrived., press [Enter] twice, type Thanks, press [Enter] twice, then type your name**
   If you are using Outlook Express, your screen should look similar to Figure C-7; if you are using Hotmail, your screen should look similar to Figure C-8.
7. **Click the Send button on the toolbar in the message window**
8. **If a dialog box opens asking you to enter your password, type your password, then click OK**
   The message window closes, and the message is sent to the mail server for delivery to Sharon and to you. In Outlook Express, the message is also copied to the Sent Items folder. If you are using Outlook Express, the mail window appears. If you are using Hotmail, a window appears with the notification that your message has been sent.

TROUBLE
If you are using Outlook Express, skip Step 9.

9. **If you are using Hotmail, click the Return to Inbox link**
   The Hotmail mail window appears.

Clues to Use

Correcting your e-mail message content

If you notice a typing error before sending an e-mail message, you can select the error with your mouse pointer and then make the required correction. You can move the insertion point between the text boxes by pressing [Tab] to move forward or [Shift][Tab] to move backward, or by clicking in the desired text boxes. To check the spelling of your e-mail message, click the Spelling button on the toolbar in Outlook Express; or click Tools on the toolbar in Hotmail, then click Spell Check.

FIGURE C-7: Completed message window in Outlook Express

Text entered in Subject text box also appears in title bar

Send button

Bcc text box does not appear by default

Sharon's e-mail address

Your e-mail address will appear here

Subject

Message body pane

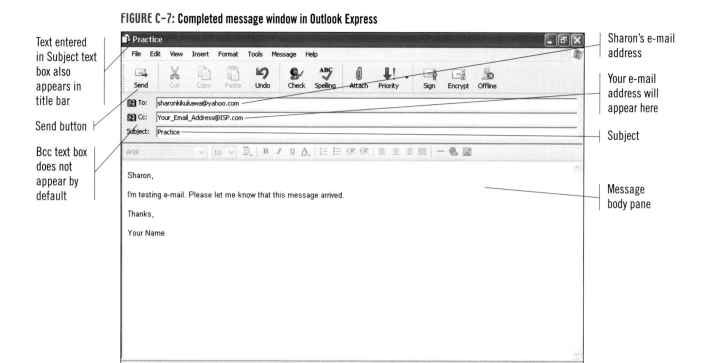

FIGURE C-8: Completed message window in Hotmail

Send button

Sharon's e-mail address

Your e-mail address will appear here

Subject

Message body pane

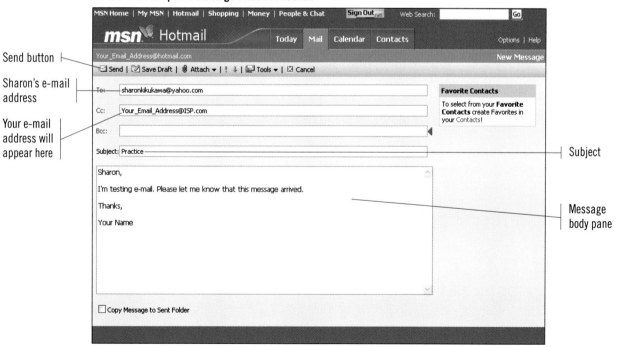

Internet

Checking Incoming E-Mail

E-mail messages sent to you are held on the mail server until you use your e-mail program to retrieve them. You receive incoming e-mail messages in your Inbox folder (also called the Inbox). When the Inbox contains unread messages, the word "Inbox" and the number of unread messages appear in bold in the folders list. A closed envelope icon appears next to the message header summary for an unread message, and the message header summary appears in bold. An open envelope icon appears next to the message header summary for each message you have read, and the message header summary is not bold.  When you sent the message to Sharon, you copied the message to yourself by typing your e-mail address in the Cc text box. You check your e-mail to see if you received the copy of the message you sent to Sharon.

STEPS

1. **View the list of messages in your Inbox**

   If you are using Outlook Express and you have set your options to check for new messages periodically, the Practice message might already appear in your Inbox. If you are using Hotmail, the Practice message appears in the list.

   TROUBLE
   If you are using Hotmail, skip Step 2.

2. **If you are using Outlook Express and if the message is not in your Inbox, click the Send/Recv button on the toolbar**

3. **If a dialog box opens asking for your password, type your password, then click OK**

   Within a few moments, your mail server transfers all new e-mail to your Inbox. The message that you copied to yourself when you e-mailed the message to Sharon appears in the message list. See Figure C-9.

   TROUBLE
   If you do not see the Practice message in your Inbox, you might be looking in the wrong folder. Be sure "Inbox" is selected in the Folders list. If you still don't see the Practice message in the message list, wait a few minutes, then repeat Steps 2 and 3.

4. **If you are using Outlook Express, double-click Practice in the message list; if you are using Hotmail, position the pointer over the sender's name (your name) in the message list so that the pointer changes to 🖑, then click the sender's name**

   The Practice message opens in a message window. If you are using Outlook Express, see Figure C-10; if you are using Hotmail, see Figure C-11.

5. **If you are using Outlook Express, click the Close button in the Practice message window title bar; if you are using Hotmail, click the Inbox link in the upper or lower-right corner of the message window**

   The message window closes and the mail window appears with the Inbox selected. If you are using Outlook Express, note that the contents of the selected message appears in the Preview pane.

Clues to Use

Saving drafts and copies of sent messages

If you write an e-mail message but you aren't ready to send it yet, you can file it in the Drafts folder. To save a draft in Outlook Express, click File on the menu bar in the New Message window, and then click Save. If a dialog box opens telling you that a copy of the message was saved in the Drafts folder, then click OK. To save a draft in Hotmail, click the Save Draft button on the toolbar in the New Message window. You can save copies of Sent messages as well. In Outlook Express, the default is to save a copy of the message in the Sent folder. To verify this, click Tools on the menu bar in the Mail window, click Options, click the Send tab, then verify that the Save copy of sent messages in the 'Sent Items' folder check box is selected. In Hotmail, you need to choose whether to save a copy of each message in the Sent Messages folder. In the New Message window, select the Copy Message to Sent Folder check box before you send the message. Note that Hotmail automatically deletes messages in the Sent Messages folder that are older than 30 days.

FIGURE C-9: Outlook Express and Hotmail mail windows containing new message

Closed envelope and bold message header summary indicate an unread message in Outlook Express

Send/Recv button in Outlook Express

Sender's name

Indicates number of unread messages (yours might differ)

Closed envelope and yellow background indicate an unread message in Hotmail

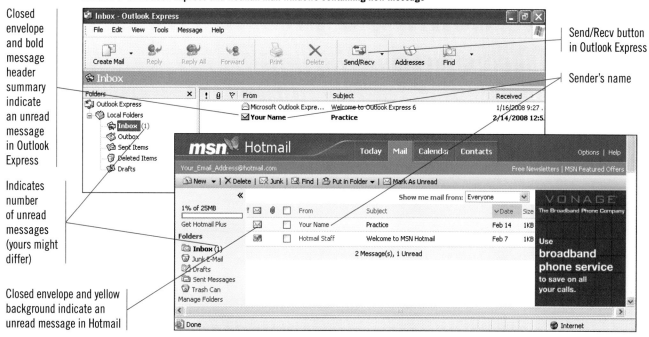

FIGURE C-10: Outlook Express message window

E-mail address of sender (your name will appear here)

Your name might appear here instead of your e-mail address

Close button

E-mail address of recipient

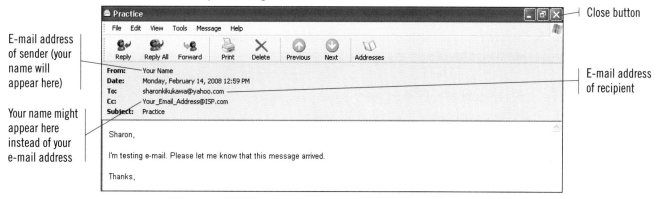

FIGURE C-11: Hotmail message window

Your name and e-mail address appear here

Your name might appear here instead of your e-mail address

Inbox link

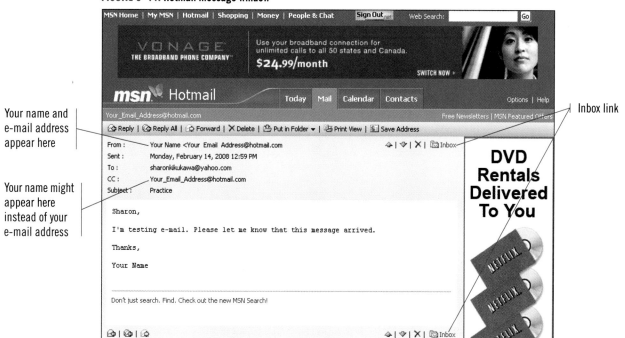

Attaching a File to an E-Mail Message

You might want to send an e-mail message that includes a file, such as a document created in a word-processing program or a spreadsheet program, or a picture. You can send any type of file over the Internet by attaching it to an e-mail message. A file linked to an e-mail message is called an attachment. 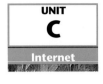 Because e-mailing attachments between employees of Kikukawa Air would be useful for sharing information, such as maintenance schedules, you decide to explore how the attachment feature works by attaching a memo reminding pilots to get their annual physicals.

STEPS

1. **Open a New Message window**

2. **Type your e-mail address in the To text box**

3. **Click in the Subject text box, then type Annual physical reminder**

4. **Press [Tab], then type Please see the file attached to this message. in the message body pane**

> **QUICK TIP**
> Most Webmail services and ISPs restrict the size of file attachments.

5. **Press [Enter] twice, then type your name**

6. **Click the Attach button on the toolbar in the message window, then, if you are using Hotmail, click File on the menu that opens**

   If you are using Outlook Express, the Insert Attachment dialog box opens. If you are using Hotmail, the Attach File window appears.

> **TROUBLE**
> If you are using Outlook Express, skip to Step 8.

7. **If you are using Hotmail, click Browse**

   The Choose File or the File Upload dialog box appears.

> **TROUBLE**
> If you don't see the file name extension rtf, Windows probably is set up to hide extensions on your computer.

8. **Click the Look in list arrow, navigate to the drive and folder where your Data Files are stored, then double-click the file Physicals.rtf**

   If you are using Outlook Express, the message window appears with the file Physicals.rtf listed as attached to the message. See Figure C-12. If you are using Hotmail, the path and file name appears in the Find File text box in the Attach File window. See Figure C-13.

9. **If you are using Hotmail, click the OK button on the toolbar in the Attach File window**

   The Hotmail New Message window appears with the file Physicals.rtf listed as attached to the message. See Figure C-14.

> **TROUBLE**
> If you are using Outlook Express, skip Step 9.

10. **Click the Send button on the toolbar in the message window, then, if you are using Hotmail, click the Return to Inbox link**

    The message window closes and the message is sent to the mail server for delivery. The mail window appears.

FIGURE C-12: Outlook Express e-mail message with attachment

Filename of attached file

Attach button

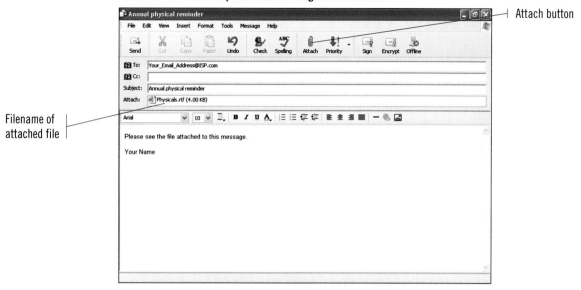

FIGURE C-13: Attach File window in Hotmail

OK button

Path and file name of file to attach (your path might differ)

Name of window

Click to browse for file

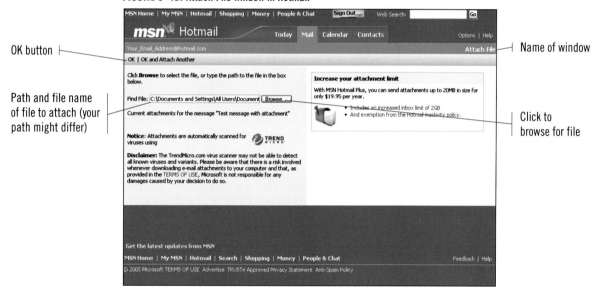

FIGURE C-14: Hotmail e-mail message with attachment

File name of attached file

Attach button

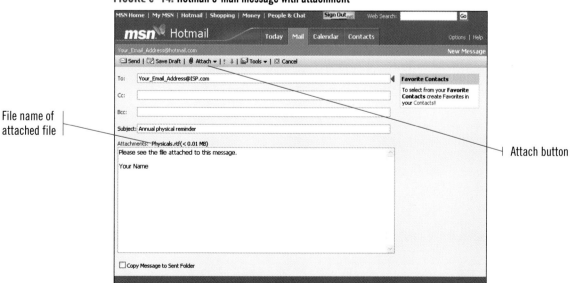

Saving an E-Mail Attachment in Outlook Express

When you receive an e-mail message with a file attached, you can open the attachment or you can save it to view later. 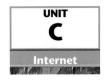 You decide to experiment with the options for working with an attached file. You save the attachment on your computer.

STEPS

1. **If you are using Outlook Express and if the Annual physical reminder message has not arrived in your Inbox yet, click the** Send/Recv button **on the toolbar**

   The paperclip next to the envelope icon in the message header summary indicates that the message contains an attachment.

2. **Click** Annual physical reminder **in the message list**

   The message appears in the Preview pane and a paperclip appears in the upper-right corner of the Preview pane.

3. **Click the** paperclip **in the Preview pane**

   A menu appears. See Figure C-15. If you click the filename in the paperclip menu in the Preview pane, the file will open in the program in which it was created, and then you can use the Save As command in that program to change the file name to one that is more meaningful to you.

4. **Click** Save Attachments **on the menu**

   The Save Attachments dialog box opens. See Figure C-16. If there were more than one file attached to the e-mail message, they would all be listed in the Attachments To Be Saved list.

5. **Click** Browse

   The Browse for Folder dialog box opens.

6. **Click** plus **and** minus signs **as needed to navigate to the drive and folder where your Solution Files are stored, click the folder where your Solution Files are stored, then click** OK

   The Browse for Folder dialog box closes.

7. **Click** Save **in the Save Attachments dialog box**

   The dialog box closes and the attachment is saved.

8. **If you changed your security options to save the attached file, click** Tools **on the menu bar, click** Options, **click the** Security tab, **select the** Do not allow attachments to be saved or opened that could potentially be a virus check box, **then click** OK

FIGURE C-15: Saving an attachment in Outlook Express

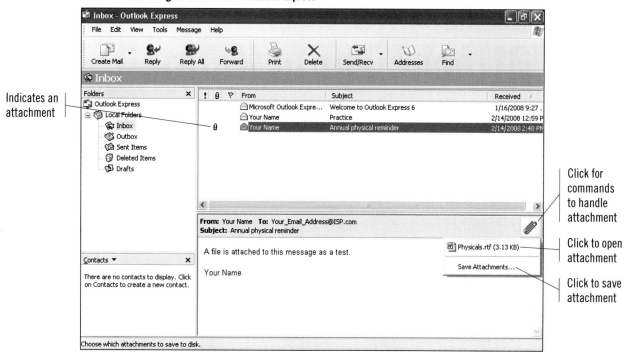

Indicates an attachment

Click for commands to handle attachment

Click to open attachment

Click to save attachment

FIGURE C-16: Save Attachments dialog box in Outlook Express

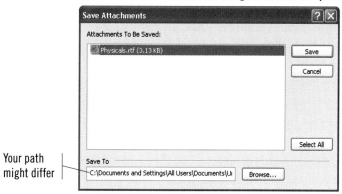

Your path might differ

Clues to Use

Understanding e-mail viruses, worms, and Trojan horses

E-mail can carry malicious programs, such as viruses, worms, and Trojan horses. A computer **virus** is a piece of software that runs without your permission and performs undesired tasks, such as deleting the contents of your hard disk. Viruses **self-replicate**, meaning that they create, and in some cases distribute, copies of themselves to infect more computers. **Worms** and **Trojan horses** are variations on this idea, and they are of special concern to e-mail users because they reproduce by using e-mail programs on infected computers to send out copies of themselves as attachments to automatically generated e-mail messages to everyone in the victim's e-mail address book. However, you can take a couple easy steps to protect yourself and those with whom you exchange e-mail. The most important precaution you can take is not opening a file attachment from a sender you don't know, because the attachment might contain a worm or Trojan horse. If you receive an e-mail message from an e-mail address that you recognize, make sure the accompanying e-mail message makes sense and is specific to you. If it is not, it might be the product of a worm. You can also install **anti-virus software**, which is software that protects your computer from these malicious programs. Some e-mail programs have built-in virus detection, and many schools and colleges distribute anti-virus software for free to students, staff, and faculty; check with your instructor, system administrator, or computing services center to see if this software is available to you.

Saving an E-Mail Attachment in Hotmail

When you receive an e-mail message with a file attached, you can save it to view later. 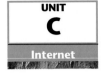 You decide to experiment with the options for working with an attached file. You save the attachment on your computer.

STEPS

TROUBLE
If you are using Outlook Express, skip to the next lesson.

1. **If the Annual physical reminder message has not arrived in your Inbox yet, click** Inbox **in the Folders list**

   The paperclip next to the envelope icon in the Annual physical message header summary indicates that the message contains an attachment. See Figure C-17.

2. **Open the** Annual physical reminder message **in a message window**

   The message appears in a message window and the attachment is listed as a link next to the word "Attachment" below the message header. See Figure C-18.

TROUBLE
If you are using Firefox and the Enter name of file to save to dialog box does not open, then Firefox is configured to save files to a pre-determined location. Click Tools on the menu bar, click Options, click Downloads on the left, then click Show Folder. The folder in which downloads are saved is opened. Locate the Physicals.rtf file, use Windows Explorer to move the file to the drive and folder where your Solution Files are stored, then skip Steps 6 and 7.

3. **Click the** Physicals.rtf link **next to Attachment**

   Hotmail automatically scans the attachment for viruses. When it is finished, a window opens telling you that the file was scanned and that no viruses were found. See Figure C-19.

4. **Click the** Download File button **on the toolbar**

   If you are using Internet Explorer, the File Download dialog box opens; if you are using Firefox, the Opening Physicals.rtf dialog box opens.

5. **If you are using Internet Explorer, click** Save**; if you are using Firefox, click the** Save to Disk option button**, then click** OK

   If you are using Internet Explorer, the Save As dialog box opens. If you are using Firefox, the Enter name of file to save dialog box opens.

6. **Click the** Look in **or** Save in list arrow**, navigate to the drive and folder where your Solution Files are stored, note that the filename in the File name text box is** Physicals.rtf**, then click** Save

   The dialog box closes and the attachment is saved. If you are using Internet Explorer, the Download complete dialog box opens. If you are using Firefox, you are returned to the window with the message that the virus scan is finished.

TROUBLE
If you are using Internet Explorer and the Download com-plete dialog box does not appear, a previ-ous user selected the Close this dialog box when download complete check box. Skip Step 7. If you are using Firefox, skip Step 7.

7. **If you are using Internet Explorer, click** Close **in the Download complete dialog box**

   You are returned to the window with the message that the virus scan is finished.

8. **Click the** Cancel button **on the toolbar**

   The Annual physical reminder message window appears.

9. **Click the** Inbox link **in the upper-right corner of the message window**

   The Hotmail mail window appears with the Inbox selected.

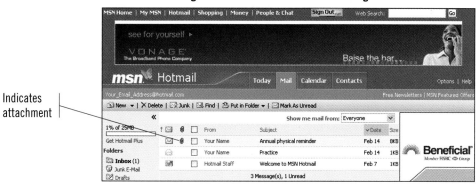

FIGURE C-17: Message with attachment in the Hotmail message list

Indicates attachment

FIGURE C-18: Attachment in Hotmail message window

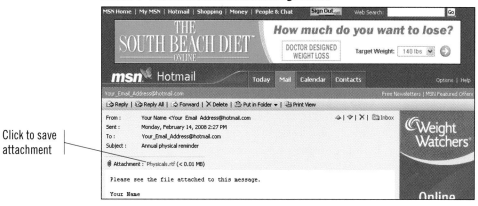

Click to save attachment

FIGURE C-19: Hotmail virus scan results on attached file

Click to download attachment

Virus scan results

Clues to Use

Understanding e-mail viruses, worms, and Trojan horses

E-mail can carry malicious programs, such as viruses, worms, and Trojan horses. A computer **virus** is a piece of software that runs without your permission and performs undesired tasks, such as deleting the contents of your hard disk. Viruses **self-replicate**, meaning that they create, and in some cases distribute, copies of themselves to infect more computers. **Worms** and **Trojan horses** are variations on this idea, and they are of special concern to e-mail users because they reproduce by using e-mail programs on infected computers to send out copies of themselves as attachments to automatically generated e-mail messages to everyone in the victim's e-mail address book. However, you can take a couple easy steps to protect yourself and those with whom you exchange e-mail. The most important precaution you can take is not opening a file attachment from a sender you don't know, because the attachment might contain a worm or Trojan horse. If you receive an e-mail message from an e-mail address that you recognize, make sure the accompanying e-mail message makes sense and is specific to you. If it is not, it might be the product of a worm. You can also install **anti-virus software**, which is software that protects your computer from these malicious programs. Some e-mail programs have built-in virus detection, and many schools and colleges distribute anti-virus software for free to students, staff, and faculty; check with your instructor, system administrator, or computing services center to see if this software is available to you.

Internet

Replying to an E-Mail Message

You can use your e-mail program's Reply option to respond to the sender of a message quickly and efficiently. When you reply to an e-mail message, the sender's name is automatically placed in the To text box, and the text of the original message appears in the body of the new message for reference. 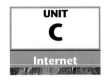 You practice using the Reply option by replying to the copy of the e-mail message you sent to Sharon.

STEPS

1. **If you are using Outlook Express, click Practice in the message list; if you are using Hotmail, click the sender's name in the Practice message header summary**

   If you are using Outlook Express, the message appears in the Preview pane; if you are using Hotmail, the message opens in its message window.

QUICK TIP

If the original sender sent the message to multiple recipients, you can reply to the sender and all recipients of the original message by clicking the Reply All button.

2. **Click the Reply button on the toolbar**

   A new message window opens. The original sender's e-mail address or name appears in the To text box (in this case, this is your name). "Re:" appears at the beginning of the original subject text, indicating that this message is a response to the original message. The insertion point appears in the message body pane above the original message. In Outlook Express, a vertical line appears to the left of the entire message, including the message header. In Hotmail, the symbol > is in front of each line of the header and body of the original message. See Figure C-20.

3. **Type I created this message using the Reply button. in the message body pane, press [Enter] twice, then type your name**

4. **Click the Send button on the message window toolbar, then, if you are using Hotmail, click the Return to Inbox link**

   The message is sent to the mail server for delivery to you, and the mail window appears.

TROUBLE

If you are using Hotmail, skip Steps 5 and 6. The RE: Practice message should be in your Inbox message list as shown in Figure C-22.

5. **If you are using Outlook Express and if the Re: Practice message is not in the message list, click the Send/Recv button on the toolbar**

   The Re: Practice message appears in your Inbox.

6. **If you are using Outlook Express, click Re: Practice**

   See Figure C-21 if you are using Outlook Express; see Figure C-22 if you are using Hotmail.

Clues to Use

Learning about netiquette

Netiquette, a term coined from the phrase "Internet etiquette," is the set of commonly accepted rules that represent proper behavior on the Internet. E-mail has its own set of rules, which have evolved over time and will continue to evolve as it gains new users. The generally accepted rules for e-mail messages are:

- Avoid writing your messages in ALL CAPITAL LETTERS BECAUSE IT LOOKS LIKE YOU ARE SHOUTING.
- Keep your messages simple, short, and focused on their topics.
- Include a descriptive subject in the Subject line and a signature, so the recipient knows the content of your message.
- Avoid sending unsolicited messages, especially those with attachments.

- Use a spell checker and read your message and correct any spelling or grammatical errors before sending it.
- Use common courtesy, politeness, and respect.
- Don't assume that all your mail is delivered and read. If you suspect that an important message did not arrive in the recipient's mailbox, either resend the message with an appropriate addition stating that you think that the message was not received, or call the person and follow up by phone. Another way to check your account is to send a message to yourself; if you do not receive it back, you can suspect a problem.

FIGURE C-20: Re: Practice message windows in Outlook Express and Hotmail

Your e-mail address might appear here

"Re:" automatically added to Subject line

Insertion point

Vertical line indicates original message in Outlook Express

> indicates original message in Hotmail

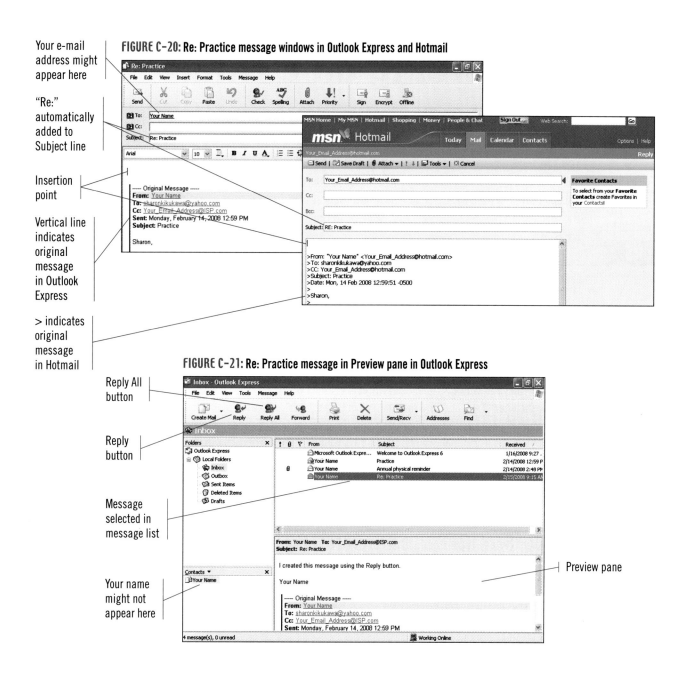

FIGURE C-21: Re: Practice message in Preview pane in Outlook Express

Reply All button

Reply button

Message selected in message list

Your name might not appear here

Preview pane

FIGURE C-22: RE: Practice message in message list in Hotmail

RE: Practice message

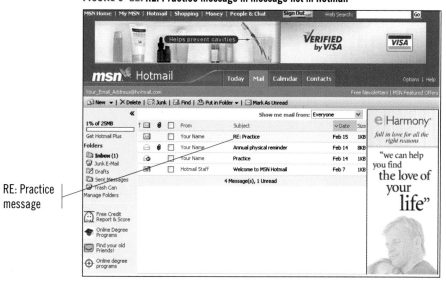

Internet

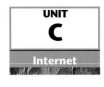

Forwarding an E-Mail Message

You can send any message you receive to someone else, which is called **forwarding**. When you use the Forward option, the original message appears in the Compose window. Forwarding is similar to replying, except that a forwarded message is not automatically addressed to the original sender; you must address the message to the desired recipients. ▰▰▰▰ To practice forwarding messages and to see how they look to recipients, you forward the Practice message to yourself and to Sharon.

STEPS

1. **If you are using Outlook Express, click** Practice **in the message list; if you are using Hotmail, click the sender's name in the Practice message header summary**

   If you are using Outlook Express, the message appears in the Preview pane; if you are using Hotmail, the message opens in its message window.

2. **Click the** Forward button **on the toolbar**

   A new message window opens and displays the text of the message to forward. Notice that the Subject text box includes "Fw:" and the original subject text. "Fw:" indicates that the message is being forwarded. In Outlook Express, the original message is in the message body pane under a heading identifying it as the original message. In Hotmail, the symbol > is in front of each line of the body of the original message. The insertion point appears in the To text box.

3. **Type** sharonkikukawa@yahoo.com **in the To text box, then type your e-mail address in the Cc text box**

4. **Click in the** message body pane **above the original message line, type** Sharon, **press** [Enter] **twice, type** I used the Forward command to send this message., **press** [Enter] **twice, then type your name**

5. **Click the** Send button **on the message window toolbar, then, if you are using Hotmail, click the** Return to Inbox link

   The message is sent to the mail server for delivery to you, and the mail window appears.

6. **If you are using Outlook Express and if the Fw: Practice message is not in the message list, click the** Send/Recv button **on the toolbar**

   The message appears in your Inbox.

7. **If you are using Outlook Express, click** Fw: Practice **in the message list**

   See Figure C-23 if you are using Outlook Express; see Figure C-24 if you are using Hotmail.

Clues to Use

Using emoticons

E-mail can be an impersonal form of communication, and as a result some writers use emoticons to express emotion. An **emoticon** is a form of electronic body language expressed by a group of keyboard characters that represent a human expression when viewed together. To see the emotion the writer is expressing, tilt your head to the left. Some examples of emoticons are :-) (the **smiley**), :-((a frown), ;-) (a smiley with a wink), and :-o (fear or surprise).

FIGURE C-23: Fw: Practice message in Preview pane in Outlook Express

Forward button

Message selected in message list

Preview pane

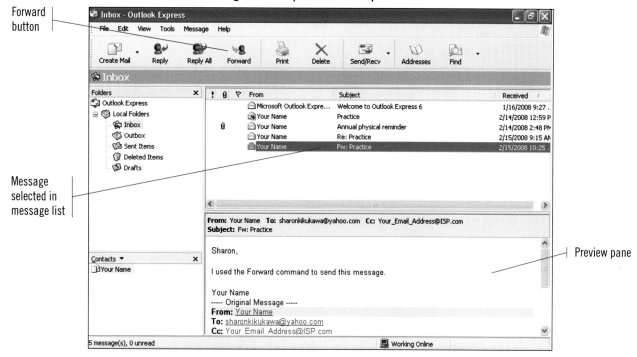

FIGURE C-24: FW: Practice message in message list in Hotmail

FW: Practice message

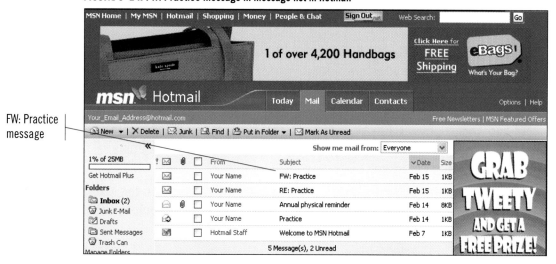

Internet

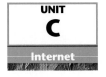

Organizing E-Mail Messages

You can organize your e-mail messages by using e-mail folders to file your messages by category. For example, you might file messages from friends in one folder and file messages concerning a certain project in a different folder. When you file a message, you move it from the Inbox to another folder. If you are using Outlook Express, you can also make copies of a message to store it in multiple folders. ▓▓▓▓ Sharon wants you to show employees of Kikukawa Air how they can organize their e-mail, so you decide to try creating a folder to hold all messages relating to Kikukawa Air, and then copy a few messages into it.

STEPS

TROUBLE

If your are using Hotmail and the New Message window opens instead of the New Folder window, you clicked the New button instead of clicking the New button list arrow. Click the Inbox link to return to the Hotmail mail window, then repeat Step 1.

1. **If you are using Outlook Express, click** File **on the menu bar, point to** Folder, **then click** New; **if you are using Hotmail, click the** New button list arrow **on the toolbar, then click** Folder

   If you are using Outlook Express, the Create Folder dialog box opens as shown in Figure C-25; if you are using Hotmail, the New Folder window opens as shown in Figure C-26.

2. **Type** Kikukawa **in the Folder Name text box**

3. **If you are using Outlook Express, click** Local Folders **in the Select the folder in which to create the new folder list; if you are using Hotmail, skip this step**

4. **Click** OK, **then click** Inbox **in the Folders list, if necessary**

   You are returned to the mail window and the new Kikukawa folder you created appears in the Folders list. See Figure C-27.

5. **If you are using Outlook Express, drag** Practice **from the message list to the Kikukawa folder in the Folders list; if you are using Hotmail, select the** check box **in the Practice message header summary, click the** Put in Folder button **on the toolbar, then click** Kikukawa

   The Practice message disappears from the Inbox message list.

6. **Click** Kikukawa **in the Folders list**

   The message list displays the contents of the Kikukawa folder. The only message in it is the message you moved from the Inbox, Practice.

7. **Click** Inbox **in the Folders list**

   You want to move the other three messages you sent in this unit as well. You can move all three of them at once.

8. **If you are using Outlook Express, press and hold** [Ctrl], **click** Re: Practice, Fw: Practice, **and** Annual physical reminder, **then release** [Ctrl]; **if you are using Hotmail, select the** RE: Practice, FW: Practice, **and** Annual physical reminder check boxes

   All three messages are selected.

9. **If you are using Outlook Express, drag the selected messages to the** Kikukawa folder; **if you are using Hotmail, click the** Put in Folder button **on the toolbar, then click** Kikukawa

   The messages disappear from the Inbox message list.

10. **Click** Kikukawa **in the Folders list**

    The four messages you moved appear in the message list.

FIGURE C-25: Create Folder dialog box in Outlook Express

FIGURE C-26: New Folder window in Hotmail

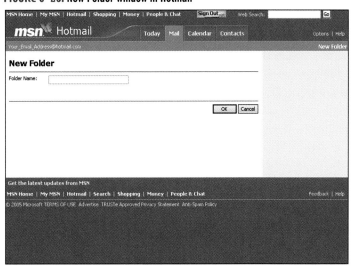

FIGURE C-27: Kikukawa folder in Folders list in Outlook Express and Hotmail

New folder

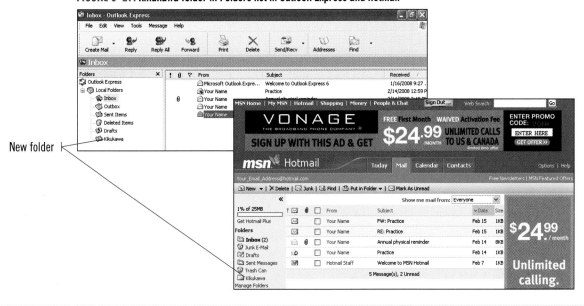

Clues to Use

Renaming folders you create

You can rename folders that you create in both Outlook Express and Hotmail. If you are using Outlook Express, right-click the folder you want to rename in the Folders list, then click Rename on the short-cut menu. If you are using Hotmail, click Manage Folders in the Folders list to open the Manage Folders window, select the check box next to the folder you want to rename, then click the Rename button on the toolbar. Type the new name for the folder in the Folder Name text box, then click OK.

UNIT
C

Internet

Deleting E-Mail Messages

Just as you can delete unnecessary files from your computer, you can also delete e-mail messages that you no longer need. When you delete a message, the message moves to the Deleted Items folder in Outlook Express and the Trash Can folder in Hotmail. To permanently delete items in the Deleted Items or Trash Can folder, you need to empty the folder. ▇▇▇▇ You practice deleting e-mail by removing some of the messages in your Inbox.

STEPS

1. **If you are using Outlook Express, click Practice in the Kikukawa folder message list; if you are using Hotmail, select the Practice check box in the Kikukawa folder message list**
   The Practice message is selected.

2. **Click the Delete button on the toolbar**
   The Practice message is moved from the Kikukawa folder to the Deleted Items folder in Outlook Express and to the Trash Can folder in Hotmail.

> **TROUBLE**
> If you accidentally deleted the wrong message, click Deleted Items or Trash Can in the Folders list, then move the message back to the Kikukawa folder.

3. **If you are using Outlook Express, click Deleted Items in the Folders list; if you are using Hotmail, click Trash Can in the Folders list**
   The Practice message you deleted appears in the Deleted Items or Trash Can folder message list. If you are using Outlook Express, you do not need to view the contents of the Deleted Items folder before you delete its contents, but opening this folder before emptying it allows you to verify that you're not about to permanently delete a message you want to keep.

4. **If you are using Outlook Express, right-click Deleted Items in the Folders list, then click Empty 'Deleted Items' Folder on the shortcut menu, as shown in Figure C-28; if you are using Hotmail, click the Empty button on the toolbar, as shown in Figure C-29**
   A warning dialog box opens asking if you are sure you want to permanently delete the contents of the folder.

5. **If you are using Outlook Express, click Yes; if you are using Hotmail, click OK**
   The e-mail message no longer appears in the Deleted Items or Trash Can folder message list. When you empty this folder, the message is permanently deleted. Now you will delete the Kikukawa folder you created and its contents.

> **TROUBLE**
> If you are using Hotmail, skip to Step 9.

6. **If you are using Outlook Express, right-click Kikukawa in the Folders list, click Delete on the shortcut menu, then click Yes in the warning dialog box**
   The Kikukawa folder and its contents are moved to the Deleted Items folder.

7. **If you are using Outlook Express, click Sent Items in the Folders list, then delete the four messages you sent in this tutorial**
   In Outlook Express, the default is for a copy of each message you send to be stored in the Sent Items folder. You should check this folder periodically and delete unneeded messages to avoid this file growing too large.

8. **If you are using Outlook Express, right-click Deleted Items in the Folders list, click Empty 'Deleted Items' Folder on the shortcut menu, then click Yes in the warning box**

> **TROUBLE**
> If you are using Outlook Express, skip Steps 9 and 10.

9. **If you are using Hotmail, click Manage Folders in the Folders list, select the Kikukawa folder check box in the folder list in the Manage Folders window, click the Delete button on the toolbar, then click OK in the warning box**
   The Kikukawa folder disappears from the list of folders, and the number of messages in the Trash Can folder changes to 3.

10. **If you are using Hotmail, click the Empty link next to the Trash Can folder in the list of folders, then click OK in the warning box**
    The Kikukawa folder and its contents are permanently deleted. Note that the number of messages in the Trash Can folder returns to 0.

FIGURE C-28: Emptying the Deleted Items folder in Outlook Express

Click this command to permanently remove items from the Deleted Items folder

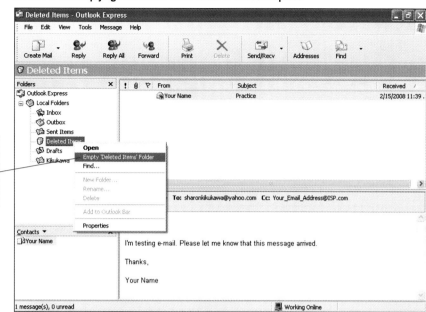

FIGURE C-29: Deleting items from Trash Can folder in Hotmail

Click to permanently delete messages in Trash Can folder

Folder name

Clues to Use

Copying messages in Outlook Express

If you are using Outlook Express, you can copy a message from one folder to another instead of moving them, so that the message appears in both folders. Select the messages you want to copy. Press and hold [Ctrl], drag the selected messages to the folder, then release [Ctrl]. A copy of the selected message is placed in the folder to which you dragged the messages, while leaving the original messages in their current location. Notice that the messages remain in the message list of the current folder. Click the folder to which you copied the messages. The messages appear in that folder as well.

Maintaining an Address Book in Outlook Express

You can save e-mail addresses and contact information, such as phone numbers and postal addresses, in the Outlook Express Address Book. You can also create **nicknames**, which are shortened names for the e-mail addresses of people you send e-mail to frequently. Each person that you add is called a **contact**, and the information about that person is collected on a **contact card**. 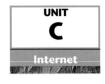 You begin to create an address book for employees of Kikukawa Air.

STEPS

1. **Click the** Addresses button **on the toolbar in the Outlook Express mail window to open the Address Book – Main Identity window, then click the** Maximize button **in the title bar**
   See Figure C-30.

2. **Click** Main Identity's Contacts **in the left pane, if necessary, click the** New button **on the toolbar in the Address Book window, then click** New Contact **on the menu that opens**
   The Properties dialog box opens. You use this dialog box or window to add contacts to the Address Book.

3. **Type** Sharon **in the First text box, press** [Tab] **twice, type** Kikukawa **in the Last text box, click in the** Nickname text box, **then type** Shar
   The Display text box changes to reflect the information you added to the First and Last text boxes.

4. **Click in the** E-Mail Addresses text box, **type** sharonkikukawa@yahoo.com, **then click** Add
   Figure C-31 shows the completed Properties dialog box for Sharon.

5. **Click** OK
   To delete an address in the Address Book, select it, then click the Delete button on the Address Book window toolbar.

6. **Create entries in the Address Book for the following Kikukawa Air employees:**

First Name	Last Name	Nickname	E-Mail Address
Chris	Breed	Chris	chrisbreed@kikukawaair.com
Jenny	Mahala	Jen	jennymahala@kikukawaair.com
Richard	Forrester	Rich	richardforrester@kikukawaair.com
Your first name	Your last name	Your nickname	Your e-mail address

7. **Click the** Close button **on the Address Book – Main Identity window title bar, click the** Create Mail button **on the toolbar in the mail window, then click the** To button **to the left of the To text box**
   The Select Recipients dialog box opens.

8. **Click** Sharon Kikukawa **in the list of contacts, then click** To
   Sharon Kikukawa's name appears in the To text box.

9. **Click** OK, **click in the** To text box **after Sharon's name, type** ; (semi-colon), **press the** [Spacebar], **type your nickname; then press** [Tab]
   Figure C-32 shows the New Message window with the two names entered.

10. **Click in the** Subject text box, **type** Address Book test, **click in the message body pane, type** I'm testing the Address Book feature in Outlook Express., **press** [Enter] **twice, type your name, click the** Send button **on the message window toolbar, then click the** Send/Recv button **on the toolbar, if necessary**
   The message arrives in your Inbox. Notice that the contacts you added are listed in the Contacts list at the bottom left of the mail window.

FIGURE C-30: Outlook Express Address Book window

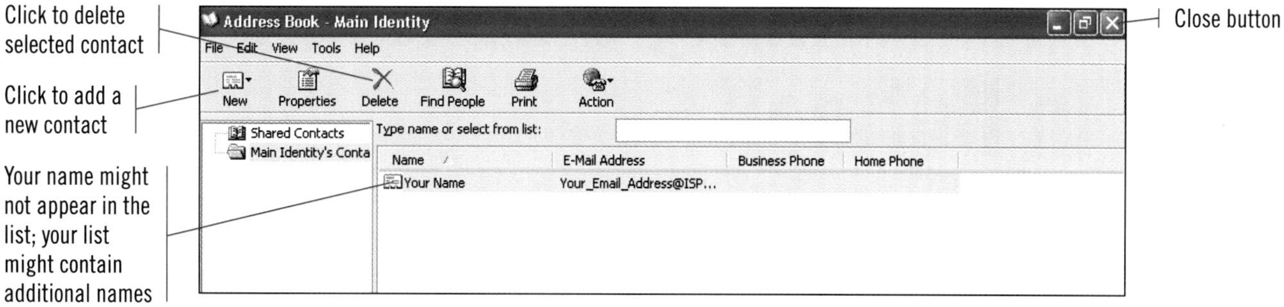

Click to delete selected contact

Click to add a new contact

Your name might not appear in the list; your list might contain additional names

Close button

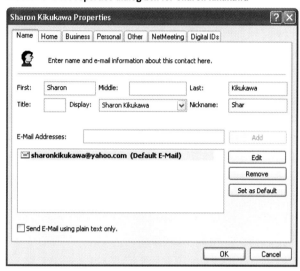

FIGURE C-31: Properties dialog box for Sharon Kikukawa

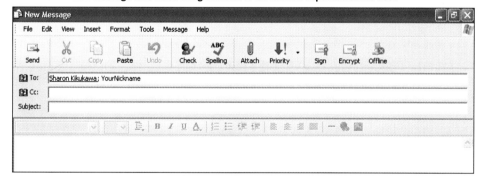

FIGURE C-32: New Message addressed using contacts in the Outlook Express Address Book

Clues to Use

Updating the Outlook Express Address Book

You can quickly add a sender's e-mail address to the Outlook Express Address Book. When you receive a message from someone who is not listed in the Address Book, right-click the person's name in the message header summary in the message list, then click Add Sender to Address Book on the shortcut menu; or open the message in its message window, right-click the sender's name in the message header, then click Add to Address Book on the shortcut menu.

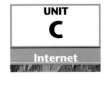

UNIT
C

Internet

Maintaining a Contacts List in Hotmail

You can save e-mail addresses and contact information, such as phone numbers and postal addresses, in the Contacts list in Hotmail. When you add a name to the Contacts list, you also create a **Quickname**, which is a shortened name for the contact. Each person that you add is called a **contact**, and the information about that person is collected on a **contact card**. ▰▰▰▰ You begin to create a contacts list for employees of Kikukawa Air.

STEPS

TROUBLE

If you are using Outlook Express, skip to the next lesson.

QUICK TIP

In Hotmail, Quicknames are required.

QUICK TIP

To add several contacts in a row, click the Save and Add Another Contact button on the toolbar.

1. **Click the** Contacts tab **in the Hotmail mail window**

   The Contacts window opens in Hotmail as shown in Figure C-33.

2. **Click the** New button **on the toolbar in the Contacts window**

   The New Contact window opens. You use this window to add e-mail addresses to the Contacts list.

3. **Click in the** First Name text box, **type** Sharon, **press** [Tab], **type** Kikukawa **in the Last Name text box, press** [Tab], **then type** Shar **in the Quickname text box**

   The Mark this contact as a favorite check box is checked; contacts marked as a favorite will appear in the Favorite Contacts list to the right of New Message windows so that you can quickly click a name in the list.

4. **Click in the** Work text box **in the Online Addresses box, then type** sharonkikukawa@yahoo.com

   Figure C-34 shows the completed Contact card for Sharon.

5. **Click the** Save button **on the toolbar**

   To delete an address in the Contacts list, select its check box in the Contacts window, then click the Delete button on the toolbar.

6. **Create contact cards for the following Kikukawa Air employees:**

First Name	Last Name	Nickname	E-Mail Address
Chris	Breed	Chris	chrisbreed@kikukawaair.com
Jenny	Mahala	Jen	jennymahala@kikukawaair.com
Richard	Forrester	Rich	richardforrester@kikukawaair.com
Your first name	Your last name	Your nickname	Your e-mail address

7. **In the Contacts window, click the** New button list arrow **on the toolbar, click** Mail Message, **then click the** To link **to the left of the To text box**

   The MSN Hotmail – Select Message Recipients – Web Page Dialog dialog box opens.

8. **Click in the** To box, **if necessary, then click** Kikukawa, Sharon **in the My Contacts list**

   Sharon Kikukawa's e-mail address appears in the To text box.

9. **Click** OK, **click in the** To text box **after Sharon's name, type** , (comma), **then type your Quickname**

   Your nickname appears next to Sharon's e-mail address in the list of recipients. Figure C-35 shows the To box with the two names entered.

10. **Click in the** Subject text box, **type** Contacts list test, **click in the message body pane, type** I'm testing the Contacts list feature in Outlook Express., **press** [Enter] **twice, type your name, click the** Send button **on the message window toolbar, then click the** Return to Inbox link

    The message arrives in your Inbox.

FIGURE C-33: Contacts window in Hotmail

Contacts tab

FIGURE C-34: Contact card for Sharon Kikukawa

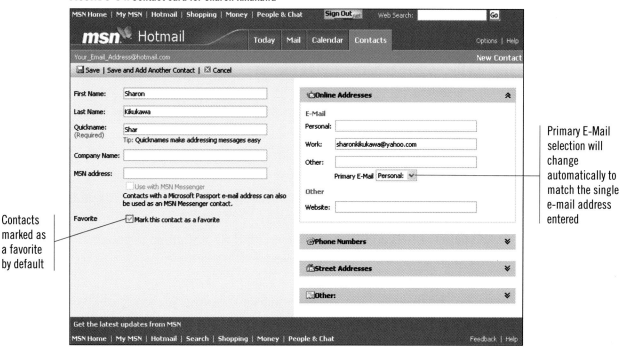

Contacts marked as a favorite by default

Primary E-Mail selection will change automatically to match the single e-mail address entered

FIGURE C-35: New Message addressed using contacts in Hotmail Contacts list

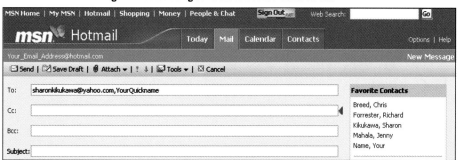

Clues to Use

Updating the Hotmail Contacts list

You can quickly add a sender's e-mail address to the Hotmail Contacts list. When you receive a message from someone who is not listed in the Contacts list, open the message in its message window, then click the Save Address button on the toolbar.

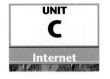

Creating a Group in Outlook Express

You can quickly send an e-mail message to a group of people by creating a **group** or **mailing list**, which is a group of two or more e-mail addresses. You create a group in the Outlook Express Address Book by creating a name for the group, and then assigning e-mail addresses to the named group. When you want to send an e-mail message to a group, simply insert the group's name in the To text box to send a single message to all the group members simultaneously. Because Kikukawa Air, like many companies, is organized into departments such as Personnel, Marketing, and Operations, you realize that groups would be useful when you want to send messages to all the employees in a particular department. You start by creating a group for the Personnel Department.

STEPS

> **TROUBLE**
>
> If you are using Hotmail, skip to the next lesson.

1. **Click the** Addresses button **on the toolbar**
   The Address Book – Main Identity window opens.

2. **Click the** New button **on the Address Book toolbar, then click** New Group
   The Properties dialog box for a new group opens as shown in Figure C-36.

3. **Type** Personnel **in the Group Name text box, then click** Select Members
   The Select Group Members dialog box opens.

4. **Select** Chris Breed's name **in the list of contacts, then click** Select **to add that name to the list of group members**

5. **Add** Jenny Mahala **and** Sharon Kikukawa **to the list of group members**
   Three names are added to the Personnel group.

6. **Click** OK
   The Personnel Properties dialog box appears with the three names you added to the Personnel group.

7. **Click** OK **in the Personnel Properties dialog box, then click** Main Identity's Contacts **in the list in the left pane in the Address Book window**
   The group is identified in the contacts list by the people icon as shown in Figure C-37.

8. **Click the** Close button **in the Address Book window title bar, open a New Message window, then click the** To button
   The Personnel group is listed in the list of contacts.

9. **Click** Cancel **in the Select Recipients dialog box, then click the** Close button **in the New Message window title bar**

10. **Click the** Close button **in the mail window title bar to exit the Outlook Express e-mail program**

FIGURE C-36: Properties dialog box for new group

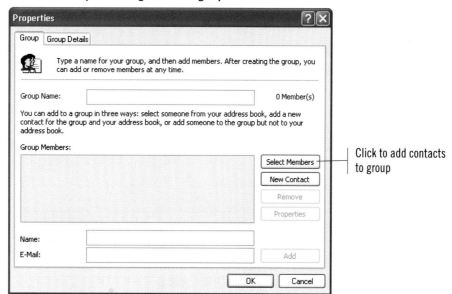

Click to add contacts to group

FIGURE C-37: Address Book window in Outlook Express after Personnel group added

Icon indicates group

Group in list of contacts

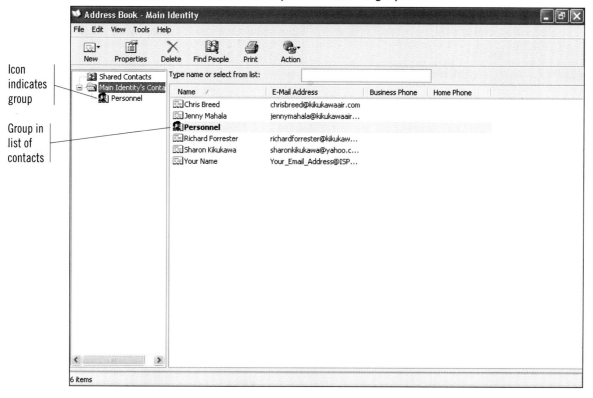

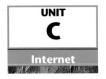

Creating a Group in Hotmail

You can quickly send an e-mail message to a group of people by creating a **group** or **mailing list**, which is a group of two or more e-mail addresses. You create a group in the Hotmail Contacts list by creating a name for the group, and then assigning e-mail addresses to the named group. When you want to send an e-mail message to a group, simply insert the group's name in the To text box to send a single message to all the group members simultaneously. ▆▆▆▆ Because Kikukawa Air, like many companies, is organized into departments such as Personnel, Marketing, and Operations, you realize that groups would be useful when you want to send messages to all the employees in a particular department. You start by creating a group for the Personnel Department.

STEPS

TROUBLE
If you are using Outlook Express, skip this lesson.

1. **Click the** Contacts tab, **then click the** Groups link **in the left pane**
   The Groups window opens.

2. **Click the** New button **on the toolbar**
   The New Group window opens as shown in Figure C-38.

3. **Type** Personnel **in the Group Name text box**

4. **Click** Breed, Chris **in the list of contacts, then click** Add **to add that name to the Group Members list**

5. **Add** Jenny Mahala **and** Sharon Kikukawa **to the Group Members list**
   Three names are added to the Personnel group.

6. **Click the** Save button **on the toolbar**
   The group is listed in the Folders list under Groups and is identified as a group by the people icon as shown in Figure C-39.

QUICK TIP
Note that groups do not show up in the My Contacts list if you click the To link.

7. **Open a New Message window**
   The group is listed below a horizontal line in the Favorite Contacts list on the right.

8. **Click the** Cancel button **on the toolbar**

9. **Click** Sign Out **at the top of the Hotmail window to sign out of your Hotmail account, then exit your browser**

FIGURE C-38: New Group window in Hotmail

Click to
save group

Click to add
selected
contact to
group

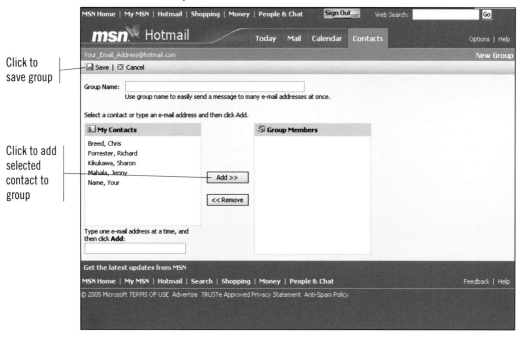

FIGURE C-39: Group window after Personnel group added in Hotmail

Icon
indicates
group

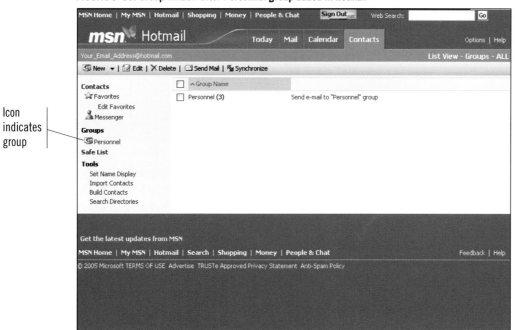

Internet

Practice

▼ CONCEPTS REVIEW

Identify the function of each element of the message window shown in Figure C-40 if you are using Outlook Express or in Figure C-41 if you are using Hotmail.

FIGURE C-40

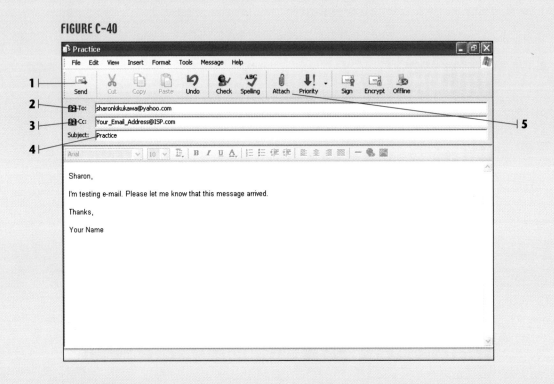

FIGURE C-41

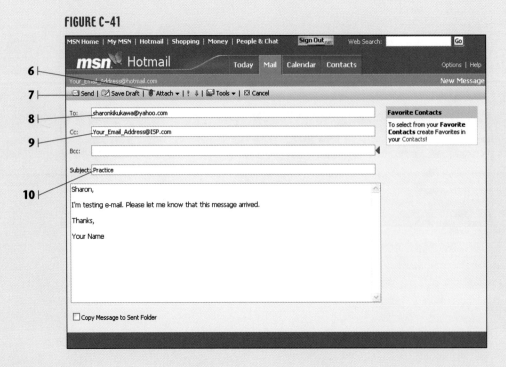

Match each term with the statement that best describes it.

11. **Attachment**
12. **Mail server**
13. **Inbox**
14. **Subject text box**
15. **New Message window**
16. **Message header summary**

a. A file that accompanies an e-mail message
b. A window used to create messages
c. A server that runs special software for handling e-mail tasks
d. The summary information about a message, including sender, subject, and date
e. A location where you type the main topic of an e-mail message
f. A folder that contains all incoming messages

Select the best answer from the list of choices.

17. **Message header summaries are listed in the:**
    a. mail window.
    b. Folders list.
    c. message body pane.
    d. message list.

18. **Sending an e-mail message you've received to a new recipient is called:**
    a. forwarding.
    b. replying.
    c. copying.
    d. messaging.

19. **You can organize your e-mail by placing messages into:**
    a. files.
    b. the Junk E-Mail folder.
    c. folders.
    d. the Address Book or Contacts list.

20. **To send a copy of an e-mail message to someone who is not the main recipient of the message, in which text box do you enter that person's e-mail address?**
    a. To
    b. Cc
    c. Subject
    d. Attachment

▼ SKILLS REVIEW

1. **Send an e-mail message.**
   a. Open your e-mail program or sign into your Webmail account, then open a New Message window.
   b. Address the message to your instructor, a friend, or a colleague.
   c. Cc the message to yourself.
   d. Type **Dinner Meeting** as the subject of your message.
   e. Type the following message:
      Hi <<name of recipient>>,
      We are planning to meet for dinner at <<a local restaurant name>> on November 30. Please bring the presentation on the Ford account.
   f. Type your name below the message.
   g. Send the message.

Internet

2. Check incoming e-mail.

   a. Retrieve your e-mail.

   b. Read the Dinner Meeting message.

3. Attach a file to an e-mail message.

   a. Open a New Message window.

   b. Address the message to your instructor, a friend, or a colleague.

   c. Cc the message to yourself.

   d. Type **Dinner Meeting Participants** the subject of your message.

   e. Type the following message:

     Attached is a list of the people we have invited to attend the dinner meeting at <<restaurant name>> on November 30. Please check the list and get back to me with any suggestions for additional participants.

   f. Add your name to the end of the message.

   g. Attach the **Dinner Meeting.rtf** file located in the drive and folder where your Data Files are stored.

   h. Send the file with the attachment.

4. Save an e-mail attachment.

   a. Retrieve your e-mail.

   b. Save the **Dinner Meeting.rtf** file attached to the Dinner Meeting Participants message in the location where your Solution Files are stored.

5. Reply to an e-mail message.

   a. Reply to the sender of the Dinner Meeting Participants message.

   b. Send a copy of the message to your instructor, a friend, or a colleague.

   c. Type the following message:

     I'd be delighted to attend the meeting on November 30.

   d. Add your name to the message.

   e. Send the message.

   f. Retrieve your e-mail.

6. Forward an e-mail message.

   a. Forward the Dinner Meeting Participants message to your instructor, a friend, or a colleague.

   b. Cc the message to yourself.

   c. Type the following message:

     I have reviewed the list of meeting participants. We should also include Juan Sanchez from the Marketing Department.

   d. Add your name to the message.

   e. Send the message.

   f. Retrieve your e-mail.

7. Organize e-mail messages.

  a. Create a new e-mail folder named **Meetings**.

  b. Move all four of the Dinner Meeting messages to the Meetings folder.

  c. View the contents of the Meetings folder to verify that all four messages appear.

8. Delete e-mail messages.

  a. Delete the Dinner Meeting message in the Meetings folder.

  b. Delete the Meeting folder and all of its contents.

  c. If you are using Outlook Express, delete the four Dinner Meeting messages you sent from the Sent Items folder.

  d. Empty the contents of the Deleted Items or Trash Can folder.

9. Maintain an Address Book or a Contacts list.

  a. Create a new contact card for Loree Erickson at lerickson@kikukawaair.com. Loree's nickname or Quickname is Lo.

  b. Create a new contact card for Lorenzo Seale at lseale@kikukawaair.com. Lorenzo's nickname or Quickname is Lor.

  c. Create a new contact card for Consuela Longue at clongue@kikukawaair.com. Consuela's nickname or Quickname is Con.

10. Create a group.

  a. Create a group called **Meetings**.

  b. Add Loree Erickson and Consuela Longue to the list.

  c. Check the Address Book or Contacts list for the Meetings entry.

  d. If you are using Outlook Express, exit the program.

  e. If you are using Hotmail, sign out of the service and exit your browser.

▼ INDEPENDENT CHALLENGE 1

Your instructor has asked you to submit your next assignment via e-mail. You are also asked to send a copy of the assignment to yourself.

  a. Locate a file in one of the folders on your computer to include as an attachment with the e-mail message to your instructor. Make sure the file contains a very short document that will not take up a great deal of disk space. For example, you could select a short essay that you completed for another course or a short letter you wrote to a friend. Alternately, you could use one of the Data Files from this unit. After you have determined which file you will attach to your e-mail, start your e-mail program or sign into your Webmail service.

  b. Add your instructor's name and e-mail address to the Address Book or Contacts list. Use an appropriate nickname or Quickname that is easy to remember.

  c. Create a new message.

  d. Type **E-Mail Assignment** for the subject.

  e. In the To text box, type your instructor's nickname.

  f. In the Cc text box, type your e-mail address.

▼ INDEPENDENT CHALLENGE 1 (CONTINUED)

g. Type the following message in the message body pane:

Here's a copy of <<describe the file>> as you requested. Please let me know as soon as you receive the file. Thanks.

h. Leave a blank line after the end of your message, then type your name, class name, class section, and e-mail address on four separate lines.

i. Attach the file you have chosen to the message.

Advanced Challenge Exercise

- Mark the message as high priority by clicking the appropriate button on the toolbar.
- Check the spelling in the message by clicking the appropriate button on the toolbar.
- If you are using Hotmail, click the option to save a copy of the message in the Sent Messages folder.

j. Send the message.

k. Check for new e-mail to download your message.

l. Delete the E-Mail Assignment message from the Inbox and the Sent Items or Sent Messages folders, if necessary, then empty your Deleted Items or Trash Can folder.

m. Exit your e-mail program or sign out of your Webmail service and exit your browser.

▼ INDEPENDENT CHALLENGE 2

You regularly send e-mail updates of what's going on in your life to several friends who don't live nearby. You want to create a group in your Address Book or Contacts list to simplify addressing the updates.

a. Start your e-mail program or sign into your Webmail service.

b. Add the names, appropriate nicknames or Quicknames, and e-mail addresses of three classmates to your Address Book or Contacts list.

c. Add your instructor's full name, nickname, and e-mail address to the Address Book or Contacts list, if necessary.

d. Create a contact card for yourself, if necessary.

e. Create a new group named **Updates**, then add your classmates, your instructor, and yourself to the group.

f. Create a new e-mail message with **Update Message** as the subject. Address the message to the Updates group.

g. Type a short message informing your classmates that your e-mail message is testing the use of your new mailing list.

h. Send the message.

i. Retrieve and open the message. (You should receive the message because you are included in the mailing list.)

j. Delete the message you just sent and received, empty the Deleted Items or Trash Can folder, then exit your e-mail program or sign out of your Webmail service and exit your browser.

▼ INDEPENDENT CHALLENGE 3

Bridgefield Engineering Company (BECO) is a small engineering firm in Somerville, New Jersey, that manufactures and distributes heavy industrial machinery for factories worldwide. Because BECO has trouble reaching its customers around the world in different time zones, the company has decided to implement an e-mail system to facilitate contact between BECO employees and their customers. BECO hired you to help employees set up and use this e-mail system. Your first task is to send a message to several of BECO's marketing staff located throughout the country.

a. Start your e-mail program or sign into your Webmail service.

b. If necessary, add your instructor and two classmates to the Address Book or Contacts list. Use an appropriate nickname for each person. Be sure you have a complete contact card for yourself.

▼ INDEPENDENT CHALLENGE 3 (CONTINUED)

c. Start a new message, and address the message to your instructor and your two classmates.

d. Send a copy (Cc) of the message to yourself.

e. Type an appropriate topic in the Subject text box.

f. Type the following message:

Please include the following at the end of all e-mail messages you send to customers. "Bridgefield manufactures machines to your specifications. We can build borers, planers, horn presses, and a variety of other machines. E-mail us for further information."

g. Sign your name.

h. Send the message.

i. Retrieve the message.

j. Delete the message you just sent and received, empty the Deleted Items or Trash Can folder, then exit your e-mail program or sign out of your Webmail service and exit your browser.

▼ INDEPENDENT CHALLENGE 4

You've recently set up office e-mail at Fiona's Hat Shop where you work. Now that clients and vendors have begun sending you e-mails, you need to set up a way of organizing the e-mail messages that you've received.

a. Start your e-mail program or sign into your Webmail service.

b. Send brief messages to four classmates, and send copies of the messages to yourself. Include the name of the store, Fiona's Hat Shop, somewhere in the body of two of the messages.

c. Retrieve and view all e-mail messages that you receive.

d. Create a folder named **Vendors** and a folder named **Clients**.

e. Move one e-mail message into the Vendors folder, then move three message into the Clients folder.

f. View the contents of both folders.

Advanced Challenge Exercise

- Return to the Inbox, then use the Find button to find the message sent to one of your classmates in the Clients folder.
- Use the Find button to find the two messages that included "Fiona's Hat Shop" in the body of the message.
- If you are using Outlook Express, use the Find button to search for all messages received after yesterday.

g. Delete the messages you sent and empty the Deleted Items or Trash Can folder, if necessary, then exit your e-mail program or sign out of your Webmail service and exit your browser.

▼ VISUAL WORKSHOP

Use the skills you learned in this unit to create the message shown in Figure C-42 if you are using Outlook Express or in Figure C-43 if you are using Hotmail. The file attachment is located in the drive and folder where your Data Files are stored. When you have completed the message and attached the file, add your name below Maleko's name, then send the message to your instructor or a colleague.

FIGURE C-42

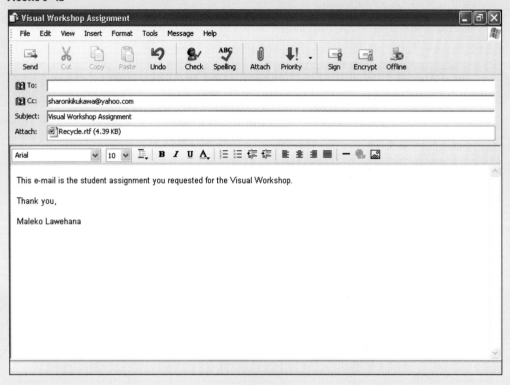

FIGURE C-43

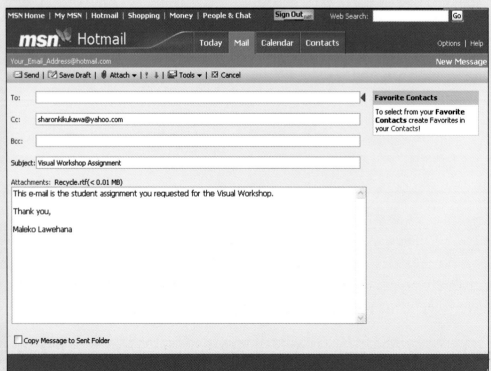

Searching the Web

OBJECTIVES

Define search engines
Develop a Web search strategy
Use a search engine
Use a Web directory
Use a meta-search engine
Use a subject guide
Understand advanced searching techniques
Conduct a search using the Advanced Search page
Conduct a search using Boolean operators

You can use the Web to access millions of Web pages, which contain information on a virtually unlimited number of topics. To find the information you want among all these Web pages, you need to learn searching methods and tools. ▓▓▓ Nancy Shand and Ranjit Singh, staff writers at the *Georgetown Journal*, a top-rated daily newspaper that serves the Georgetown metropolitan area, have hired you as their assistant. They want you to use the Web to help them gather information for their stories.

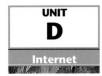

Defining Search Engines

A **search engine** is a Web site (or part of a Web site) that finds Web pages containing the word or phrase you specify. For example, you could enter the word "Louisiana" into the appropriate location in a search engine, and then click the Search button to get a list of Web pages that might contain information about Louisiana. ▓▓▓▓▓ Before you accept your first research assignment from Ranjit and Nancy, you decide to learn some of the terms associated with Web searching and search engines.

DETAILS

The following terms are associated with searching the Web:

- **Keywords and Search Expressions**

  A **search expression** or **query** is the words or phrases you enter when you conduct a search. A search expression can be composed of one or several words; each word in a search expression is called a **keyword**.

QUICK TIP
Many search engines include information about their search engines, robots, and databases on their Help or About pages.

- **Search Engine Databases**

  A search engine does not search the Web to find a match to the search expression you enter; it only searches its own database of Web content that it has catalogued. Each search engine database indexes the information it collects from the Web differently. Some search engines store the entire content of every Web page they index; other search engines collect information only from a Web page's title, description, keywords, or HTML tags; and others read only a certain amount of the text in each Web page. If the terms you use in your search expression are not in the part of the Web page that the search engine stores in its database, the search engine will not return a hit for that page. Therefore, if you enter the same search expression into different search engines, you will get some results that are the same and some that are different because each search engine contains a different set of information in its database and each search engine uses different procedures to search its database. You get the best results by entering keywords that don't have multiple meanings and are not articles or prepositions.

- **Web Robot**

  Each search engine uses a Web robot to build its database. A **Web robot**, also called a **bot** or a **spider**, is a program that automatically searches the Web to find new Web sites and updates information about old Web sites that are already in the database. A Web robot also deletes information in the database when a Web site no longer exists. The main advantage of using an automated searching tool is that it can examine far more Web sites than an army of people ever could. However, the Web changes every day and even the best search engine sites cannot keep their databases completely updated. When you click links on a search engine results page, you will find that some of the Web pages no longer exist.

- **Hits**

  A **hit** is a Web page that is indexed in the search engine's database and contains text that matches your search expression.

- **Results Pages**

  All search engines provide a series of **results pages**, which include links to Web pages that match your search expression. Figure D-1 shows a results page using the Google search engine for the search expression *modern art*.

- **Narrowing the Search Results**

  To narrow your search results, create a search expression that contains more than one keyword; most search engines will search for pages that contain all of the words in your search expression, although in no particular order. If you want to search for pages that contain a specific phrase, you enclose the phrase in quotation marks in the search expression. For example, if you search for pages that contain the keyword *rice*, one search engine returns over 18 million hits, and the pages cover topics ranging from a page for Rice University to a page about someone who's last name is Rice to pages having something to do with rice, the grain. But if you search using the search expression *brown rice*, the number of hits decreases to about a 7.5 million; and if you search with *"brown rice"* (enclosed in quotation marks) the number of hits decreases to about 1 million. Finally, if you add the keyword *recipe* so that the complete search expression is *"brown rice" recipe*, the number of hits decreases again to about a half million.

FIGURE D-1: One search engine's results page for a search on keywords "modern" and "art"

Sponsored links

Keywords appear in this Web page title

List of search results

Keywords appear in this Web page description

Clues to Use

How search engines are financed

The organizations that operate search engines often sell advertising space on the search engine Web site and on the results pages. An increasing number of search engine operators also sell paid placement links on results pages. For example, Toyota might want to purchase rights to the keyword *car*. When you enter a search expression that includes the keyword *car*, the search engine creates a results page that has a link to Toyota's Web site at or near the top of the results page. Most, but not all, search engines label these paid placement links as **sponsored links**. If the advertising appears in a box on the page (usually at the top, but sometimes along the side or bottom of the page), it is called a **banner ad**. Search engine Web sites use the advertising revenue to generate profit after covering the costs of maintaining the computer hardware and software required to search the Web and create and search the database. The only price you pay for access to these tools is that you see advertising banners on many of the results pages and you might have to scroll through some sponsored links at the top of results pages; otherwise, your usage is free.

Internet

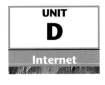

Developing a Web Search Strategy

UNIT
D
Internet

You can use the Web to quickly find answers to specific questions or as a resource to explore interesting concepts and ideas. Each of these question types, specific and exploratory, requires a different search strategy. Before you start accepting research requests from Nancy and Ranjit, you decide to familiarize yourself with a searching strategy.

DETAILS

Consider the following as you develop a search strategy:

- **Specific Question**

    A **specific question** is a question that you can phrase easily and has only one answer. Specific questions might require you to start with broad categories of information and then gradually narrow the search until you find the answer to your question. Figure D-2 shows this process of sequential, increasingly focused questioning. As you narrow your search, you might find results that do not lead you to the answer of your question. If that happens, you need to choose the result (or path) that will lead you to the correct answer as shown in Figure D-2.

- **Exploratory Question**

    An **exploratory question** starts with a general, open-ended question that leads to other, less general questions, which result in multiple answers. The answers to the questions at each level should lead you to more information about the topic you are researching. This information then leads you to more questions and answers. Figure D-3 shows how this questioning process broadens the scope of results as you gather information pertinent to the exploratory question.

- **Conducting a Search**

    Once you determine the type of question you need to use in your search, you can begin the actual Web search process. After you carefully formulate and state your question, you select the appropriate tool or tools to use in your search, and then conduct the search.

- **Evaluating the Results**

    After obtaining your results from a Web search tool, you need to evaluate these results to determine if they answer your question. If they do not, you continue the search by refining or redefining your question and then selecting a different search tool to see if you get a different result. The first three steps are the same for both specific and exploratory questions, but the determination of when your search process is completed is different for the each type of question. For specific questions, you repeat this process as many times as necessary until you obtain the specific answer you seek; for exploratory questions, you repeat it until you have found a satisfactory range of information regarding your topic.

- **Refining the Search**

    After evaluating your results, you might decide that your question was not answered. If the results do not answer the question to your satisfaction, you need to redefine or reformulate the question and reconsider the search expression you used. Then you need to conduct a second search using a different question or search expression.

FIGURE D-2: Specific research question search process

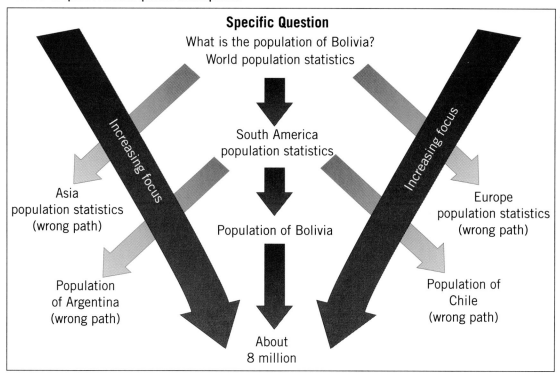

Specific Question
What is the population of Bolivia?
World population statistics

South America
population statistics

Population of Bolivia

About
8 million

Increasing focus

Asia
population statistics
(wrong path)

Population
of Argentina
(wrong path)

Increasing focus

Europe
population statistics
(wrong path)

Population of
Chile
(wrong path)

FIGURE D-3: Exploratory research question search process

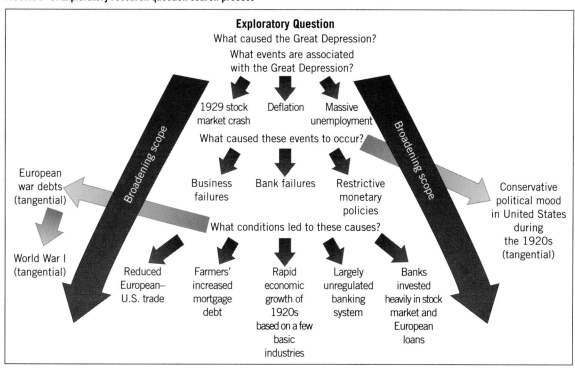

Exploratory Question
What caused the Great Depression?
What events are associated
with the Great Depression?

1929 stock
market crash

Deflation

Massive
unemployment

What caused these events to occur?

Business
failures

Bank failures

Restrictive
monetary
policies

What conditions led to these causes?

Broadening scope

European
war debts
(tangential)

World War I
(tangential)

Reduced
European–
U.S. trade

Farmers'
increased
mortgage
debt

Rapid
economic
growth of
1920s
based on a few
basic
industries

Largely
unregulated
banking
system

Banks
invested
heavily in stock
market and
European
loans

Broadening scope

Conservative
political mood
in United States
during
the 1920s
(tangential)

Using a Search Engine

No one knows how many Web pages exist on the Web, but the number is now in the billions. Each of these Web pages might contain thousands of words, images, or links to downloadable files. Unlike the content of a library, the content of the Web is not indexed in any standardized way. Fortunately, you can use search engines to help you find the information you need. ▓▓▓▓ Nancy needs to know the average temperature on Mars for a story that she is writing. This search question is a specific question, not an exploratory question, because you are looking for one specific answer—the average temperature on Mars.

STEPS

TROUBLE

If the results page contains a message that the search engine couldn't find any results that matched your search expression, return to the Student Online Companion, choose a different search engine, then repeat Steps 2 and 3.

1. **Start your Web browser, go to the Student Online Companion at** www.course.com/illustrated/internet4, **click the** Unit D link, **then click one of the links to a search engine under Lesson 3**

   Your browser opens the home page of the search engine you chose.

2. **Type** Mars average temperature **in the search expression text box**

   Figure D-4 shows the search expression entered in the Search text box on the home page of the AlltheWeb search engine.

3. **Click the appropriate button to start the search (this button is usually labeled "Search," "Go," or "Find")**

   The search results appear on a new results page, which states that there are thousands of Web pages that might contain the answer to your query.

TROUBLE

If you do not find any useful links on the first page of search results, click the numbers at the bottom of the results page to open additional results pages.

4. **Scroll down the results page, examine your search results, then click links until you find a Web page that provides the average temperature of Mars**

   The average temperature on Mars is -63° Celsius, -81° Fahrenheit. (Some Web sites might report a slightly different number.)

5. **Return to the Student Online Companion at** www.course.com/illustrated/internet4, **click the** Unit D link, **then click a link to another of the search engines listed under Lesson 3**

   The home page of the search engine you chose opens.

6. **Type** Mars average temperature **in the search expression text box**

   Figure D-5 shows the search expression entered in the search expression text box in the AOL search engine.

7. **Click the appropriate button to start the search**

   The search results appear on a new results page. Figure D-6 shows the results page in MSN Search.

8. **Scroll down the results page, examine your search results, then click links until you find the average temperature of Mars**

   Once again, you should find that the average temperature on Mars is -63° Celsius, -81° Fahrenheit. Your specific search was successful.

Clues to Use

Word variants in search engines

Most major search engines search for variants of keywords automatically. For example, if you search using the keywords *Canada travel guide*, most search engines will return hits that include the keywords "Canadian" as well as "Canada" as well as pages containing the plural form of the word "guide." Unfortunately, you cannot dictate which variant of your keywords the search engine will use.

FIGURE D-4: Search expression entered in the AlltheWeb search engine

Search expression

Click to conduct search

FIGURE D-5: Search expression entered in the AOL search engine

Search expression

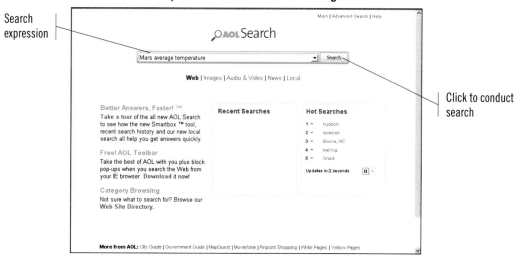

Click to conduct search

FIGURE D-6: Results page in MSN Search

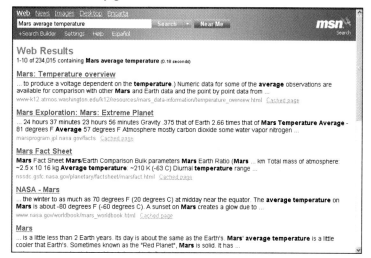

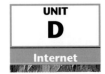
Using a Web Directory

A **Web directory** is a list of links to Web pages that is organized into hierarchical categories. Web directories and search engines both use a database of links to Web pages to enable users to search for information in different ways. Rather than using a database compiled by Web bots, however, a Web directory uses human editors or computers to decide which Web pages will be included in the directory and in which category to store the link to selected Web pages. Users can browse for information by general categories, rather than by using specific search terms. Many Web directories now include search engines, and you need to click a link on the site's home page to view the directory. Ranjit wants to know the latest news and information about his profession. He asks you to provide him with a set of links to Web sites about the media industry. You use a directory to identify Web sites based on the category of information that Ranjit needs.

STEPS

1. **Go to the Student Online Companion at** www.course.com/illustrated/internet4, **click the** Unit D link, **then click one of the links to a Web directory under Lesson 4**

   The directory you selected opens. The home page contains a list of categories into which the directory links are organized. The Netscape Search directory is shown in Figure D-7.

> **QUICK TIP**
> A category that contains the term "Media," "Professions," or "Jobs" would be a good choice.

2. **Examine the categories on the directory's home page and click a link that is likely to contain information about the journalism profession**

   The page you selected opens, showing links to lower levels in the hierarchy, links in the hierarchies of other categories, and, usually, some sponsored links.

3. **Examine the page that loads in your browser and search for links to subcategories that include words such as "industry news" or "industry updates"**

   You might need to search several levels down in the directory to find the information you are looking for.

> **QUICK TIP**
> In some Web directories, you can search within a category.

4. **When you find a link to a subcategory that seems like it contains information about the media industry, click it**

   The LookSmart Web directory, after following the Work & Money/Industries/Entertainment & Media links, is shown in Figure D-8.

5. **Examine the links on the page that opens in your browser, then, if the category doesn't seem narrow enough or the links are not appropriate, click additional subcategories until you see links that might contain the information you are searching for**

6. **Click one of the links listed in the subcategory and examine the Web page**

7. **Navigate back to the subcategory page, click a different subcategory link, then examine the Web page**

Clues to Use

Understanding hybrid search engine directories

Most Web directories today are part of Web sites that also include search engines; for example, Google, Yahoo!, and LookSmart offer standard search engines as well as directories. You can click the More link at the top of the Google home page, then click the Directory link to view the Google directory; scroll down the Yahoo! home page to the Yahoo! Web Directory section, then click the More Yahoo! Web Directory to view the Yahoo! directory; or click the Web or Directory tab in the LookSmart home page to alternate between the search engine and the directory. This **hybrid search engine**, a combination of search engine and directory, provides a powerful and effective tool for searching the Web. You can use the directory in a hybrid search engine to help you identify which category in the directory is likely to contain the information you need. After you enter a category, you can use the search engine to narrow the search even further by entering a search expression and limiting the search to that category.

FIGURE D-7: Netscape Search directory categories

Main categories in the Netscape Search directory

Subcategories in Netscape Search directory

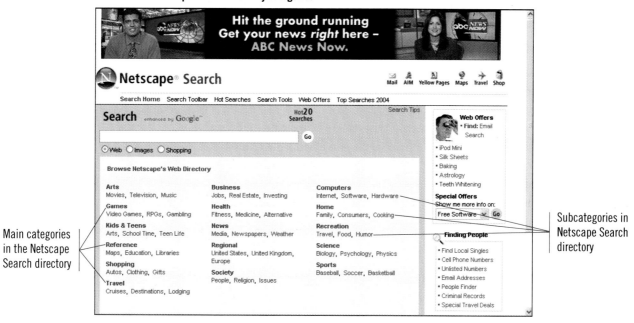

FIGURE D-8: LookSmart Entertainment & Media directory page

LookSmart directory hierarchy

Additional subcategories to search

Related links on other sites

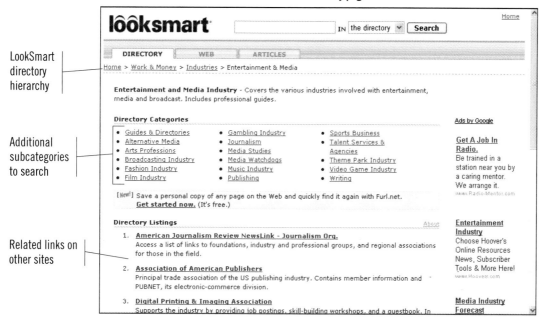

Internet

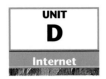

Using a Meta-Search Engine

A **meta-search engine** is a tool that uses multiple search engines. Using a meta-search engine, you can search several search engines simultaneously, so you don't have to conduct the same search in different search engines. Most meta-search engines forward your queries to a number of major search engines and directories, including Google, Lycos, MSN Search, Teoma, and several others. After a meta-search engine sends your search expression to several search engines, the search engines compare the search expression against their databases of Web page information and return results to the results page of the meta-search engine for you to view. Some meta-search engines identify the search engine they retrieve the links from; others do not. ▓▓▓▓ You want to learn how to use meta-search engines so that you can access information more quickly. You decide to use Nancy's question about the average temperature on Mars to test a meta-search engine.

STEPS

1. **Go to the Student Online Companion at** www.course.com/illustrated/internet4, **click the Unit D link**, **then click one of the links under Lesson 5**

   The home page of the meta-search engine you chose opens.

QUICK TIP

Mamma.com was one of the first meta-search engines on the Web.

2. **Type** Mars average temperature **in the search expression text box**

   Figure D-9 shows the search expression entered in the Mamma.com meta-search engine.

3. **Click the appropriate button to start the search**

   A results page appears showing the hits for each search engine that the meta-search engine searched. If you used the Turbo10 meta-search engine, you might see results similar to the results page shown in Figure D-10.

4. **Examine your search results, then click appropriate links to find the average temperature on Mars**

   As you scroll through the results pages in a meta-search engine, you might see a wide variation in the number and quality of the results provided by each search engine or directory. Although most of the Web pages returned by one search tool will not be returned by any other search tool, you also might notice duplicate hits.

Clues to Use

Using natural language queries

A few search engines, such as the Ask Jeeves search engine, use natural language querying. A **natural language query** allows users to enter a question exactly as they would ask a person that question. The search engine analyzes the question using knowledge it has been given about the grammatical structure of questions and then uses that knowledge to convert the natural language question into a search query. This procedure of converting a natural language question into a search expression is sometimes called **parsing**.

FIGURE D-9: Search expression entered in the Mamma.com meta-search engine

Search expression

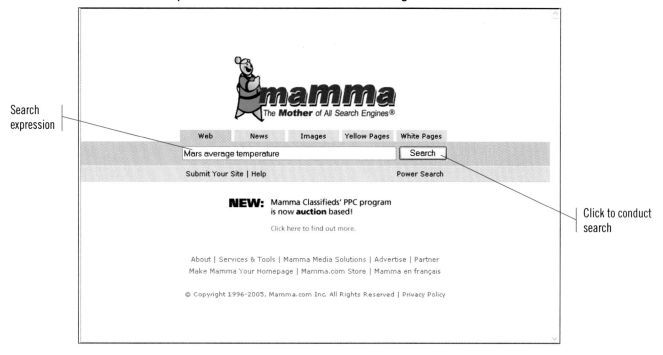

Click to conduct search

FIGURE D-10: Turbo10 meta-search engine results

Indicates number of results pages

Search results returned by A9.com

Search results returned by Ask.com (also called Ask Jeeves)

Search results returned by WiseNut.com

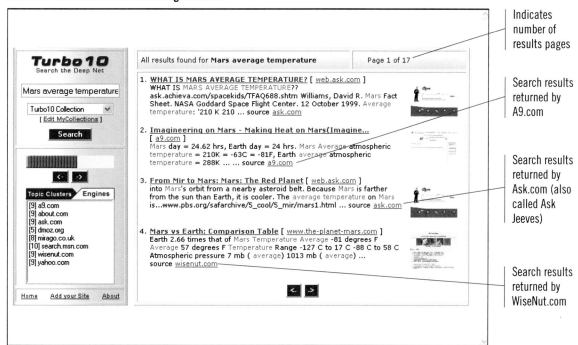

UNIT
D

Internet

Using a Subject Guide

A **subject guide** (also called a **Web bibliography, clearinghouse,** or **virtual library**) organizes references into categories and subcategories. In a subject guide, each reference is a link to a Web page. Some subject guides include **annotations** (summaries or reviews) of Web pages. This information can help you identify Web pages that fit your level of knowledge or interest. ████ Ranjit informs you that he needs information about the business and economic effects of current trends in biotechnology and the potential effects of genetic engineering research. He asks you to find some Web sites that he can explore to learn more about biotechnology trends in general and genetic engineering research in particular. You know that biotechnology is a branch of the biological sciences, so you identify three keywords, *biotechnology*, *genetic engineering*, and *biology*, to use as you browse the subject guide's categories. You decide to use a subject guide so that you can use the provided reviews to help you determine the best links to give to Ranjit.

STEPS

1. **Go to the Student Online Companion at** www.course.com/illustrated/internet4, **click the Unit D link, click one of the links to a Web bibliography under Lesson 6, then scroll down the Web page and read the category links**

2. **Examine the page for links that might lead to information about biotechnology, genetic engineering, or biology, and then click one of the links**

   A list of subcategories opens.

3. **Click an appropriate subcategory link, then click links as necessary to find the information that Ranjit requested; again, look for categories that mention biotechnology, genetic engineering, or biology**

   A list of keywords in the selected subcategory appears.

4. **Click the biotechnology link**

   A list of links appears, or you might need to click additional subcategories. The list of links that appear after following the Science/Technology/Biotechnology links in the Librarian's Index to the Internet is shown in Figure D-11. Some bibliographies, like Argus Clearinghouse, evaluate a Web site on a separate page. Figure D-12 shows the links in the Argus Clearinghouse after following the Science & Mathematics/biology/biotechnology links; Figure D-13 shows the guide information page in Argus Clearinghouse for the National Biotechnology Information Facility Web site.

Clues to Use

Subject guides vs. search engines

Subject guides are compiled by reference experts or experts in the categorized fields, so they naturally do not list as many references as a search engine would. So why would you want to use a subject guide when you are given fewer results in response to a search? Subject guides are useful when you want to obtain a broad overview or a basic understanding of a complex subject area. For example, using a search engine or directory to find information about quantum physics could give you millions of hits to technical papers and Web pages devoted to current research issues in quantum physics. In contrast, a subject guide page can offer hyperlinks to specific information about quantum physics at various levels so you can quickly find pages that give you a basic introduction to the subject or offer the latest news about the subject.

FIGURE D-11: Biotechnology subcategory in the Librarian's Index to the Internet

Indicates total number of results

Subject category selected

Review of site

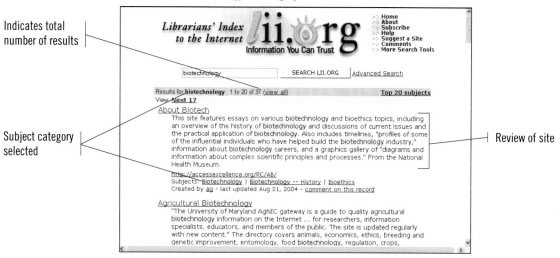

FIGURE D-12: Biotechnology subcategory in Argus Clearinghouse

Subcategory

Navigation path through the category-subcategory-keyword hierarchy

Five check marks indicate a highly rated site

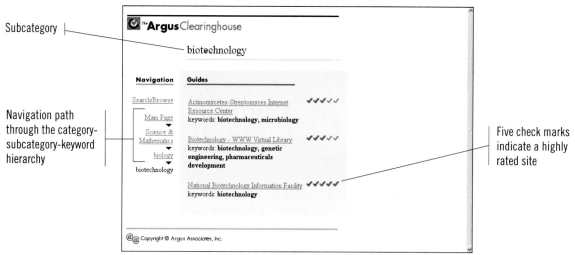

FIGURE D-13: Argus Clearinghouse guide information for National Biotechnology Information Facility Web site

Biotechnology Information Facility Web site

Selected keyword

Author information

Rating information

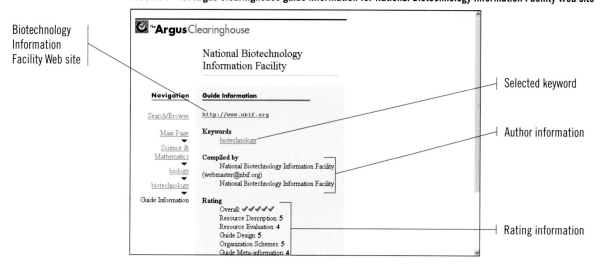

Understanding Advanced Searching Techniques

To get reliable results from a search engine or a meta-search engine, you must select your keywords carefully. When the objective of your search is straightforward, you can choose one or two words that will work well. More complex search questions require more complex queries to broaden or narrow your search expression. Recall that you can restrict the search to pages that contain a specific phrase by enclosing your search expression in quotation marks. You can also use various additional techniques to perform advanced searches that will give you results pages more relevant to your search question. Some of the questions Ranjit and Nancy ask require you to find specific information. You decide to learn about techniques for formulating complex queries to reduce the number of irrelevant hits in your search results.

DETAILS

The following terms are associated with advanced Web searching:

- **Advanced Search Pages in Search Engines**

  Most search engines use an Advanced Search page to provide users with a step-by-step process for conducting an advanced search. You use menus, option buttons, and text boxes to make selections that identify your search criteria. Figure D-14 shows the Advanced Search page in Teoma.

QUICK TIP

Note that typing a phrase in the text box that restricts the search to all of the keywords is not the same as using quotation marks around the search expression; in the first case, using the keywords *holiday cards*, results pages are not restricted to pages that contain the phrase "holiday cards," just pages that contain the word *holiday* and the word *cards* somewhere in the page.

- **Search Filters**

  A **search filter** eliminates Web pages from a search. You can access search filter options for a search engine on its Advanced Search page. You can use the filter to specify a language, date, domain, host, or page component (such as a URL, link, image tag, or title tag). For example, you could search for a term, such as *exports*, in Web page titles and ignore Web pages in which the term appears in other parts of the Web page. You can also use the keywords to filter your results by typing the keywords in a text box that indicates that the results pages will contain *all* of the keywords or in a text box that indicates that the results pages will contain *any* of the keywords. For example, if you wanted to find pages about holiday cards, you would type the keywords *holiday cards* in the text box that restricts the search to all of the keywords; but if you wanted to find information about the holidays and cards but not necessarily "holiday cards," you would type the keywords *holiday cards* in the text box that opens up the search to include Web pages that contain only the keyword "holiday" or only the keyword "cards."

- **Boolean Operators**

  If you want, you can conduct an advanced search from the start page in a search engine by using Boolean operators. **Boolean operators**, also called **logical operators**, specify the logical relationship between the elements they join, just as the plus sign specifies the mathematical relationship between the two elements it joins. Most search engines recognize at least three basic Boolean operators: AND, OR, and NOT. You can use these operators in many search engines by simply including them in the search expression.

- **Precedence Operators**

  When you join three or more search terms with Boolean operators, you can easily become confused by the expression's complexity. To reduce the confusion, you can use precedence operators along with the Boolean operators. A **precedence operator**, also called an **inclusion operator** or a **grouping operator**, clarifies the grouping within a complex expression and is usually indicated by parentheses. Table D-1 shows several ways to use Boolean operators and precedence operators in more complex search expressions that contain the words *exports*, *France*, and *Japan*.

- **Location Operators**

  A **location operator**, or **proximity operator**, lets you search for terms that appear close to each other in the text of a Web page. The most common location operator offered in search engines is the NEAR operator. For example, if you are interested in French exports, you might want to find only Web pages in which the terms *exports* and *France* are close to each other, so to perform this search you would type *exports NEAR France*.

FIGURE D-14: Advanced Search page in Teoma search engine

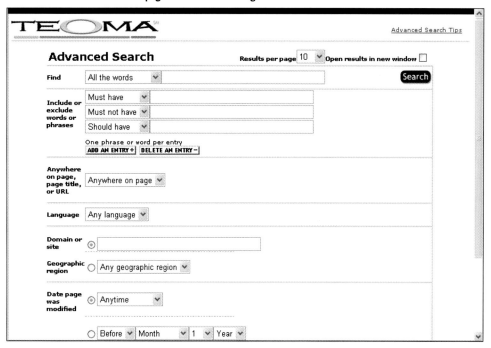

TABLE D-1: Use of Boolean and precedence operators in search expressions

search expression	search returns web pages that include	use to find information about
exports AND France AND Japan	All of the three search terms	Exports from France to Japan or from Japan to France
exports OR France OR Japan	Any of the three search terms	Exports from anywhere, including France and Japan, and all kinds of information about France and Japan
exports AND France NOT Japan	Exports and France, but not Japan	Exports to and from France to anywhere else, except exports shipped to and from Japan
exports AND (France OR Japan)	Exports and either France or Japan	Exports from or to either France or Japan
exports AND (France NOT Japan)	Exports and France, but not if the Web page also includes Japan	Exports to and from France, except exports to and from Japan

Clues to Use

Understanding search engine assumptions

When you enter a single word into a search engine, it searches for matches to that word. When you enter a search expression that includes more than one word, the search engine makes assumptions about the words that you enter. Most search engines assume that you want to match all of the keywords in your search expression (as if you had used the AND operator); however, a few search engines assume that you want to match any of the keywords (as if you had used the OR operator). These differing assumptions can make dramatic differences in the number and quality of hits returned. You can always override the assumptions the search engine makes by using the advanced search page or Boolean operators. The best way to determine how a specific search engine interprets search expressions is to read the Help pages on the search engine Web site. Read these Help pages regularly because search engines change the way they interpret search expressions from time to time.

Internet

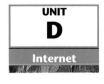

UNIT D
Internet

Conducting a Search Using the Advanced Search Page

The Advanced Search page in a search engine provides users with a step-by-step process for conducting an advanced search. You use menus, option buttons, and text boxes to make selections that identify your search criteria. ▓▓▓▓ Nancy is writing an article about Finland and would like to interview a professor she once met who taught graduate business students there. She does not remember the professor's name or the name of the university at which the professor teaches, but she does remember that the professor was part of the School of Economics at a university in Finland. She asks if you can search the Web to find the names of some Finnish universities that have a School of Economics. You decide to use the Advanced Search page of a search engine to conduct your search.

STEPS

1. **Go to the Student Online Companion at** www.course.com/illustrated/internet4, **click the** Unit D link, **then click one of the links under Lesson 8**
   The home page of the search engine you chose opens.

2. **Click the** Advanced Search link **on the Web page**
   First, you want to restrict the search to Web pages in English since you don't speak Finnish.

3. **Look for the section that restricts the search to Web pages in a specific language, then select the option to restrict the search to only Web pages written in English**
   Next you want to restrict your search to the domain .fi because schools in Finland use that domain.

TROUBLE
If the search engine you chose does not allow you to restrict the search to a domain, skip Step 4.

4. **Look for the section that restricts the search to a specific domain, then select the appropriate option or type in the appropriate text box to restrict the search to Web pages in the Finland country domain (.fi)**

TROUBLE
If the search engine you chose does not offer a text box to restrict the search to searching to an exact phrase, type "School of Economics" (including the quotes) in the same text box you used in Step 5 to enter the word "Finland."

5. **In the section that provides options for identifying whether you want the search engine to search for all or any of the keywords you specify, look for options such as "Any of the words" or "All of the words," select the option for** All of the words, **then type** Finland **in the appropriate text box**

6. **Look for an option that restricts the search engine to searching for an exact phrase, then type** School of Economics **in the appropriate text box**
   Figure D-15 shows the completed Advanced Search page in Goggle.

TROUBLE
If a message appears telling you that you didn't enter any search terms, type **Finland** in the search expression text box at the top of the Advanced Search page, then repeat the search.

7. **Click the appropriate button to start the search**
   The search results page opens. Figure D-16 shows the search results in AOL Search.

FIGURE D-15: Completed advanced search page in Google

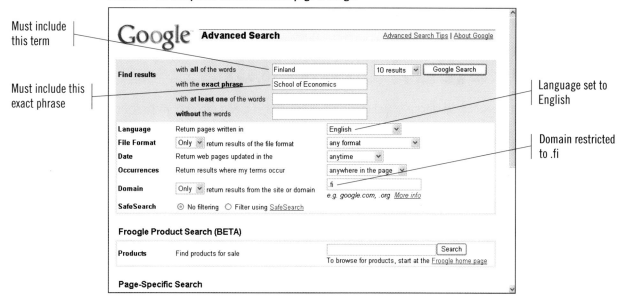

Must include this term

Must include this exact phrase

Language set to English

Domain restricted to .fi

FIGURE D-16: Search results page in AOL Search

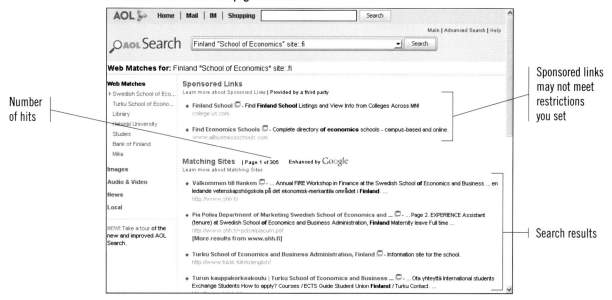

Number of hits

Sponsored links may not meet restrictions you set

Search results

Clues to Use

Using search engines with clustering features

One problem with using search engines is that they often generate thousands (or even millions) of hits. Scrolling through hundreds of results pages looking for useful links is not very efficient. Some search engines use an advanced technology to group search results into clusters. The clustering of results provides a filtering effect; however, the filtering is done automatically by the search engine after it runs the search. Figure D-17 shows the search results for weather patterns in the past six months in Southeast Asia in Vivisimo, a search engine that clusters results.

FIGURE D-17: Search results page in Vivisimo clustered search

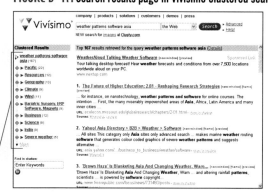

Search results collected into clusters of related links

Internet

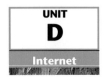

Conducting a Search Using Boolean Operators

Sometimes the Advanced Search page does not offer you enough options to structure your search expression the way that you want. In that case, you can try searching using Boolean operators. ▓▓▓▓ Ranjit is writing about fast-food franchises in various developing countries around the world. He would like to feature this industry's experience in Indonesia in an upcoming story and asks you for help. You recognize this request as an exploratory question and decide to use Boolean operators in a search engine to conduct a complex search for Web pages that Ranjit can use for his research.

STEPS

1. **Go to the Student Online Companion at** www.course.com/illustrated/internet4, **click the Unit D link, then click one of the links under Lesson 9**

   The home page of the search engine you chose opens.

2. **Type** "fast food" franchises Indonesia OR Thailand **in the search expression text box**

   This query instructs the search engine to look for Web pages containing the following characteristics: the exact phrase "fast food"; the word "franchises"; and either the word "Indonesia" or the word "Thailand." You don't need to type the Boolean operator "AND" because all of the search engines listed under Lesson 9 use all the keywords in the search expression by default. Figure D-18 shows the search expression in the Yahoo! search engine.

3. **Click the appropriate button to start the search**

   The search results appear in the window. Figure D-19 shows the search results in the Lycos search engine.

4. **Note the number of hits at the top of the list of links, then examine some of the descriptions of the first 10 results**

   You may need to go to several results pages to find the information you are looking for.

5. **Exit your Web browser**

FIGURE D-18: Search expression with Boolean operators in Yahoo!

Search expression as you typed it

FIGURE D-19: Search results of Boolean search in Lycos

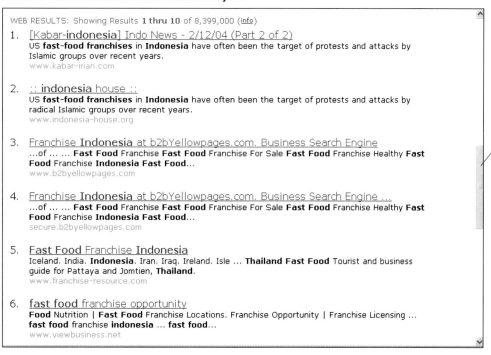

Page scrolled down to see search results

Practice

▼ CONCEPTS REVIEW

Describe the function of each element in the Netscape Search window shown in Figure D-20.

FIGURE D-20

Match each term with the statement that best describes it.

5. Search engine *b*
6. Web robot *d*
7. Subject guide *g*
8. Boolean operator *c*
9. Meta-search engine *e*
10. Boolean expression *f*
11. Hit *g*

a. A Web page that is indexed in the search engine's database and contains text that matches the search expression
b. A Web site that finds other Web pages containing the word or phrase you specify
c. Describes the relationship between words in a search expression
d. Often called a spider
e. Provides search results from several search engines
f. Japan AND (food OR sushi)
g. A search engine that organizes references into categories and subcategories

Select the best answer from the list of choices.

12. **What is the term that describes a Web page found by a search engine that matches your search expression?**
    - **a.** Results pages
    - **b.** Hit *(circled)*
    - **c.** Bot
    - **d.** Query

13. **Which of the following is a list of links to Web pages organized into hierarchical categories?**
    - **a.** Advanced search page
    - **b.** Meta-search engine
    - **c.** Web bibliography *(circled)*
    - **d.** Search engine

14. **Mamma.com is an example of a:**
    - **a.** Web spider.
    - **b.** meta-search engine. *(circled)*
    - **c.** search engine.
    - **d.** Boolean operator.

15. **Which of the following allows you to search for terms that appear close to each other in the text of a Web page?**
    - **a.** Boolean operator
    - **b.** Location operator *(circled)*
    - **c.** Precedence operator
    - **d.** Search filter

16. **Which of the following Boolean expressions will search for Web pages that contain the words "ranking" or "rating" as well as the word "college"?**
    - **a.** College OR ranking OR rating
    - **b.** College AND ranking AND rating
    - **c.** College AND ranking NOT rating
    - **d.** College AND ranking OR rating *(circled)*

▼ SKILLS REVIEW

1. **Use a search engine.**
   - **a.** Go to the Student Online Companion at **www.course.com/illustrated/internet4**, click the **Unit D link**, then click one of the search engine links under Skills Review 1.
   - **b.** Use **capital Bulgaria** as a search expression.
   - **c.** Perform the search.   *all the web . com*
   - **d.** Examine the search results to find the capital of Bulgaria.
   - **e.** Record the number of hits. (*Hint*: This is usually noted at the top of the search results page.)
   - **f.** Use a different search engine to search for the same information.
   - **g.** Record the number of hits on this page.
   - **h.** Note which of the two search engines found more hits.
   - **i.** Briefly explain which search engine provided the information you were searching for closer to the top of the search results.

2. **Use a Web directory.**
   - **a.** Go to the Student Online Companion at **www.course.com/illustrated/internet4**, click the **Unit D link**, then click one of the directory links under Skills Review 2.
   - **b.** Follow the category and subcategory links that you think will lead you to lists of museums and art galleries.
   - **c.** Note which Web directory you used and the category path to the page that lists categories for museums and art galleries. (*Hint:* You might find that museums and art galleries are listed in different subcategories.)

3. **Use a meta-search engine.**
   - **a.** Go to the Student Online Companion at **www.course.com/illustrated/internet4**, click the **Unit D link**, then click one of the meta-search engine links under Skills Review 3.
   - **b.** Use **Olympics 2004 gymnastics gold men** as a search expression, then perform the search.
   - **c.** Scroll through the results and look at the first result returned from five search engines shown on the results page.
   - **d.** Read the descriptions of the links returned. You are looking for the name of the man who won the all-around gymnastics gold medal at the 2004 Summer Olympics.
   - **e.** Follow the links to find the winner's name, keeping a list of the links you follow.
   - **f.** When you find the gold-medal winner, record his name. Did you go down any wrong paths? Were you surprised at any of the hits that resulted from your search expression?

Internet

4. **Use a subject guide.**

   a. Go to the Student Online Companion at www.course.com/illustrated/internet4, click the Unit D link, then click one of the subject guide links under Skills Review 4.

   b. Starting with a link that is likely to contain links to information about health and fitness, follow the appropriate links to find a list of links that contain general information about fitness.

   c. Record the URL of two of the sites you find.

5. **Conduct a search using the Advanced Search page.**

   a. Go to the Student Online Companion at www.course.com/illustrated/internet4, click the Unit D link, then click one of the search engine links under Skills Review 5.

   b. Go to the Advanced Search page.

   c. Specify the last 3 months as the search time frame.

   d. Specify Oceania as the region.

   e. Enter marsupials as a term that must be included and numbats as a term that must not be included.

   f. Perform the search.

   g. Record how many hits your search turned up (even if it's zero).

6. **Conduct a search using Boolean operators.**

   a. Go to the Student Online Companion at www.course.com/illustrated/internet4, click the Unit D link, then click one of the search engine links under Skills Review 6.

   b. Use the following Boolean expression to search for information about Scotland, Edinburgh or Glasgow, bagpipes, and folk groups: Scotland AND (Edinburgh OR Glasgow) AND bagpipes AND folk groups. (*Hint*: Although you do not need to use the AND operator in many search engines, it is fine to do so even if the search engine includes all of the search terms by default.)

   c. Refine the search further by specifying to exclude pages with the word "accommodations." Use the following Boolean expression: Scotland AND (Edinburgh OR Glasgow) AND bagpipes AND folk groups NOT accommodations

   d. Find a Web page listing Scottish folk groups and folk bands and note the URL.

   e. Exit your browser.

▼ INDEPENDENT CHALLENGE 1

A friend is putting together a Web site on rural living. She wants you to help her find additional Web sites on rural living so she can create a page of links to these Web sites as a resource to her visitors. You use Web search tools to find Web sites on this topic and select a small number of links that seem particularly useful.

   a. Go to the Student Online Companion at www.course.com/illustrated/internet4, then click the Unit D link. The links under Independent Challenges are for search engines, directories, and meta-search engines. Use these links as a starting point for your search.

   b. Choose at least one search tool from each category and conduct a search using the keywords rural and living.

   c. Extend or narrow your search using each tool until you find five Web sites that you believe are comprehensive guides or directories that your friend should link to on her Web site.

   d. For each Web site, record the URL and note why you believe the Web site would be useful to someone looking for information and resources on rural life. Identify each Web site as a guide, directory, or other resource.

▼ INDEPENDENT CHALLENGE 2

A friend who's never used the Web finds it hard to believe that you can find information about almost anything on the Web. You show him some of the resources that are available on the Web. To put the Web to the test, he asks five specific questions that he wants answers to during your session together.

   a. Go to the Student Online Companion at www.course.com/illustrated/internet4, click the Unit D link, then click one of the links under Independent Challenges.

▼ INDEPENDENT CHALLENGE 2 (CONTINUED)

b. Ask questions and perform searches to find the following pieces of information:

- The current temperature in Varberg, Sweden
- A picture of the flag of the state of Washington
- The telephone area code for New Orleans, Louisiana
- The number of miles in 30 kilometers
- The capital of British Columbia in Canada (*Hint*: Include the word "city" in your question.)

Advanced Challenge Exercise

- Use Boolean logic to search for a page in which the terms *republican* and *democrat* are near the term *libertarian*.
- Find a Web directory devoted to politics.
- Find a subject guide devoted to political science.

c. When you have found the answer to a question, record the search expression you used, the name of the search engine you used that led you to the Web site that contained the answer, the URL of the Web site that contained the answer, and the answer to the question.

▼ INDEPENDENT CHALLENGE 3

You are a manager at Key Consulting Group, a firm of geological and engineering consultants who specialize in earthquake-damage assessment. When an earthquake strikes, Key Consulting Group sends a team of geologists and structural engineers to the quake's site to examine the damage to buildings and determine what kinds of reconstruction will be needed. In some cases, the buildings must be demolished. Because an earthquake can occur without warning in many parts of the world, Key Consulting Group needs quick access to information about local conditions in various parts of the world, including the temperature, rainfall, and currency exchange rates. It is early July when you receive a call that an earthquake has just occurred in Japan. You decide to use the Web to obtain information about local midwinter conditions there.

a. Use a search tool to search for information on weather conditions in Japan in July and current exchange rates.

b. Record the daily temperature range, average annual rainfall, and current exchange rate for your currency to Japanese currency.

▼ INDEPENDENT CHALLENGE 4

You work as a marketing manager for Lightning Electrical Generators, Inc., a firm that has built generators for more than 50 years. The generator business is not as profitable as it once was, and John Delaney, the firm's president, asked you to investigate new markets for the company. John mentioned the fuel cell business, and explained that a fuel cell creates energy from gasoline through a chemical reaction, rather than burning it like a car does. John wants you to study the market for fuel cells in the United States. He wants to know which firms currently make and sell these products, and he wants to get some idea about the power ratings and prices for individual units.

a. Use a search tool to search for information about fuel cells. Design your searches to find the manufacturers' names and information about the products they offer.

Advanced Challenge Exercise

- Narrow your search to find Web pages that contain the exact phrase "negative impact on the environment."
- Narrow your search further by excluding pages that contain the term *fossil*.
- Narrow the search further by excluding Web pages whose domain name is .edu.

b. Prepare a short report that describes the information you have gathered, including the manufacturer's name, model number, product features, and suggested price for at least three fuel cells.

▼ VISUAL WORKSHOP

Go to the Student Online Companion at **www.course.com/illustrated/internet4**, click the **Unit D link**, then click the **Google link** under Visual Workshop. Set up the Google Advanced Search page so that it appears similar to the search page shown in Figure D-21. (*Hint*: Scroll up and down the search page if necessary so that you have the same information in the text boxes.) After you have set up the search page to search for Web pages related to coffee production in Costa Rica or Nicaragua, run the search and record the number of hits you receive. Then rewrite the search expression using Boolean operators.

FIGURE D-21

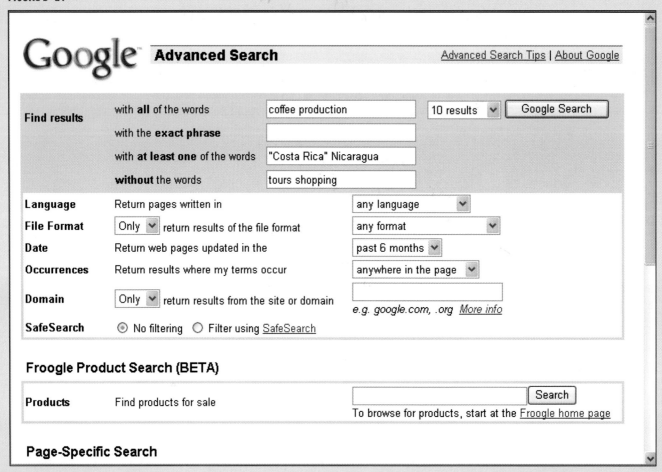

Getting Information from the Web

OBJECTIVES

Get the news
Obtain weather reports
Obtain maps and city guides
Find businesses and people
Find online reference tools
Evaluate Web resources
Understand copyrights and cite Web resources

For both businesses and individuals, the Web can be a valuable source of up-to-date information. You can get the latest news, print a map of your neighborhood, find a local business, and even reconnect with long-lost friends. In this unit, you will learn how to search the Web for current information, how to evaluate Web pages, and how to cite Web resources. 🖘🖘 You have just been hired by Cosby Promotions, a public relations firm. You are responsible for helping staff members stay current on news items and for providing up-to-date travel information to staff and clients.

Getting the News

You can easily find current news stories on the Web by using a news search engine. A **news search engine** searches only online news sites. All the major U.S. broadcasters, including ABC, CBS, CNN, Fox, MSNBC, and National Public Radio (NPR), maintain Web sites that carry news features. Broadcasters in other countries, such as the BBC, also provide news reports on their Web pages. Major newspapers, such as *The New York Times, The Washington Post,* and *The Times* in London, offer Web sites that include current news and many other features from their print editions. Marti Cosby, the president of Cosby Promotions, wants you to find recent news stories about NASA because a technical company heavily involved with the space program might become a client of Cosby Promotions. You decide to use a news search engine to look for recent news articles that mention NASA.

STEPS

1. **Go to the Student Online Companion at** www.course.com/illustrated/internet4, **click the Unit E link, then click one of the links to a news search engine under Lesson 1**

QUICK TIP
On the results pages of some news search engines, you can click a link to sort the results by date instead of by relevance.

2. **Type** NASA **in the search expression text box, then click the appropriate button to start the search**

   The search results page returned by the news search engine you chose lists articles related to NASA. See Figure E-2 for the results page for this search in the AltaVista news search engine.

3. **Explore two links that you believe will provide interesting information about NASA**

   When you click one of the links, a story opens from the publication's Web site, similar to the one shown in Figure E-3.

Clues to Use

Understanding RSS

Really Simple Syndication (RSS) is a file format that makes it possible to share updates, such as headlines, weather updates, and other Web site content, via a **newsfeed**, which is simply a file containing summaries of stories and news from a Web site. Most RSS newsfeeds must be read through a program called an **aggregator** that lets you receive newsfeed content. Some browsers, such as Firefox, and some e-mail programs, such as Thunderbird and Opera, have a built-in aggregator. You can use an RSS search engine to search the Web for newsfeeds relevant to your search expression. Figure E-1 shows the page from which you can subscribe to a newsfeed from the Reuters news service. When you subscribe to a newsfeed, you can accept the default update schedule or choose the frequency with which to download messages. Most newsfeeds update their content throughout the day. If you choose to download stories frequently, such as hourly, you'll receive notices of new stories being posted throughout the day without having to check the source.

FIGURE E-1: Subscribing to an RSS newsfeed from Reuters

Newsfeeds you can subscribe to

FIGURE E-2: AltaVista news search results for NASA

FIGURE E-2: AltaVista news search results for NASA

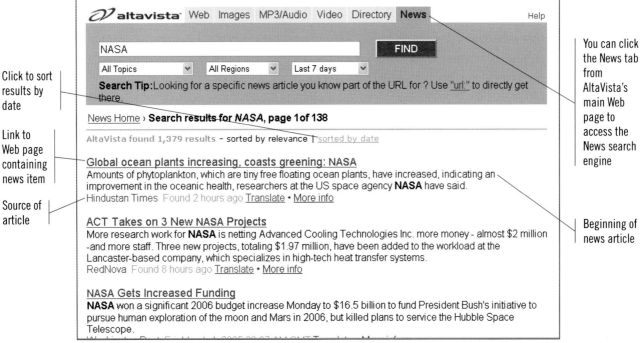

Click to sort results by date

Link to Web page containing news item

Source of article

You can click the News tab from AltaVista's main Web page to access the News search engine

Beginning of news article

FIGURE E-3: NASA-related news story on the Science Daily Web site

Clues to Use

Searching the archives on a news Web site

You can search the archives of most online news sources. Look for a search text box on the home page of the news Web site. Usually the site will return a list of links to relevant articles. Most online news sources allow you to view recent articles without registering or paying, but many require that you register or pay a fee for access to older articles. This is often indicated in the list of results.

Internet

Obtaining Weather Reports

You can obtain up-to-the-minute weather reports in destinations all over the world. This information is particularly useful for travelers. You can use the Web to check the weather report to find current local weather conditions and forecasts. ▆▆▆▆ Marti is planning two trips in the near future. First, she is going to Nashville later in the week to meet with some new country music artists whom she hopes to sign as clients for the agency. Next week, she is going to Europe where she will visit clients in Venice. She wants you to check the local weather conditions in both cities.

STEPS

1. **Go to the Student Online Companion at** www.course.com/illustrated/internet4, **click the** Unit E link, **then click one of the links to a weather service under Lesson 2**

TROUBLE
If a page appears telling you that no locations matched your search, click the Back button on the browser toolbar, then try typing simply "Nashville."

2. **Type** Nashville, TN **in the text box labeled "Forecast," "City, State," or something similar, then click the button next to that text box or press** [Enter] **to start your search**
   Depending on the Web site you chose, the current forecast for Nashville, TN, or a list of cities appears.

3. **If a list of cities appears, click the** Nashville, TN **or the** Nashville, Tennessee link
   A Web page showing current weather conditions in Nashville appears. Figure E-4 shows this information on the Weather.com Web site. Now you need to find the local weather conditions in Venice, Italy.

4. **Return to the Student Online Companion at** www.course.com/illustrated/internet4, **click the** Unit E link, **then click one of the links to a weather service under Lesson 2**

5. **Type** Venice **in the text box labeled "Forecast," "City, State," or something similar, then click the button next to that text box or press** [Enter]
   Depending on the Web site you chose, you may see a page showing the current weather conditions in Venice, Italy; a page showing the current weather conditions in a U.S. city named Venice; or a page listing links to weather conditions for a number of cities named Venice.

6. **If the page that opened shows current the weather conditions for a city named Venice in the U.S., click a link on the page for** World Forecasts **then select** Europe **from a list or click the** Europe link **on the page; type** Venice, Italy **in a text box labeled "City, Country," or something similar or select** Italy **and then** Venice **(or** Venezia**) from lists; and finally click the appropriate button or press** [Enter]

7. **If the page that opened shows a list of links to weather conditions for a number of cities named Venice, click the** Venice, Italy link

8. **Compare your screen to Figure E-5, which shows the weather for Venice, Italy on AccuWeather.com**

Clues to Use

Searching for Web sites that have been modified recently

Sometimes you might want to find information about a topic on sites that have been recently modified because you want only the latest and most up-to-date information. Many search engines allow you to choose a date range when you enter a search expression. Some search engines let you choose preset time range options, such as "in the last week" or "in the last 3 months," to limit your search to sites that were last modified within the selected time period. Other search engines let you limit searches to dates before or after a specific date. And some search engines provide a way to search for sites within a specified date range; for example, you could limit a search to sites modified between April 24, 2006 and November 11, 2006.

FIGURE E-4: Weather.com results for Nashville, TN

Type city here
to get forecast

Click for
extended
forecasts

FIGURE E-5: AccuWeather results for Venice, Italy

Type city here
to get forecast

Click for
forecasts in
countries
other than
the U.S. and
Canada

Scroll down to
see extended
forecast

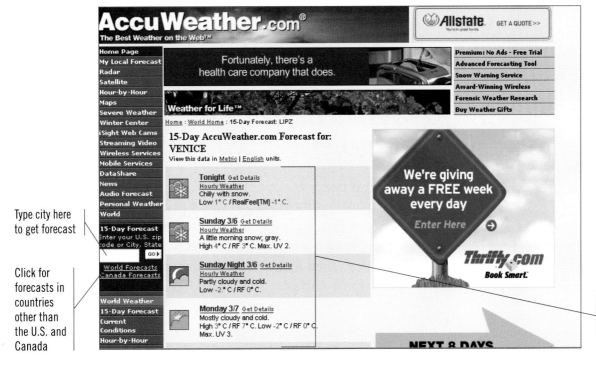

Internet

Obtaining Maps and City Guides

The Web includes a number of Web sites that provide maps and driving directions. Although the information provided by these sites is not perfect (new roads and detours caused by current construction work are not included), many people find them to be helpful travel aids. You can also use the Web to find a wealth of travel information, such as hotel and restaurant listings and sightseeing guides. ▰▰▰ While Marti is in Nashville, she wants to stop at Ryman Auditorium, the original home of the Grand Ole Opry. Marti gives you the address, 116 Fifth Avenue North, and asks you to find a map of Nashville on the Web that shows the location of Ryman Auditorium. She also asks you to look for additional information about Ryman Auditorium.

STEPS

TROUBLE

On an international Map site, click United States in the country list before typing the address.

TROUBLE

If a page opens telling you that the address could not be found, click the Back button, then change the address to "116 5th Avenue North".

1. **Go to the Student Online Companion at** www.course.com/illustrated/internet4, **click the** Unit E link, **then click one of the links under Map Sites in Lesson 3**
   The home page of the site you chose appears.

2. **Type** 116 Fifth Avenue North **in the text box labeled Address or something similar**

3. **Type** Nashville, **the city, and** TN, **the state, in the appropriate text boxes**
   The completed page on the MapQuest Web site is shown in Figure E-6.

4. **Click the appropriate button to start the search, usually** Get Map, Go, **or** Find
   The map appears for the address you entered. If you used MSN Maps, you will see a map similar to the one shown in Figure E-7. The exact location of the address you searched for, Ryman Auditorium, is marked on the map, on some sites with a red star, circle, or other indicator, and on other sites with a text box containing the address. Most maps include navigation tools that you can use to zoom in or out on the map, a link you can click to view a printable version of the map, and a link you can click to obtain directions to the address. Now you will use a city guide to obtain additional information about Ryman Auditorium.

5. **Return to the Student Online Companion at** www.course.com/illustrated/internet4, **click the** Unit E link, **then click one of the links under City Guides in Lesson 3**

6. **If necessary, click** North America **as the region you are interested in, then, if necessary, select** United States **as the country**

7. **Click the** Nashville link **if there is one (you may need to look for a** Tennessee link **first), or type** Nashville, TN **in a search text box then click the appropriate button to start your search**

8. **Click the** Attractions **or** Things to Do link **or type** Ryman Auditorium **in a search text box to search for more detailed information about Ryman Auditorium**
   Figure E-8 shows information about Ryman Auditorium in the Citysearch guide.

FIGURE E-6: Address entered in MapQuest

Address entered

Click to see map

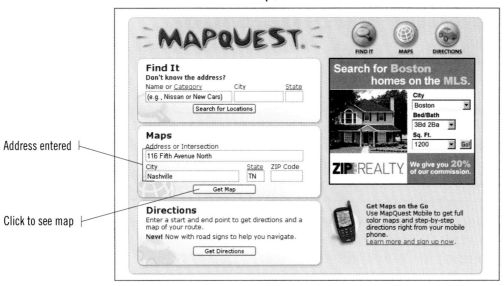

FIGURE E-7: Map from MSN Maps showing the location of Ryman Auditorium

Click to print map

Click links to get driving directions

Navigation tools to zoom in or out on map

Location of 116 Fifth Avenue North

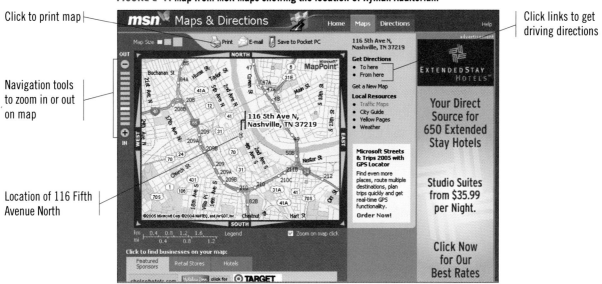

FIGURE E-8: Citysearch guide for Ryman Auditorium

Citysearch rating

Related attractions

Scroll down to read review

Finding Businesses and People

Yellow page directories are search engines that specialize in finding businesses; the businesses are grouped by type and location as in the yellow pages phone book. **White page directories** are search engines that enable you to search for addresses and telephone numbers for individuals as you would in a white pages phone book. In fact, this information is usually based on the printed telephone directory. Most sites that offer these types of directories offer both yellow and white pages directories. In addition, you can search for information about a person by simply typing the person's name into the search expression text box in a search engine. ▓▓▓▓ Marti needs to develop reciprocal relationships with public relations firms in Nashville. She wants to contact a few of them on her trip so she asks you to use a yellow pages directory to find public relations firms in Nashville. She also asks you to become more familiar with methods of searching for people on the Web.

STEPS

1. **Go to the Student Online Companion at** www.course.com/illustrated/internet4, **click the Unit E link, then click one of the links under Yellow & White Pages Directories in Lesson 4**
   All of these links are to sites that offer both yellow and white pages searches.

TROUBLE

If you chose a site whose home page asks you to choose a country, click the United States link, then perform Step 2.

2. **Click the** Yellow Pages **or** Business link, **if necessary**
   The page that contains search text boxes for the yellow pages directory on the site you chose opens.

3. **Click the** Category option button **or** Category link, **if necessary, then type** public relations **in the Category, Business Type, or Keyword text box**

4. **Type** Nashville **in the City text box, click the** State list arrow **and click** TN **or type** TN **in the State text box, then click** Search **(or something similar)**
   A Web page opens displaying a list of categories that most closely match the one you entered.

TROUBLE

If you chose a site whose home page asks you to choose a country, click the link for your country. If you choose a site that assumes you are searching only the U.S. or the U.S. and Canada and you need to search another country, click the International or World Directories link, click the link for your country, then perform Step 7.

5. **Click** Public Relations Counselors **or** Communications & Public Relations Consultants **in the list of categories**
   Figure E-9 shows the results page with listings from the SuperPages Communications & Public Relations Consultants category. The listings include a name, address, telephone number, and link to a map and driving directions. Most yellow pages directories also provide links to the Web sites of firms (if the firm has one).

6. **Return to the Student Online Companion at** www.course.com/illustrated/internet4, **click the Unit E link, then click one of the links under Yellow & White Pages Directories in Lesson 4**

7. **Click the** White Pages **or** People Pages link, **if necessary, then type your first and last names, address, city, and state or province in the appropriate text boxes**
   Figure E-10 shows the search page on the WhitePages.com People Search page.

8. **Click** Search **(or something similar)**
   Look for your name in the results pages.

9. **Return to the Student Online Companion at** www.course.com/illustrated/internet4, **click the** Unit E link, **then click one of the links under Search Engines in Lesson 4**

QUICK TIP

Due to the popularity and robustness of the Google search engine, searching for information about someone by using a search engine is often referred to as "googling" the person.

10. **Type your name in the search expression text box of the search engine you chose, then click the appropriate button to start the search**
    A search on your name might result in many hits or no hits at all.

FIGURE E-9: Results page for SuperPages search

Click to see phone number

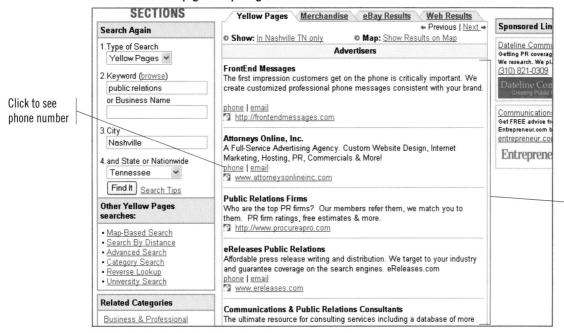

Business that paid for placement at the top of the category list

FIGURE E-10: Personal information entered in WhitePages.com

Your information will appear here

Click to start search

Clues to Use

Privacy concerns

Many people expressed concerns about privacy violations when white pages information became easily accessible on the Web. (In fact, in the Google search engine, you can type a phone number in the search text box and get the white pages listing and a link to a map to the person's address.) Some Web sites make unpublished and unlisted telephone numbers available for public use. In response to these privacy concerns, many white pages sites now offer individuals ways to remove their listings. If you want to remove your listing from a white pages site, check out the Web site's Help or FAQs (Frequently Asked Questions) links. Of course, many companies allow anyone who pays for their services to access more information about individuals than most people ever imagined would be available to the paying public. Even if you don't purchase goods or services online, credit card companies store consumer information in computers that are connected to the Internet. Also, businesses, whether online or in the mall, are using more sophisticated technology to track and record what consumers buy and sell. Consumers should be vigilant about guarding their personal information and periodically check their credit reports for errors.

Internet

Finding Online Reference Tools

The Web is full of pages that contain many useful items of information; these pages form an online library of sorts. Some Web sites collect links to many references in one place. For example, the LibrarySpot and Internet Public Library Web sites are collections of hyperlinks to reference materials, electronic texts, and other library Web sites. Another useful resource is the U.S. Library of Congress Web site, which includes links to a huge array of research resources, ranging from the Thomas Legislative Information site to the Library of Congress archives. In addition, the Web contains many text resources, including dictionaries, thesauri, encyclopedias, glossaries, grammar checkers, rhyming dictionaries, and language-translation pages. In preparation for her trip to Venice, Marti asks you to find some information for her. First, she wants to know how Venice is connected to Italy's mainland. She also wants you to find some general information about the culture and history of Italy. Finally, she would like to know how to say "I don't speak Italian" in Italian. You decide to use some of the Web's library and text resources to find this information.

STEPS

TROUBLE
If there is more than one Encyclopedias link, click the one for general information.

QUICK TIP
Some sites offer information for no charge as long as you register with them and provide your name, address, phone number, and e-mail address. This might result in you receiving much more junk e-mail than you had before. Check the privacy policy on the Web site before you register to make sure that they do not sell your information to other Web sites.

TROUBLE
If you don't see the links specified in Step 7, the Web site was probably redesigned since this book was printed. Look for similar links, or find the Web site's search text box, then type Italy in it to try to find the relevant page.

1. **Go to the Student Online Companion at** www.course.com/illustrated/internet4, **click the Unit E link, then click one of the links under Internet Libraries in Lesson 5**
   The home page of the Web site you chose opens.

2. **Click the** References link **(or something similar), if necessary, then click the** Encyclopedias link
   The Encyclopedias page opens.

3. **Click one of the links to a general encyclopedia**
   The home page for the encyclopedia you chose opens.

4. **If there is an option to search the encyclopedia you chose or another source, click the option to search the encyclopedia, type** Venice **in the search expression text box, then click the appropriate button to start the search**
   A list of articles appears. Some will be labeled as available only to paid subscribers or members of the site.

5. **Click an article that is not labeled as a subscriber or member article and that contains general information about Venice**
   The article opens. Somewhere in the article, it should state that Venice is connected to Italy's mainland by a railroad and highway bridge.

6. **Return to the Student Online Companion at** www.course.com/illustrated/internet4, **click the** Unit E link, **then click the** U.S. Library of Congress link **under Lesson 5**
   The home page of the U.S. Library of Congress Web site opens. See Figure E-11.

7. **Click the** Research Centers link, **click the** European link, **click the** Portals to the World: Europe link, **then click the** Italy link
   A page containing a list of links to general information about Italy in several categories opens. You note the URL for Marti.

8. **Return to the Student Online Companion at** www.course.com/illustrated/internet4, **click the** Unit E link, **then click one of the links under Translation Tools in Lesson 5**
   The home page of the Translation site you chose opens.

9. **Type** I don't speak Italian **in the appropriate text box**
   Figure E-12 shows the phrase typed in the SYSTRAN site.

10. **Click** English to Italian **in the list box or click** English **as the source language and** Italian **as the target language, then click** Translate **(or something similar)**
    The phrase "I don't speak Italian" is "Non parlo italiano" in Italian.

FIGURE E-11: U.S. Library of Congress Web site home page

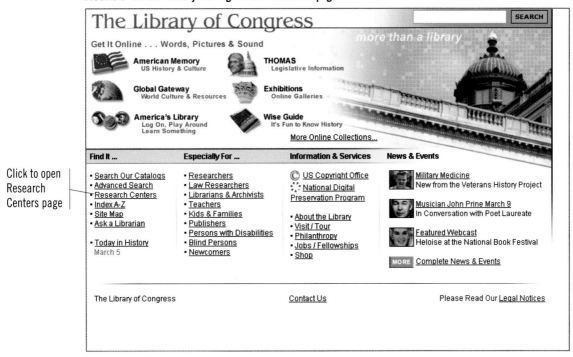

Click to open Research Centers page

FIGURE E-12: Phrase typed in SYSTRAN translation Web site

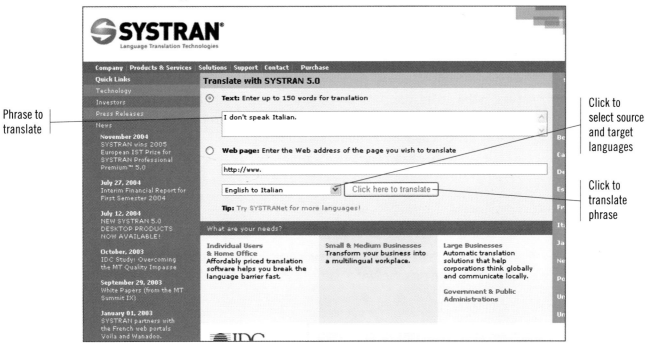

Phrase to translate

Click to select source and target languages

Click to translate phrase

Clues to Use

Archiving the Web

The Web itself has become the subject of archivists' attention. The Internet Archive's Wayback Machine (*www.archive.org*) provides researchers a series of snapshots of Web pages as they were at various points in the history of the Web. The name "Wayback Machine" is from an old cartoon in which the characters used the Wayback Machine to journey to a historical event. The archive has over a petabyte (a **petabyte** is approximately 1,000,000,000,000,000, or 10^{15}, bytes) of data stored and is growing at the rate of 20 terabytes (one **terabyte** is approximately 1,000,000,000,000, or 10^{12}, bytes) per month. To use the Wayback machine, you type a URL, and then select a date from a list that opens. The archived version of the Web page you selected opens in your browser.

Internet

Evaluating Web Resources

Like a library, the Web makes a huge variety of information readily available without a standard for differentiating reliable data from less reliable data. As a result, it's important to evaluate and verify the information you view. Table E-1 summarizes how you can evaluate Web pages. Based on your evaluation, you can decide if the information presented on the page is credible. A client of Cosby Promotions is a nonprofit group that is concerned about global warming. You are assigned to do research for this organization. You have found two Web sites that appear to contain relevant information. Before you pass along your findings, you need to evaluate the quality of the Web sites.

STEPS

1. **Go to the Student Online Companion at** www.course.com/illustrated/internet4, **click the** Unit E link, **click the** NRDC Global Warming page link **under Lesson 6, then evaluate the Web page based on the criteria presented in Table E-1**

   The Web page shown in Figure E-13 has a simple, clear design. The .org domain in the URL verifies that the publisher is a nonprofit organization. The grammar and spelling are correct, and the content is clearly presented. The reputable references and the consistent style of the Web page suggest that this Web site is a quality resource. The author or publisher of the Web page is identified at the bottom of the page as Natural Resources Defense Council.

2. **Scroll to the bottom of the Web page, then click the** About Us link

   The About Us page lists information about the organization, including links to its annual report. This page also identifies the president and the executive director. This organization appears to be well-established.

3. **Click the** Contact us link **at the bottom of the page**

   You see the organization's address, telephone and fax numbers, and e-mail addresses for various departments at NRDC are listed on the Contact Us page.

   QUICK TIP
   On well-designed Web sites, you can usually find a link to click to bring you to the site's home page, but it is useful to know how to do this using the URL.

4. **Click in the** Address **or** Location bar, **click to the right of the URL, then press** [Backspace] **as many times as necessary to delete all of the text to the right of the .org/ domain name so that the URL appears as** *http://www.nrdc.org/*

   It can be helpful to view the home page of a Web site you are trying to evaluate to see if the sponsoring organization has anything to do with the page you are viewing.

5. **Press** [Enter]

   The NRDC home page appears. This page includes links to information about the organization, including current news and activities, directors, and membership. You want to view an additional resource.

   QUICK TIP
   A balanced approach to a topic can be a sign of a good Web site.

6. **Return to the Student Online Companion at** www.course.com/illustrated/internet4, **click the** Unit E link, **then click the** NASA Earth Observatory Global Warming page link **under Lesson 6**

   This page on the NASA Earth Observatory Web site includes an article written to explain global warming. See Figure E-14. The article includes information supporting the contention that the earth is getting warmer as well as information or sources that express doubts about the phenomenon.

7. **Scroll to the bottom of the page**

   You'll see an e-mail contact link, and the name of the NASA official responsible for the page content.

8. **Delete all of the URL in the Address or Location bar after .gov/, then press** [Enter]

   The home page of the NASA Earth Observatory opens. Again, you notice that there is an e-mail contact and an author listed for the page.

9. **Click the** About the Earth Observatory link

   A page listing the mission statement and the people responsible for the site opens. Based upon the evaluation criteria listed in Table E-1, you decide that you have two credible resources to give to the client.

10. **Exit your browser**

FIGURE E-13: Global Warming page on NRDC Web site

Clicking logo brings you to site's home page

Appropriate graphics

Easy-to-understand organization

FIGURE E-14: Global Warming page on NASA Earth Observatory Web site

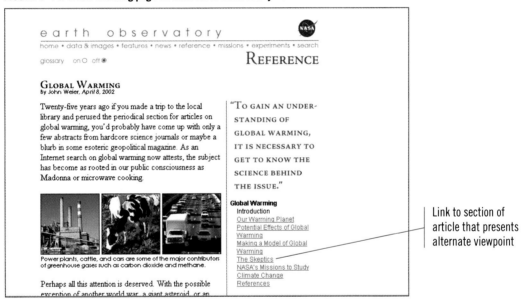

Link to section of article that presents alternate viewpoint

TABLE E-1: Web page evaluation guidelines

Component	Evaluation
Authorship	*Author affiliations:* Check universities or companies associated with the author to verify a relationship. *Author qualifications:* Determine if the author's qualifications relate to the material that appears on the Web site. *Author contact information:* Make sure you can telephone or e-mail the author directly. *Domain identifier:* Examine the domain identifier in the URL. If the Web site claims affiliation with an educational or research institution, then the domain should be .edu or .ac for educational or academic institution. A nonprofit organization would most likely use the .org domain, and a government unit or agency would use the .gov domain.
Content	Read the content critically and evaluate if the included topics are relevant to the Web site.
Appearance	Look at the design critically; Web page design elements that often suggest low quality include loud colors that distract the user, graphics that serve no purpose, flashing text, grammatical and spelling errors, and poor organization.
Objectivity	Evaluate how the Web site presents its information. Does it describe factual information with emotional language in an effort to sway your opinion?
Currency	Check to see when the Web page was created or revised. Older Web pages might contain outdated information.

Understanding Copyrights and Citing Web Resources

If you use portions of Web page text or an image from a Web page as support for a topic in a research or business document, you must treat it like any other published source and cite it appropriately. Some files on the Web are in the **public domain**, which means that you can freely copy them without requesting permission from the source. Even though you can use public domain information without obtaining permission, you should check the Web site carefully for requirements that you acknowledge the source of the material when you use it. If you cannot find a clear statement of copyright terms or a statement indicating that the files are in the public domain, you should not use them. ▓▓▓ Marti reminds you to collect information about the sites you visit so you can include a proper reference to your sources in any report you write. You decide to learn more about how to properly cite Web resources.

DETAILS

Things to consider when citing Web resources are described below:

QUICK TIP

In the U.S., works created after 1977 are protected for the life of the author plus 70 years; works copyrighted by corporations or non-profit organizations are protected for 95 years from the date of publication or 120 years from the date of creation, whichever is earlier.

- **Copyrights**

  A **copyright** is a right granted by a government to the author or creator of a literary or artistic work, which is defined as the tangible expression of an idea. This right gives the author or creator the sole and exclusive right to print, publish, or sell the work. Creations that can be copyrighted include virtually all forms of artistic or intellectual expression, including books, music, artworks, recordings (audio and video), architectural drawings, choreographic works, product packaging, and computer software.

- **Obtaining a Copyright**

  In the United States, the creator of a work does not need to register that work to obtain copyright protection. In other words, a work that does not include the words "copyright," "copyrighted," or the copyright symbol (©), and that was created after 1977 is copyrighted automatically by virtue of the copyright law.

- **Copyrights and Ideas**

  The idea contained in a product is not copyrightable; instead, the particular form of expression of the idea is what creates a work that can be copyrighted. For example, you cannot copyright the idea to write a song about love, but you can copyright the song you write. If an idea cannot be separated from its expression in a work, that work cannot be copyrighted. For example, mathematical calculations cannot be copyrighted. A collection of facts, however, can be copyrighted, but only if the collection is arranged, coordinated, or selected in a way that causes the resulting work to rise to the level of an original work.

QUICK TIP

If you are unsure whether your use is indeed fair use, the safest course of action is to contact the copyright owner and ask for permission to use the work.

- **Fair Use and Plagiarism**

  The **fair use** of a copyrighted work includes copying it for use in criticism, comment, news reporting, teaching, scholarship, or research. When you make fair use of a copyrighted work in your school assignments or research, you should always provide a citation to the original work. Acknowledging a source can be especially important when you use public domain material in papers, reports, or other school projects. Failure to cite the source of material that you use (whether it is in the public domain or it is protected by copyright) is called **plagiarism** and can be a serious violation of your school's academic honesty policy. There is plenty of information online about respecting copyrights. One of the most useful of these sites is the Stanford University Copyright & Fair Use site shown in Figure E-15.

QUICK TIP

Always check to see if your instructor (for classroom work) or editor (for work you are submitting for publication) has established citation guidelines that you should use.

- **Citation Formats**

  For academic research, the two most widely followed standards for print citations are those of the American Psychological Association (APA) and the Modern Language Association (MLA). Their formats for Web page citations are similar to each other and both include the following elements: name of the author or Web page creator (if known), title of the Web site in italics or a description of an untitled page (not in italics), name of the site's sponsoring organization (if any), date the page was retrieved, and the URL enclosed in chevron symbols (< >). Figure E-16 shows examples of Web page citations that conform to the APA and MLA citation styles.

FIGURE E-15: Stanford University Copyright & Fair Use home page

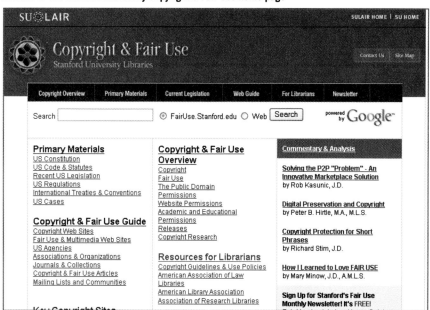

FIGURE E-16: Commonly-used formatting style for references to Web pages

> ## Web page with a title and an author but no copyright or creation date
>
> Hinman, L.M. *Ethics Updates*. University of San Diego. Retrieved 12 Feb. 2005 <http://ethics.sandiego.edu>.
>
> ## Web page with a title, but no author
>
> *Java Technology*. Sun Microsystems, Inc. 2005. Retrieved 15 Feb. 2005 <http://java.sun.com/>.
>
> ## Web page with no title and no author
>
> United States Postal Service home page. 2005. Retrieved 18 Mar. 2005. <http://www.usps.com>.

Clues to Use

Moving and disappearing URLs

Any method of citing Web pages faces one serious and yet unsolved problem—moving and disappearing URLs. The Web is a dynamic medium that changes constantly. A Web page exists only in an HTML document on a Web server computer. If that file's name or location changes or if the Web server is disconnected from the Internet, someone looking up your reference will not be able to locate the page at the URL you listed. When a page does not exist on a Web site, a page displaying an error message appears when the URL for that page is typed into a browser. These error messages are called 404 error messages, because 404 is the status code in HTTP that tells a user the requested Web page was not found. Some Web sites put a custom message on their 404 message page giving suggestions for finding the page you are looking for. If the Web site you are on does not give you this information, try going to the home page of the Web site by deleting all the text after the domain name in the Address or Location bar and then pressing the Enter key. You can also use a search engine to search for the page you want.

Practice

▼ CONCEPTS REVIEW

Identify the purpose of each Web page shown in Figures E-17 through E-20.

FIGURE E-17

1.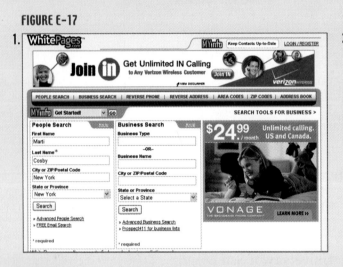

FIGURE E-18

2.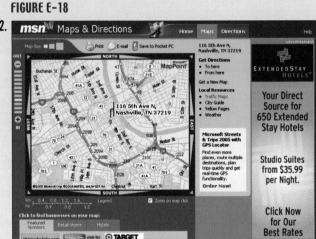

FIGURE E-19

3.

FIGURE E-20

4.

Match each term with the statement that best describes it.

5. **Public domain** b
6. **Yellow pages directory** c
7. **News search engine** a
8. **White pages directory** e
9. **Copyright** d

a. Searches news stories in multiple publications
b. Works that can be freely copied and reproduced
c. A directory of business names and addresses
d. A right granted by a government to an author or creator
e. A directory of personal information such as address and phone number

Select the best answer from the list of choices.

10. Which of the following is generally available on a Web site that provides maps?

   a. Driving directions

   b. Navigation tools to zoom in on the map

   c. Printable map

   d. All of the above

11. Which of the following is the best way to find out how to say "Good Morning" in another language?

   a. Use an online encyclopedia.

   b. Use the U.S. Library of Congress Web site.

   c. Use an online language-translator.

   d. Use a search engine.

12. Which of the following characteristics might identify a Web page as unreliable?

   a. Use of the .org domain

   b. Spelling errors

   c. Author's e-mail address

   d. References

13. Which of the following describes using a copyrighted work for use in news reporting or teaching?

   a. Plagiarism

   b. Fair use

   c. Copyright

   d. Public domain

14. Which of the following is not one of the elements you should include when you cite a Web resource?

   a. Web page creator

   b. Web site ranking in a search engine

   c. Date the Web page was accessed

   d. URL of the Web page

▼ SKILLS REVIEW

1. Get the news.

   a. Go to www.course.com/illustrated/internet4, click the Unit E link, then click one of the links to a news search engine under Skills Review 1.

   b. Search for recent news stories about Russia.

   c. Return to www.course.com/illustrated/internet4, click the Unit E link, then click another link to a news search engine under Skills Review 1.

   d. Search for recent news stories about Russia.

   e. Note whether you found links to different stories in each news search engine.

2. Obtain weather reports.

   a. Go to www.course.com/illustrated/internet4, then click the Unit E link.

   b. Use two of the weather forecasting sites listed under Skills Review 2 to find and enter the current temperatures for each of the cities listed in Table E-2.

TABLE E-2

	Stockholm, Sweden	Tokyo, Japan	Santiago, Chile	Cairo, Egypt
Weather Site 1 URL				
Weather Site 2 URL				

3. Obtain maps and city guides.

   a. Go to www.course.com/illustrated/internet4, click the Unit E link, then click one of the links under Map Sites in Skills Review 3.

   b. Find a map of Howard University in Washington, DC. The address is 2400 Sixth St. NW.

   c. Return to www.course.com/illustrated/internet4, click the Unit E link, then click one of the links under City Guides in Skills Review 3.

   d. Find and open the city guide to Washington, DC.

   e. Find the date and time of one upcoming event in the city.

4. Find businesses and people.

   a. Go to www.course.com/illustrated/internet4, click the Unit E link, then click one of the links under Yellow & White Pages Directories in Skills Review 4.

   b. Conduct a yellow pages search for art in New Orleans, Louisiana.

   c. Select a category that might include art galleries from the list of possible categories.

   d. Return to www.course.com/illustrated/internet4, click the Unit E link, then click one of the links under Yellow & White Pages Directories in Skills Review 4.

Internet

    e. Conduct a white pages search of a family member.

    f. Return to **www.course.com/illustrated/internet4**, click the **Unit E link**, then click one of the links under Search Engines in Skills Review 4.

    g. Conduct a search of a classmate's name.

5. Find online reference tools.

    a. Go to **www.course.com/illustrated/internet4**, click the **Unit E link**, then click the **LibrarySpot link** under Skills Review 5.

    b. Click the **Quotations link**, then click one of the links under General Quotations.

    c. Search for a quote about education by using the search expression text box or by using links to categories. Write down one quote and the source.

    d. Return to **www.course.com/illustrated/internet4**, click the **Unit E link**, then click the **US Library of Congress link** under Skills Review 5.

    e. Click the **Thomas link** to open a database containing information about Federal legislation.

    f. Click the **Latest Daily Digest link** in the Congressional Record, then write down one of the items listed under Highlights.

    g. Return to **www.course.com/illustrated/internet4**, click the **Unit E link**, then click one of the links under Translation Tools in Skills Review 5.

    h. Write down the translation of **Good morning** in Swedish and Portuguese.

6. Evaluate Web resources.

    a. Go to **www.course.com/illustrated/internet4**, click the **Unit E link**, then click the About.com link under Skills Review 6.

    b. Click the **Health & Fitness link**, then click the **Diabetes link**.

TABLE E-3

	author contact	author affiliation	.edu, .org or .gov domain	reputable references
Web site 1 URL:	Yes/No	Yes/No	Yes/No	Yes/No
Web site 2 URL:	Yes/No	Yes/No	Yes/No	Yes/No

    c. Click a link that you think will bring you to links to articles that explain the causes of diabetes.

    d. Explore two of the Web sites in the list, then evaluate them using Table E-3.

▼ INDEPENDENT CHALLENGE 1

You have decided to take a vacation to a city in the United States or Canada. To help plan your trip, you will use the Web to find maps, hotel and restaurant listings, and sightseeing suggestions.

    a. Decide on a city to visit.

    b. Go to **www.course.com/illustrated/internet4**, click the **Unit E link**, then click one of the links under City Guides in Independent Challenge 1 and search for information about the city you plan to visit.

    c. Note the names of two restaurants in the city you plan to visit.

    d. Note the name of a hotel in the city you plan to visit.

    e. Find an upcoming event in the city you plan to visit.

    f. Print the first page of the Web page. Be sure to include the URL in the header or footer information.

    g. Return to **www.course.com/illustrated/internet4**, click the **Unit E link**, then click one of the links under Weather Sites in Independent Challenge 1 and find the current temperature in the city you plan to visit.

    h. Summarize the information you have found about the city you plan to visit. Include the names and addresses of the two restaurants, the URL for the Web page with information about the hotel, a description of the upcoming event, and a brief description of the current weather conditions.

▼ INDEPENDENT CHALLENGE 2

You are a sales representative for Portland Concrete Mixers, a company that makes replacement parts for concrete mixing equipment. You have been transferred to the Olympia area in Washington and want to plan your first sales trip there. Because you plan to drive to Olympia, you need information about the best route as well as a map of the city. You hope to generate some new customers and, therefore, need to identify sales-lead prospects in the Olympia area. Companies that manufacture ready-mixed concrete are good prospects for you.

    a. Go to **www.course.com/illustrated/internet4**, click the **Unit E link**, then click one of the links under Map Sites in Independent Challenge 2.

Advanced Challenge Exercise

- Click the link for driving directions on the home page of the site you chose.
- Type **Portland, OR** as your starting address, then type **Olympia, WA** as your destination address.
- Click **Get Directions** (or something similar).
- Zoom in on the map to obtain a more detailed map of the route from Portland to Olympia.
- Print the map.

    b. Return to **www.course.com/illustrated/internet4**, click the **Unit E link**, then click one of the links under Yellow Pages Directories in Independent Challenge 2.

    c. Search for businesses connected to ready-mixed concrete in Olympia, WA.

    d. Select three companies that you think would be good prospects.

    e. Outline your travel plans and list the names and addresses of the three companies you've identified.

▼ INDEPENDENT CHALLENGE 3

You are the owner of a popular nightclub, Ragtime Tonight, which is located near a convention center. An increasing number of your patrons are travelers who make airline, hotel, and car-rental reservations using the Web, and you want to create a Web site that reaches them. While designing the Web site, you decide you'd like to add some ragtime audio clips that play when the Web site is opened using a Web browser. However, you need to know more about allowable usage, copyright restrictions, and licensing before proceeding.

    a. Go to **www.course.com/illustrated/internet4**, click the **Unit E link**, then click one of the links under Independent Challenge 3 to learn about allowable use and limitations of copyrighted work.

    b. Write a summary of the information you find. Describe what you can do, what you can't do, and ideas for how you might legally include ragtime music on your Web site at the lowest cost.

▼ INDEPENDENT CHALLENGE 4

You are conducting research on politics in Mexico. Currently, you are studying the history of land ownership in this country. In your report, you want to tie this history together with relevant recent events.

    a. Go to **www.course.com/illustrated/internet4**, click the **Unit E link**, then click one of the links to a news search engine under Independent Challenge 4.

    b. Search for recent news articles mentioning land ownership issues in Mexico.

    c. Read and summarize the two articles.

Advanced Challenge Exercise

- Use the style shown in the unit to write down the citations for the two articles.
- Use a search engine to find examples of the MLA and APA citation styles for Web sources, then rewrite the citations for the two articles in each of these two styles.
- Write a few sentences explaining the difference between the MLA and APA citation styles for Web sources.

    d. Use your favorite search engine and search for two Web sites that contain information about the history of land ownership in Mexico.

    e. Evaluate each of the two Web sites you found. Write a brief explanation describing why the sites can be considered reliable or questionable.

Internet

▼ VISUAL WORKSHOP

Go to www.course.com/illustrated/internet4, click the Unit E link, then click the MSN Maps link under Visual Workshop. Find the map illustrated in Figure E-21. The address entered is 25 Thomson Place, Boston, Massachusetts. When you have found the map, print a copy.

FIGURE E-21

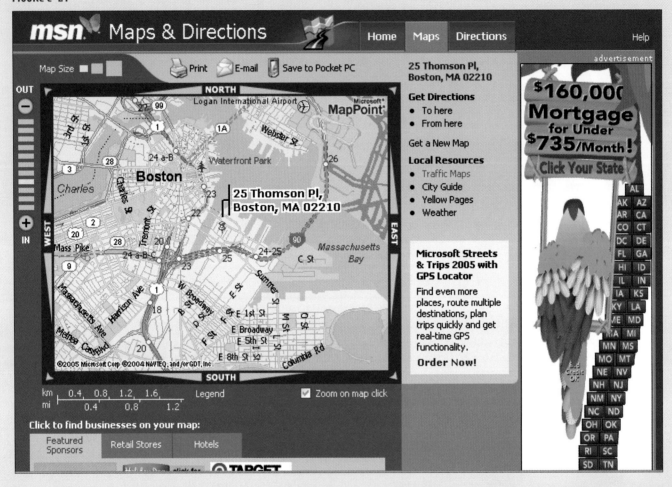

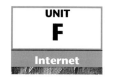
Communicating on the Web

OBJECTIVES

Define mailing lists
Locate a mailing list
Subscribe to a mailing list
Monitor a mailing list
Unsubscribe from a mailing list
Find a newsgroup
Understand chat
Participate in a chat session
Use instant messaging
Learn about virtual communities

You can build on your Internet knowledge by taking advantage of more advanced Internet communication tools, such as mailing lists, newsgroups, chat groups, and instant messaging. These tools enable you to easily exchange ideas and information with other people interested in common topics or areas. Lincoln Art Glass Company (LAG) is a small art glass company located in Nebraska. From its combined showroom and studio, LAG sells stained glass, glass supplies, and books to the public. Your job is to investigate how your manager, Mike DeMaine, can use mailing lists, chat groups, instant messaging, and newsgroups to learn about new industry techniques and trends, as well as to make contact with colleagues in the industry and potential customers.

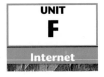

Defining Mailing Lists

As you learned in Unit A, a mailing list, sometimes called an **e-mail list**, is a list of names and e-mail addresses for a group of people who share a common interest in a subject or topic and exchange information by subscribing to the list. An **announcement list** is a mailing list that is similar to a newsletter in that it sends messages to subscribers, but does not allow subscribers to post to the list. When a list member posts a message to the list, the member sends the message to the **list address**, or the **list name**, and the message is sent to all members of the list. ▰▰▰ You want to find out if mailing lists provide information about art glass and art glass dealers. You start your research by learning some common terms associated with mailing lists.

DETAILS

Some common terms associated with mailing lists are listed below:

- List Server

  A **list server** is a server that runs mailing list software. **Mailing list software** is software that runs on the list server and maintains a database containing the e-mail addresses for all members, manages each user's request to join or leave a mailing list, receives e-mail messages posted to the list, and sends mailing list messages to list members. The **administrative address** is the e-mail address to which you send **commands**, requests to the list server to take a prescribed action. Unlike messages posted to the list, commands are not forwarded to other list members.

- Subscribing

  To **subscribe** to, or **join**, some mailing lists, you send an e-mail message to the administrative address. Some mailing lists also provide a form on a Web page to subscribe to a list. To subscribe by sending an e-mail message to a list server, the message usually contains a command that the server understands, such as "subscribe," along with the name of the mailing list and your e-mail address. To subscribe to a mailing list using a form on a Web page, you are often required to **register** and provide more information than just your e-mail address, such as your name, birth date, and possibly your postal address. When you no longer want to receive messages from a mailing list, you **unsubscribe** (or **drop**) from the list.

- Moderated and Unmoderated Lists

  Posts sent to a **moderated mailing list** are read and evaluated by a **list moderator** before they are sent to members of the mailing list. The list moderator is responsible for discarding any messages that are inappropriate for or irrelevant to the list's members. All members of an **unmoderated mailing list** automatically receive all messages, regardless of content.

- Open and Closed Lists

  Most lists are **open lists** that automatically accept all members; a **closed list** is one in which membership is *not* automatic. In a closed list, the **list administrator**, a person assigned to oversee one or more mailing lists, can either reject or accept your request to become a list member. The list administrator might reject your membership request if the list has too many members or if you are not part of the group's specified community. Figure F-1 shows a mailing list description of an unmoderated, open list.

- Frequently Asked Questions (FAQ)

  A **Frequently Asked Questions (FAQ)** document contains the answers to common questions that users ask about a mailing list and its subject. Users who want information about a mailing list, or potential members who want to find out if the mailing list seems appropriate for their interests, can find answers in the mailing list's FAQ. New list subscribers should always read the FAQ to be sure they understand the list rules and conventions and to check the answers to any common questions that have been asked before. Figure F-2 shows the FAQ Web page for a mailing list.

FIGURE F-1: Description of an unmoderated, open list

Identifies list as unmoderated

Identifies list as open

Shows how active the list is

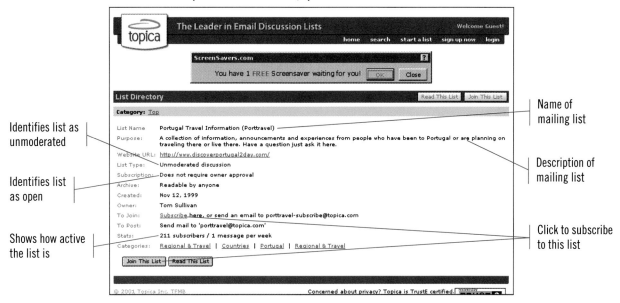

Name of mailing list

Description of mailing list

Click to subscribe to this list

FIGURE F-2: Mailing list FAQ Web page

Links to answers

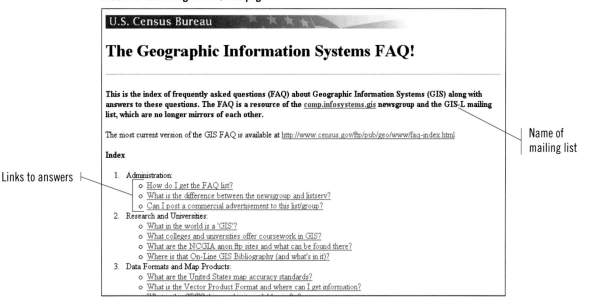

Name of mailing list

Clues to Use

Warnings about mailing lists

Mailing lists are valuable tools for receiving current and useful information. However, if you subscribe to a mailing list, you need to check your e-mail regularly. Depending on a mailing list's activity, you might receive many messages every day. In fact, some mailing lists can generate hundreds of messages each week. By checking your e-mail frequently, you can respond to, file, or delete messages in a timely fashion. Also, because the list server forwards the e-mail message that you post to every person subscribed to the mailing list, you expose yourself to potential privacy problems because the message you send contains your name and e-mail address. In addition, if you include your signature with your message, you might also be providing your mailing address and phone number to all list members. To protect your privacy, make sure you don't include a signature or any personal information in e-mail messages you post to the mailing list and use a free e-mail account address for your subscriptions (such as Yahoo! Mail or Hotmail). Finally, if your e-mail program and ISP allow you to send auto-replies (an automatic e-mail message that gets sent as a reply to every message you receive) when you are away—for example, on vacation—remember to suspend your mailing list subscriptions so that you don't send your auto-reply message to every member of the mailing list every time one of them posts a message. If this happens, you will probably be unsubscribed from the list by the list owner and you may not be allowed to resubscribe.

Internet

Locating a Mailing List

You can use search engines to search for mailing lists by using a search expression such as "*topic* e-mail list," where *topic* is the topic you are interested in. Several Web sites index mailing lists and can help you locate mailing list resources. You can also issue a command to a list server to send you a list of mailing lists. Table F-1 lists some common commands processed by list servers. Once you find a mailing list on the topic in which you are interested, it's a good idea to read a description of the list and see how active and current the list is. ░░░░░ You start working on Mike's request by searching for mailing lists related to art glass.

STEPS

1. **Go to the Student Online Companion at** www.course.com/illustrated/internet4, **click the** Unit F link, **then click the** Yahoo! Groups link **under Lesson 2**

   Yahoo! Groups is a list of mailing lists organized into categories.

QUICK TIP

You can also use a search engine to find a mailing list that interests you. Go to the search engine you want to use, then type the topic in which you are interested in followed by the words *mailing list* or *discussion group*.

2. **Click in the** Find a Group text box, **type** art glass **as the search expression, then click** Search

   A list of mailing lists that match your search criteria appears. A brief description and link for each list appears below the list name.

3. **Read the description for a few of the groups, then click the link to a mailing list that might interest Mike**

   The Web page that opens provides information about the mailing list, including the mailing list's name and description, the number of members (subscribers), an indicator showing the number of messages per month so that you can determine how active the list is, a description of the group settings (whether the group is open or closed, moderated or unmoderated, etc.), and a link to join the group (subscribe). Figure F-3 shows the information page of the cameo-glass mailing list.

4. **Return to the Student Online Companion at** www.course.com/illustrated/internet4, **click the** Unit F link, **then click the** Topica link **under Lesson 2**

   The Topica home page opens, similar to Figure F-4.

5. **Locate the search text box on the page, type** art glass **as the search expression, then click** Search

   A list of categories and mailing lists that match your search criteria appears. The search results are too broad and include lists that contain only the word "art" or the word "glass."

TROUBLE

New lists appear and old lists disappear from time to time. If you do not get any results from the search in Step 6, click the Back button on the toolbar, then skip to Step 7.

6. **Locate the search text box on the page, type** "art glass" **(including the quotation marks) as the search expression, and then click** Search

   A much shorter list is returned this time.

7. **Click the link to a mailing list that might interest Mike**

   Read the list information. You can also send a command to a list server to locate lists that contain specific words in their names.

8. **Start your e-mail program or log in to your Web-based e-mail account, start a new message, address it to** listserv@listserv.net, **type** global glass **in the Subject text box, type** list global glass **in the message body, then send the message**

   The "list global" command followed by "glass" returns a list of mailing lists whose name contains the word "glass."

QUICK TIP

To obtain information about a specific list, send an e-mail message to the administrative address with "list global *listname*" in the message body.

9. **Retrieve your messages, then open the** File: "LISTSERV LISTS" message

   A list of mailing lists is contained in this e-mail message.

10. **Close the message window**

FIGURE F-3: Information page for the cameo-glass mailing list on Yahoo! Groups

Click to read archived messages

Click to subscribe to mailing list

Number of members

Mailing list information

Recent messages would appear here

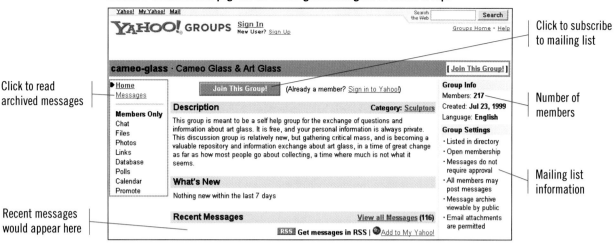

Reproduced with permission of Yahoo! Inc. © 2005 by Yahoo! Inc. YAHOO! and the YAHOO! logo are trademarks of Yahoo! Inc.

FIGURE F-4: Topica home page

Categories of mailing lists on Topica

TABLE F-1: Common mailing list commands

command	description
subscribe *listname your name* subscribe *listname*	Adds your e-mail address to the mailing list named *listname*
unsubscribe *listname* signoff *listname*	Removes your e-mail address from the mailing list named *listname*
review *listname*	Retrieves the names and e-mail addresses of members of the mailing list
list global *search terms*	Retrieves a list of mailing lists on the list server with the search terms in the list name
index *listname*	Retrieves a list of archive filenames for the mailing list named *listname*
get *filename*	Retrieves the file named *filename* from the archive
info *listname*	Requests information about the list
set *listname* conceal set *listname* conceal yes	Conceals your name and e-mail address from other subscribers of the mailing list named *listname* when a subscriber issues the review command
set *listname* no conceal set *listname* conceal no	Reveals your name and e-mail address to other subscribers of the mailing list named *listname* when a subscriber issues the review command

Subscribing to a Mailing List

You subscribe to a mailing list by sending an e-mail message to a list server's administrative address with a request to join the list's membership or by visiting the mailing list sponsor's Web site and using a form to enter your name and e-mail address. When you subscribe to a moderated mailing list, the list's moderator must accept you as a member before you can send and receive messages; when you subscribe to an unmoderated mailing list, your acceptance is automatic as long as you have typed the command in the e-mail message properly or filled in the required information on the form on the Web site. Some mailing lists provide an option for receiving **message digests**, in which several postings are grouped into a single e-mail message to help reduce the number of messages you receive from the list. After you subscribe to a mailing list, you receive a **welcome message**, which informs you that you have been subscribed. Often, the welcome message tells you how to unsubscribe from the list, how to request a list of commands from the list server, how to temporarily suspend your subscription, or how to access older messages. It's a good idea to file the welcome message in an e-mail folder for future reference. ▰▰▰▰▰ While Mike checks with colleagues on which art glass mailing lists would be the best to join, you join a mailing list for practice.

STEPS

1. **Start your e-mail program or log in to your Web-based e-mail account, then start a new message**

2. **Address the message to** listserv@listserv.gsa.gov

   This address is the administrative e-mail address for the Federal Citizen Information Center general information mailing list. This mailing list is an announcement list that provides updates on consumer issues, tips to help consumers get the most for their money, and special offers.

3. **Enter** subscribe **as the message subject**

   Although some mailing list software requires that you type commands in the Subject text box, the listserv mailing list server software does not. However, using a subject can make it easier to identify messages that you have sent.

4. **In the message body, type** subscribe fedinfo, **press** [Spacebar], **then type your full name**

   Figure F-5 shows the subscribe message in Outlook Express.

5. **Send your message, wait a few minutes, check for new messages, then open the message from** L-Soft list server

   After the mailing list server has accepted and processed your subscription request, you receive a message that informs you that you were subscribed to the mailing list. Figure F-6 shows the message received in Outlook Express.

6. **Read the e-mail message**

   Sometimes the welcome message will provide directions for unsubscribing from the list using the unsubscribe command; other times, a link is provided that you can click to access a form on a Web page to manage your subscription.

7. **Close the message window**

FIGURE F-5: Request for mailing list subscription

Administrative e-mail address for mailing list

"Subscribe" command

List name

Your name will appear here

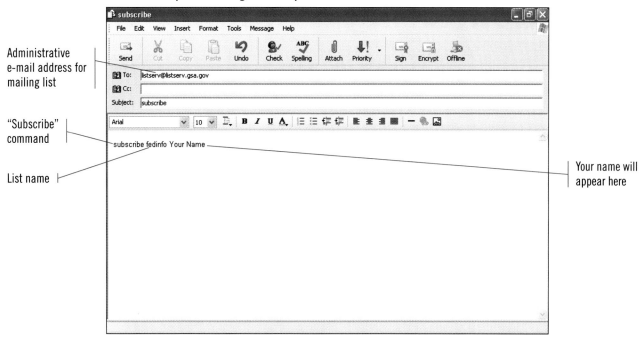

FIGURE F-6: Welcome message from FEDINFO mailing list in Outlook Express

Administrative address

Subscription information from the list server (this complete message might not appear in all e-mail programs)

Click this link to manage your subscription (might not appear in all e-mail programs)

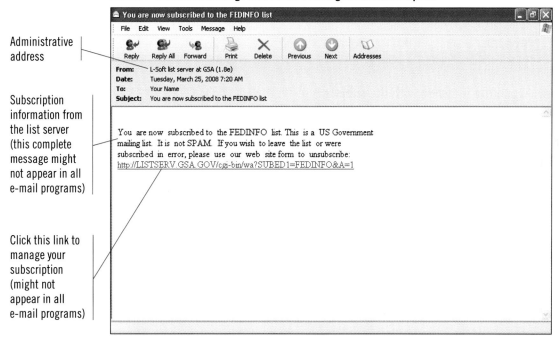

Clues to Use

Confirming subscriptions

Some mailing lists require you to confirm that you want to subscribe to the list. If you subscribe to this type of mailing list, you might receive a message telling you that your subscription request was received. You will also receive a message from the list requesting that you confirm your subscription. The message might ask you to reply to the message and send it; click a link to open a new Web page; or follow similar instructions. Read the confirmation message and carefully follow the instructions. If you receive a confirmation message, read it and follow the directions to confirm your subscription. Often, you will receive another message after you have confirmed your subscription officially welcoming you to the list. These mailing lists will usually ask you to send a confirmation e-mail when you unsubscribe from the list as well.

Monitoring a Mailing List

Many mailing lists are lists to which you can post messages. If you subscribe to a mailing list that allows you to post messages, you should **lurk**, or observe messages without posting any new messages, for a little while. Lurking allows you to become familiar with the list's culture and to research any basic questions in the list's FAQ to avoid filling up other members' e-mail boxes with questions that you might be able to answer yourself. In addition to lurking, you might also want to review past messages from the list. The list server stores past messages in a file called an **archive**. To access the archives, you can go the Web site associated with the list, or you can submit a command to the list server. ▇▇▇▇ You continue to work with mailing lists by requesting and viewing archived messages for the FEDINFO mailing list.

STEPS

1. **Address a new e-mail message to** listserv@listserv.gsa.gov

   You are sending this message to the administrative address because you are sending a command rather than posting a message.

2. **Type** index request **as the subject, then type** index fedinfo **in the message body**

   Make sure that nothing else appears in the message body. The word "index" is the command that you use to ask the mailing list server to send the list of archives for the FEDINFO mailing list.

3. **Send your message, wait a few seconds, then check for new messages**

   The mailing list server sends an e-mail message that contains a list of archive filenames. If the message doesn't arrive after a few seconds, wait a minute and check for messages again. You receive two messages from the list server. One informs you that the information you requested is being mailed to you under separate cover (that is, in another e-mail). The other is the list of archives you requested. See Figure F-7.

4. **Open the message with the subject** File: "FEDINFO FILELIST"

   Figure F-8 shows an archive list; the list in your e-mail message will probably be different. The message lists monthly archives for all e-mail messages posted to the FEDINFO mailing list.

5. **Close the message window, address a new e-mail message to** listserv@listserv.gsa.gov, **enter** Month of 1/27/05 list **as the subject, then type** get fedinfo LOG0501 **in the message body**

   This command retrieves the messages sent to the mailing list during the month of January 2005. These messages are contained in an archive named LOG0501. To retrieve the file, you use the "get" command followed by the filename.

6. **Send your message, wait a few seconds, then check your e-mail for new messages**

   Again, two messages are received, one informing you that the file you requested is being mailed to you under separate cover.

7. **Open the message with the subject** File: "FEDINFO LOG0501"

   This message contains the text of all messages sent to the list during the month of January 2005. There should also be a link to the archives at the bottom of the e-mail message.

8. **Scroll to the bottom of the message, then click the link** http://www.pueblo.gsa.gov/maillist.htm

   Your browser opens to the page on which you manage subscriptions from the Federal Citizen Information Center.

9. **Click the** FCIC FEDINFO archives link

   The page containing the list of FEDINFO archives opens. From here, you can click the link to any of the monthly archives.

FIGURE F-7: Messages from list server

Message containing the list of archive files

Message telling you that the file is being mailed under separate cover

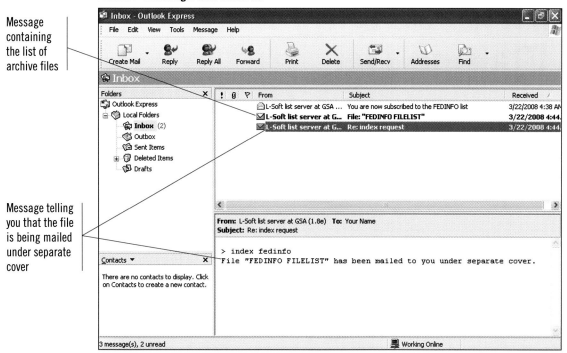

FIGURE F-8: List of available archive files for FEDINFO mailing list

Confirms postings are archived monthly

Filename of archive created January 2003

Date and time LOG0301 archive file was created

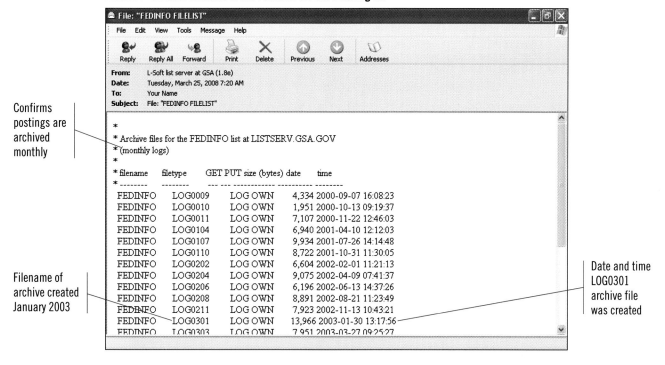

Clues to Use

Dealing with objectionable posts

Unfortunately, some posts are potentially offensive to mailing list readers. If you subscribe to a moderated mailing list, the likelihood of objectionable material is low because the list's moderator can delete objectionable material or postings that do not contain content relevant to the list. In an unmoderated list, however, there is no moderator to handle the disposition of objectionable material, so you must assume that job yourself. Keep in mind that people have different impressions of information posted to a mailing list. If you have subscribed to a list and find many posts about objectionable topics, your course of action might be either to avoid reading the objectionable messages or unsubscribe from the list. Fortunately, there are many lists on every topic, so if you are unhappy with your participation in one list, unsubscribe from the list and try another one.

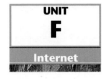

Unsubscribing from a Mailing List

When you unsubscribe from a mailing list, you stop receiving messages. Typically, the command to leave a mailing list is either "unsubscribe" or "signoff" followed by the mailing list's name. As with all administrative requests, you send your unsubscribe or signoff message to the mailing list's administrative address. Often the welcome message from a mailing list and each message received from the list also includes a link or directions for unsubscribing to the list. ▰▰▰ Now that you've learned how to join and use mailing lists, you leave the FEDINFO mailing list to reduce the number of e-mail messages that you receive each day.

STEPS

1. **Click the** Back button **in your browser window to return to the Web page on which you manage subscriptions from the Federal Citizen Information Center**

2. **Click the** Unsubscribe option button **next to FEDINFO in the table**

3. **Click in the** Your e-mail address text box, **type your e-mail address, click in the** Your name text box, **then type your name**
   See Figure F-9. Make sure you type the same e-mail address that you used to subscribe to the list.

4. **Click** SUBMIT
   A new Web page opens with a message thanking you for visiting the FCIC mailing list subscription page. See Figure F-10.

5. **Check your e-mail**
   You should receive an e-mail message confirming that you have been removed from the FEDINFO mailing list.

6. **Open the message with the subject** Re: Federal CIC Mailing Lists
   The message, similar to the one shown in Figure F-11, confirms your removal from the FEDINFO mailing list.

7. **Close any open message windows and exit your e-mail program or sign out of your Webmail account**

> **QUICK TIP**
> You can also send a message to the administrative address with "unsubscribe" in the message body, followed by the list name (fedinfo, in this case), followed by your name.

FIGURE F-9: Unsubscribing from the FEDINFO mailing list on the FCIC mailing list Web page

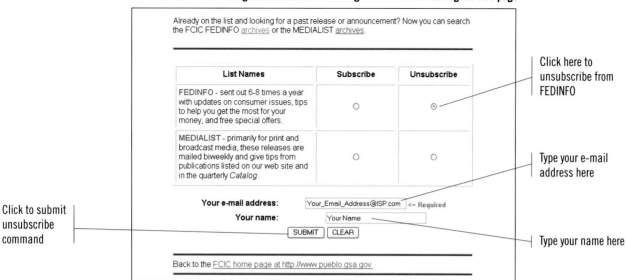

Click here to unsubscribe from FEDINFO

Type your e-mail address here

Click to submit unsubscribe command

Type your name here

FIGURE F-10: FCIC mailing list thank you Web page

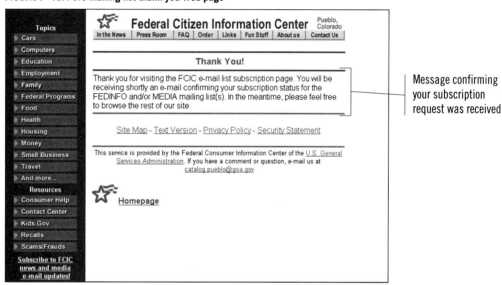

Message confirming your subscription request was received

FIGURE F-11: Signoff confirmation

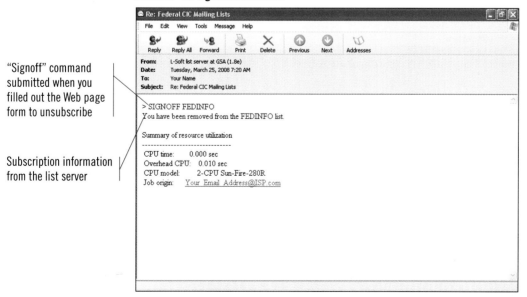

"Signoff" command submitted when you filled out the Web page form to unsubscribe

Subscription information from the list server

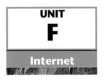

UNIT
F

Internet

Finding a Newsgroup

As you learned in Unit A, a newsgroup is a system in which messages are stored on Internet servers, sorted by topic. Newsgroups are part of the Usenet database. A server that stores a Usenet newsgroup is called a **news server**. Usenet was one of the first large, distributed information databases in the world. A **distributed database** is stored in multiple physical locations, with portions of the database replicated in different locations. Each of these multiple physical locations does not, however, store a complete copy of the database. You need to use a newsreader to access the messages in a newsgroup. Most mail client software, such as Outlook Express, have a newsreader built-in. If you use Webmail, Outlook Express, which is installed with Windows, will open as the default newsreader if another one is not specified. In addition, some Web sites allow you to read newsgroup messages using a browser. ▓▓▓ You start learning about newsgroups by investigating newsgroups that Mike might be interested in.

STEPS

1. **Go to the Student Online Companion at** www.course.com/illustrated/internet4, **click the** Unit F link, **then click the** Harley Hahn's Master List of Usenet Newsgroups link **under Lesson 6**

   The Web page opens.

2. **Click in the** Search for text box

3. **Type** glass, **then click** Go

   A list of links to newsgroups containing the key term "glass" opens in a results page. See Figure F-12. The category indicates that this newsgroup is about crafting with glass.

4. **Click the** Newsreader link **next to rec.crafts.glass**

   Your default newsreader opens with the rec.crafts.glass newsgroup listed as a newsgroup, and the list of messages appears in the message list. Figure F-13 shows the newsgroup in the newsreader in Outlook Express. Note that the messages in a newsgroup are arranged in **threads**; that is, they are arranged by discussion. You can click the plus sign next to the first message in a topic, then read all the replies to that topic.

5. **Exit your newsreader**

6. **Return to the Student Online Companion at** www.course.com/illustrated/internet4, **click the** Unit F link, **then click the** Google Groups link **under Lesson 6**

   The home page for Google Groups opens. The Google Groups directory offers useful tools for accessing Usenet newsgroups. Most news servers regularly delete articles after a period of time. Google Groups does not delete newsgroup articles; it has stored over 800 million newsgroup articles dating from 1981 in its database. Google Groups also includes a search engine that allows you to search newsgroup articles by subject, name, or article author.

7. **Type** art glass **in the Search Groups text box, then click** Search Groups

   Google Groups returns a list of links in various newsgroups. The newsgroup to which each article was originally posted is included at the end of each article summary as a link. See Figure F-14.

8. **Click a** rec.crafts.glass link **under one of the article summaries**

   The Google Groups site enables you to use your browser to read newsgroup messages, so your newsreader doesn't open. Instead, the messages in the group appear in the browser window with the newsgroup name at the top. The messages are arranged chronologically.

> **TROUBLE**
>
> If a dialog box opens asking for a password, type your password in the text box, then click OK. If you don't have a newsreader account set up, a dialog box or a wizard might open prompting you to set up an account. If you don't want to do this right now, click Cancel, and then skip Step 6.

> **QUICK TIP**
>
> Like mailing lists, newsgroups can be moderated or unmoderated, and open or closed.

FIGURE F-12: Description page for rec.crafts.glass newsgroup on Tile.net

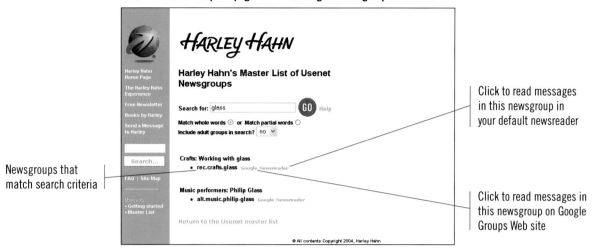

Newsgroups that match search criteria

Click to read messages in this newsgroup in your default newsreader

Click to read messages in this newsgroup on Google Groups Web site

FIGURE F-13: Outlook Express newsreader with the rec.crafts.glass newsgroup open

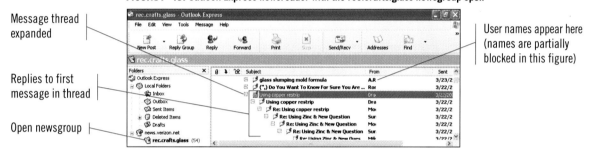

Message thread expanded

Replies to first message in thread

Open newsgroup

User names appear here (names are partially blocked in this figure)

FIGURE F-14: List of messages in Google Groups that match search expression

Search expression

Name of newsgroup

Topic name

Clues to Use

Mailing lists, newsgroups, and forums

As online discussions and mailing lists grow more popular, new software and Web sites are being developed to make it easier for users to create and participate in a discussion. As these discussions grow more popular, the terminology referring to them is blurring and the three terms are often used interchangeably. Generally, mailing lists refer to discussions or information transmitted via e-mail; newsgroups refer to Usenet groups that require a newsreader to read; and a **forum** refers to a mailing list that is stored and read on a Web site, so you use the Web site's interface instead of your e-mail program to post and read messages. Some sites, such as Delphi Forums (*www.delphiforums.com*), and Coollist (*www.coollist.com*), provide forums on a variety of topics in many categories. Many Web sites use forum software to allow users to discuss topics associated with the Web site; for example, CNET (*www.cnet.com*) hosts several forums for users on a variety of topics associated with computers.

Understanding Chat

Chat is instantaneous (or **real-time**) communication on the Internet or on the Web. Chats can be continuous, with participants entering and leaving ongoing discussions, or they can be planned to occur at a specific time and to last for a specific duration. Some chats are open to discussion of any topic, whereas other chats are focused on a specific topic or category of participants. Chatting requires participants to type quickly, therefore, chat participants often omit capitalization and do not worry about proper spelling and grammar. They frequently use emoticons and the acronyms listed in Table F-2 as shortcuts for common expressions. ░░░░░ Mike has recently heard about chat from some colleagues at an art glass conference. He asks you to learn how to use Web-based chat tools to communicate in real-time with individuals or groups of people. You begin by reviewing basic chat terms.

DETAILS

Following are a few terms common to chatting:

QUICK TIP

Some chats feature participation by a celebrity or an authority on the chat topic. These chats give worldwide users an opportunity to join discussions with people they would never have the chance to meet otherwise.

- **Public and Private Chats**

  A **private chat** occurs between individuals who know each other and are invited to participate in the chat. A **public chat** occurs in a public area, sometimes called a **chat room**, in which anyone who is registered with the chat service can come and go.

- **Internet Relay Chat**

  Internet Relay Chat (IRC) is a communications program that was developed by Jarkko Oikarinen of the University of Oulu in Finland in 1988. IRC is popular with businesses, which use it for virtual meetings with clients and employees at worldwide branch offices. You use IRC client software to connect to an IRC server.

- **Instant Messaging**

  With instant messaging (IM), users chat in real time over the Internet. Instant messages usually occur between two people who know each other, but can occur between a group of people. To chat using IM, both users must have the same IM software or IM software that lets users with different instant messaging software talk to each other. Popular IM programs are ICQ, AIM, MSN Messenger, and Yahoo! Messenger.

QUICK TIP

Although many Web chat sites have chat rooms designated for specific topics, in practice the conversations are open-ended and rarely follow the prescribed topic.

- **Web Chat Sites**

  Web chat sites offer the same capabilities as text-based IRC chat networks; however, a Web chat site is often easier to use and doesn't require users to download and install any special software. Figure F-15 shows the sign-in page for MSN Chat. The primary difference between instant messaging and Web-based chat is the people you talk with during the conversation. In a Web-based chat, some users lurk and others have multiple conversations going at the same time. When you join a chat room, your user name usually appears in a list so other chat participants can see how many people are in the room. Rules for each site vary, but in general, most Web-based chat sites prohibit spam messages, the use of automated programs to send messages to multiple chat rooms simultaneously, profane and vulgar language, and threats to individuals (called **flaming**). When reported, a chat site has the option of prohibiting the offending participant from entering any chat rooms at the site again.

- **User Names**

  Chatters often choose to register with a user name that is not their given name. For example, someone who's proud of his Irish ancestry might choose "shamrock" as a user name, or someone who is an avid collector of antique quilts might choose "I_Love_Quilts" as a user name.

Clues to Use

Using netiquette while chatting

In addition to avoiding all capital letters, most chat participants frown on flaming. Another unwanted practice is **spamming**, in which someone or an organization sends unsolicited and irrelevant messages to a chat room, just as an organization might send you e-mail spam, or unwanted and unsolicited e-mail messages. Although many chat rooms don't enforce the rules of the Internet (netiquette), as you use the Internet to communicate, you should exercise common courtesy and respect as you would when speaking in person with other people.

FIGURE F-15: Sign-in page for MSN Chat

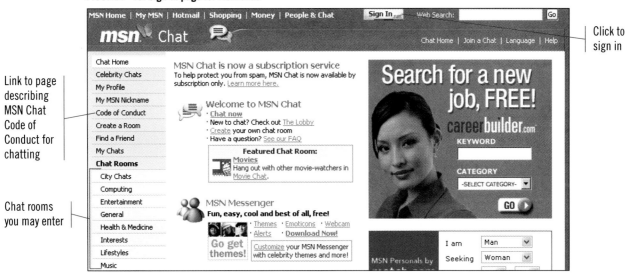

Click to sign in

Link to page describing MSN Chat Code of Conduct for chatting

Chat rooms you may enter

TABLE F-2: Commonly used chat acronyms

acronym	meaning	acronym	meaning
afk	Away from keyboard	irl	In real life (contrasted with one's online existence)
atm	At the moment	jk	Just kidding
bbl	Be back later	lol	Laughing out loud
brb	Be right back	np	No problem
btw	By the way	oic	Oh, I see
cul8r	See you later	rotfl	Rolling on the floor laughing
c-ya	See you	eg	Evil grin
ttfn	Ta-ta (goodbye) for now	wb	Welcome back
imho	In my humble opinion	imnsho	In my not so humble opinion

Participating in a Chat Session

You can find chat groups at many Web sites. After you find a Web chat site, you typically need to register before you can use the Web chat facilities. You should carefully consider whether to provide detailed personal information when you register because most current laws do not require a Web site administrator to maintain confidentiality of your information. If one Web chat site requires information that you do not want to disclose, you can simply look for another Web chat site with a less intrusive registration page. To see if chatting will be useful for Mike, you decide to evaluate a chat session. You sign on to a popular Web chat site and try using chat.

STEPS

1. **Start your Web browser, go to** www.course.com/illustrated/internet4, **click the** Unit F link, **then click the** Yahoo! Chat link **under Lesson 8**

   The Yahoo! sign in page opens.

> **TROUBLE**
> If you already have a Yahoo! ID, enter your ID and password, click Sign In, then skip to Step 5.

2. **Click the** Sign up now link

   A form opens.

3. **Complete the form, then click** Submit This Form

   Yahoo! processes your information, and then a welcome message appears. If messages appear asking you to reenter information, follow the directions, then resubmit the form. Sometimes, you will be asked to choose a different user name if the name you have chosen has already been used.

4. **Click** Continue to Yahoo!

   The Yahoo! Chat Web page appears, similar to Figure F-16.

> **TROUBLE**
> If a message appears telling you that Chat has not loaded properly, you may need to download and install Yahoo! Chat software. Check with your instructor or technical support person before downloading and installing any programs. (Note that you can chat without loading Voice Chat.)

5. **Click the link to a subject area of your choice**

   From this Web page, you can select a general chat topic and then enter the chat room for that topic. Figure F-17 shows the room in the Hobbies & Crafts category.

6. **Click the link for the topic of your choice, then click the desired chat room on the menu that appears**

   A message appears in the browser window informing you that Yahoo! Chat is loading.

7. **When Chat has finished loading, click** Continue, **if necessary, then, if necessary, click** Start Chat Now

   The chat screen opens for the room you picked.

8. **Click the** Exit link, **click the** Home link **to return to the main Yahoo! Chat Web page, then click the** Sign Out link

   A Web page opens with the message that you have signed out of Yahoo! network.

Clues to Use

Understanding unmoderated chat rooms

Although Web sites that provide chat rooms usually have rules of appropriate conduct, you might encounter conversations taking place that are offensive to you. Rules for each site vary, but in general, most Web-based chat sites prohibit spam messages, the use of automated programs to send messages to multiple chat rooms simultaneously, profane and vulgar language, and flaming. Some Web sites have a link that lets you identify participants who are not following the agreed-upon rules for the chat room. When a participant is reported, a chat site has the option of prohibiting the offending participant from entering any chat rooms at the site again. Fortunately, there are many different Web-based chat rooms available on the Internet, so if your first attempt does not provide a satisfactory experience, simply exit from that chat room and try another one.

FIGURE F-16: Yahoo! Chat Web page

Your user name appears here

Chat room categories

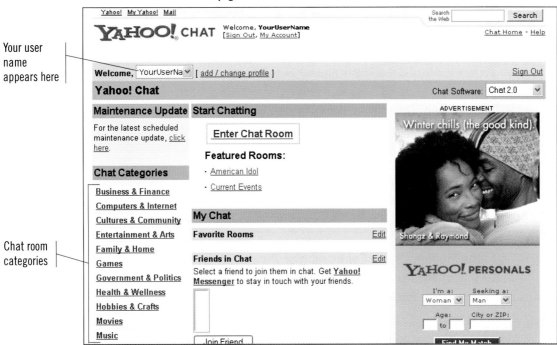

FIGURE F-17: Chat rooms in Hobbies & Crafts category in Yahoo! Chat

Current category

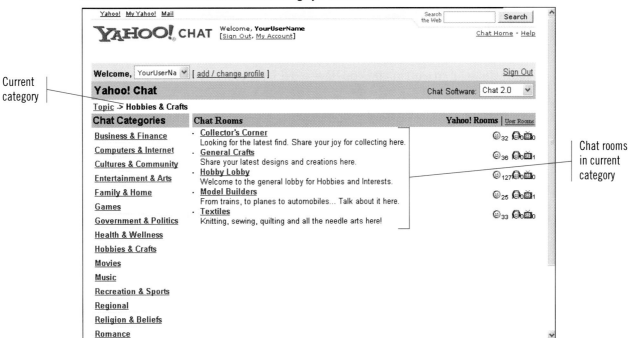

Chat rooms in current category

Internet

Using Instant Messaging

In order for two people to exchange instant messages, both people must be using the same instant messaging software or at least one of them must be using IM software, such as **Trillian**, that allows people with different instant messaging software to talk to each other. **ICQ** (pronounced "I seek you") is one of the most popular instant messaging software programs available, with over 220 million worldwide users. **AOL Instant Messenger (AIM)** was created a few years after the introduction of ICQ. AOL originally created AIM to allow its members to chat with each other, but AOL subsequently made AIM available to anyone (even those people without AOL accounts) for use on the Web. Microsoft developed **Windows Messenger**, which is installed with Windows. 🔲🔲 You think instant messaging will be useful for Mike to stay in touch with his colleagues, so you investigate various IM software.

STEPS

1. **Go to the Student Online Companion at** www.course.com/illustrated/internet4, **click the** Unit F link, **then click the** ICQ link **under Lesson 9**

   The ICQ home page appears in your browser window.

2. **Click the** What is ICQ link

   The What is ICQ page opens, providing you with general information about ICQ.

3. **Return to the Student Online Companion at** www.course.com/illustrated/internet4, **click the** Unit F link, **then click the** AOL Instant Messenger link **under Lesson 9**

   The home page for AOL Instant Messenger (AIM) appears.

4. **Click the** FAQ link

   The FAQ page opens, providing you with answers to frequently asked questions about AIM.

> **TROUBLE**
> If you do not have a .NET Passport, you will need to get one, so click the Get a .NET Passport link, then follow the instructions.

5. **Exit your browser, click the** Start button, **point to** All Programs, **then click** Windows Messenger

   Windows Messenger starts. A dialog box opens asking you to sign into your .NET Passport, or the Windows Messenger window opens with you already signed in.

6. **If you need to sign in and you have a .NET Passport, type your e-mail address in the E-mail address text box, type your password in the Password text box, then click** OK

   The Windows Messenger window opens. See Figure F-18.

> **TROUBLE**
> If a message appears telling you that the operation could not be completed, click Cancel and try again later.

7. **Click the** Add a Contact link **to open the Add a Contact wizard, click the** Search for a contact option button **to select it, click** Next, **type the name of a classmate who has signed up for Windows Messenger in the First Name and Last Name text boxes, click** Next, **then click** Finish

   Your friend is added as a contact to your contact list. (Some IM software packages refer to contacts as **buddies**.)

8. **Click the** Send an Instant Message link **to open the Send an Instant Message window, click your classmate's name, then click** OK

   The Conversation window opens with the insertion point in the text box at the bottom of the window. (In some instant message programs, this window is the Instant Message window.)

9. **Type** Hi! Want to chat?, **then click** Send

   Your message appears in the Conversation window under your name or e-mail address, and your classmate's message appears in the window under his or her name or e-mail address. See Figure F-19. (The message from the person who clicked Send first will appear first in the window.)

10. **Click the** Close button **in the Conversation window, click** File **on the menu bar in the Windows Messenger window, click** Sign Out, **then click the** Close button **in the Windows Messenger window**

FIGURE F-18: Windows Messenger window

Your name or e-mail address will appear here

Your contacts will appear here

Click to add a contact

Click to send an instant message

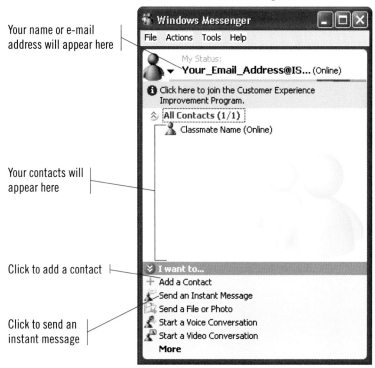

FIGURE F-19: Conversation window with an instant message session

Your message appears under your name or e-mail address

Your classmate's message appears under his or her name or e-mail address

Type your message here

Click to send your message

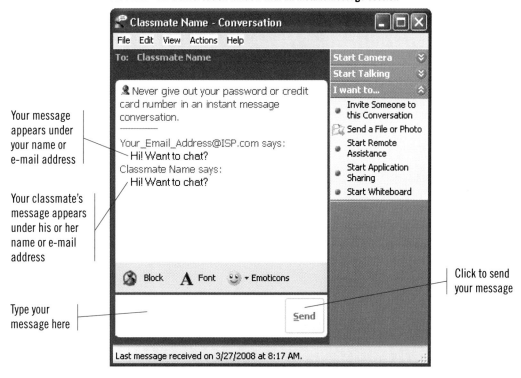

Clues to Use

IM alerts

Because both users must be online for an instant message to occur, IM software has built-in tools that let you identify your friends and alert you when your friends are online, as long as you are signed into the service. If someone sends you a message, a Conversation or Instant Message window opens and its corresponding button on the taskbar blinks.

Learning about Virtual Communities

The Web is home to many virtual communities, also known as online social groups, that have become useful tools for people who want to make new friends, establish acquaintances before moving to a new location, discuss politics, obtain advice, or make any number of other types of connections. Most of these sites provide a directory that lists members' locations, interests, and qualities. One member of the community can contact any other member, but the recipient is not required to respond. Usually the recipient will review the sender's directory information, and then, if the recipient wants, the recipient responds to the sender. The sites that host these communities rely on advertising to generate the revenue they need to operate the site. Some sites also charge members a monthly membership fee. Other sites charge for access to specific site features. ▰▰▰ You want to find out if there is a virtual community that would help Mike stay in touch with his colleagues in the industry. You start your search by learning more about virtual communities.

DETAILS

Different types of virtual communities are discussed below:

- **General Virtual Communities**

  One of the first online communities was craigslist, an information resource for San Francisco area residents that was created in 1995 by Craig Newmark. That community has grown to include communities for most major cities in the United States and in several other countries. Figure F-20 shows the craigslist San Francisco Bay Area page. Another community is Friendster. Members of Friendster post profiles with information about themselves and upload their photos. Members can post information about their interests and activities on a virtual bulletin board that is available for other members to read.

- **Targeted Community Networks**

  A targeted virtual community tries to attract people who have specific interests. For example, MySpace is a virtual community targeted at a young audience of music fans. Members can post and download digital music files, play games, create blogs, and send instant messages to each other. MySpace can charge more for the advertising it sells because it can identify characteristics of its members for its advertisers.

- **Business Networks**

  Some sites, including LinkedIn, Ryze, Tribe.net, and ZeroDegrees, focus on business networking. People use these sites to look for a new job, find potential business partners, hire someone, and conduct other activities related to business. Members of virtual communities devoted to business connections are looking for solutions to their business problems, whether it is a company looking for an employee with specific talents, a business hoping to place its product in a retail store, or an organization looking for a consultant who can provide training on a specific topic. Figure F-21 shows the LinkedIn home page.

- **Political Networks**

  In the 2004 U.S. elections, many political organizations used the Internet in a variety of ways to rally supporters, raise funds, and get their messages out to voters. People and political organizations set up Web sites to provide information for people interested in a particular candidate. These sites allowed people to discuss issues, plan strategies, and arrange in-person meetings called **meetups**.

FIGURE F-20: San Francisco Bay Area craigslist page

FIGURE F-21: LinkedIn home page

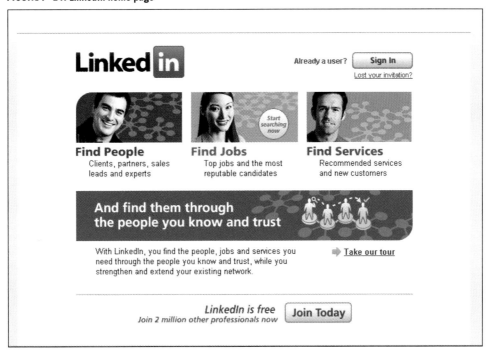

Clues to Use

Blogs and politics

During the campaign for U.S. president in 2004, candidates for U.S. president started using blogs as a way to organize their supporters and provide a forum in which candidates could freely discuss campaign issues. People with strong opinions about candidates or campaign issues started their own blogs to challenge candidates and discuss their policies during the campaign. It is important to keep in mind that although blogs are a popular and easy way to disseminate information, the information presented in them are the bloggers' personal opinions, and you should check any information presented as a fact in another source.

Practice

▼ CONCEPTS REVIEW

Identify the communication tool in use in Figures F-22 through F-25.

FIGURE F-22

1.

FIGURE F-23

2.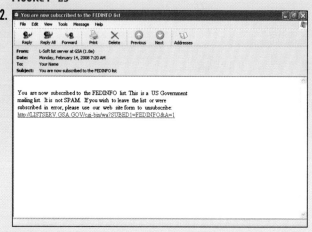

FIGURE F-24

3.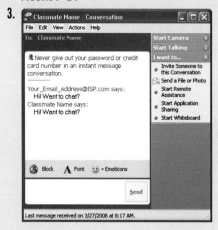

FIGURE F-25

4.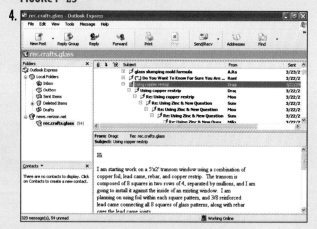

Match each term with the statement that best describes it.

5. **Posting**

6. **Administrative address**

7. **IRC**

8. **List server**

9. **Newsgroups**

10. **Subscribe valert-l**

11. **List moderator**

12. **Message digest**

a. A computer that manages mailing lists

b. Several postings from a mailing list grouped into a single e-mail message

c. A real-time communication program

d. Sending a message to a mailing list

e. A command that mailing list software can read

f. Another term for Usenet groups

g. The e-mail address to which you send mailing list commands

h. A person assigned to oversee one or more mailing lists

Select the best answer from the list of choices.

13. **In which type of mailing list are messages reviewed before being distributed?**
    a. Public mailing list
    b. Moderated mailing list
    c. Unmoderated mailing list
    d. Administered mailing list

14. **You post mailing list messages using which type of mailing address?**
    a. List address
    b. Majordomo address
    c. Administrative address
    d. Announcement address

15. **Which type of mailing list is used to send information to the mailing list but does not accept posts from members?**
    a. Closed list
    b. Moderated list
    c. Announcement list
    d. Newsletter list

16. **Silently observing postings on a mailing list is called:**
    a. peeking.
    b. lurking.
    c. watching.
    d. observing.

17. **A public chat occurs in an area known as a(n) _____.**
    a. chat room
    b. Internet Relay Chat
    c. chat session
    d. instant message window

18. **In order to read newsgroup messages, you need to use _____.**
    a. a distributed database
    b. a news server
    c. a newsreader
    d. Usenet

19. **Which of the following describes face-to-face meetings that are arranged online, usually on a political site?**
    a. Meetup
    b. Closed list
    c. Social networking
    d. Lurk

Internet

1. Locate a mailing list.

    a. Start your Web browser, go to www.course.com/illustrated/internet4, click the Unit F link, then click the Topica link under Skills Review 1.

    b. Search for mailing lists related to literature.

    c. Scroll through the results and explore links.

    d. Return to www.course.com/illustrated/internet4, click the Unit F link, then click the Yahoo! Groups link under Skills Review 1.

    e. Search for mailing lists related to literature.

    f. Follow links to find a mailing list that interests you.

    g. Start your e-mail program, create a new message, and then send a message to listserv@listserv.net with global literature in the Subject text box and list global literature in the message body.

    h. Retrieve your messages, then examine the list of mailing lists about literature.

2. Subscribe to a mailing list.

    a. Start your e-mail program, create a new message, and then use the administrative address and the subscribe command to subscribe to one of the lists you found in Step 1h; or use the Web form associated with the list to subscribe to the list.

    b. Send the message if you are subscribing via e-mail.

    c. Retrieve your messages.

    d. If necessary, send a confirmation message.

    e. Read the welcome message.

3. Monitor a mailing list.

    a. If the welcome message from the list you chose includes a command for getting an index of the mailing list's archives, make a note of that command.

    b. Create a new e-mail message addressed to the list's administrative address.

    c. If the welcome message contained a command for getting an index of the list's archives, type that command in the message body; otherwise, type index *<LISTNAME>* in the message body, where *<LISTNAME>* is the name of the mailing list you chose.

    d. Send the message.

    e. Wait several minutes, then retrieve your messages.

    f. If the index lists any files, send a message to the administrative address requesting the archives for a particular week or month (using the get command).

    g. Open the message that contains the index, and scroll down to read some of the messages that have been sent to the mailing list.

4. Leave a mailing list.

    a. Read the welcome message from your mailing list to find the command required to leave the mailing list you have joined.

    b. Create a new e-mail message, address it to the administrative address of the list you chose, and then enter the required command to leave the mailing list in the message body; or click the unsubscribe link or the link that brings you to the list's Web page in the welcome message.

    c. If you are unsubscribing by sending an e-mail message, send the message; if you are unsubscribing using the Web page form, fill out and submit the form.

    d. Wait several minutes, then retrieve your messages.

e. Read the messages from the mailing list server to confirm that you have been removed from the mailing list; or, read the message on the list's Web page confirming your removal from the mailing list.

f. Close all message windows and exit your e-mail program.

5. Find a newsgroup.

a. Go to www.course.com/illustrated/internet4, click the Unit F link, then click the Tile.net link under Skills Review 5.

b. Search for newsgroups related to landscape design.

c. Explore the links to find articles related to landscape design.

d. Return to www.course.com/illustrated/internet4, click the Unit F link, then click the Google Groups link under Skills Review 5.

e. Search for newsgroups related to landscape design.

f. Explore the links in some of the articles that appear to find other related articles about setting up a landscape design business.

6. Participate in a chat session.

a. Go to www.course.com/illustrated/internet4, click the Unit F link, then click the Yahoo! Chat link under Skills Review 6.

b. Click the link for a category that interests you, then follow links to open a chat room on a topic you choose.

c. Participate in the chat session, if you want.

d. Exit the chat room.

7. Use instant messaging.

a. Go to www.course.com/illustrated/internet4, click the Unit F link, then click the Yahoo! Messenger link under Skills Review 7.

b. Click the Features link, then read about the features that come with Yahoo! Messenger.

c. Return to www.course.com/illustrated/internet4, click the Unit F link, then click the Trillian link under Skills Review 7.

d. Click Learn about Trillian, then read about the features of Trillian.

e. Start Windows Messenger, log in, if necessary, then add a classmate to your list of contacts.

f. Send the following message to your classmate: IMing is much faster than e-mail!

g. After receiving your classmate's message, close the Conversation window, sign out of Windows Messenger, then close the Windows Messenger window.

h. Exit your browser.

▼ INDEPENDENT CHALLENGE 1

Big Island Coffee Company (BICC) grows and ships coffee beans to many of the Hawaiian Islands and parts of mainland North America. Manoa Kileahu, BICC's owner, wants to find mailing lists that might be relevant to a coffee bean supplier's marketing efforts. You will send a message to a mailing list to retrieve the names of other known mailing lists.

a. Start your e-mail program, then create a new message.

b. Address the message to listserv@listserv.net.

c. Type global marketing in the Subject text box.

d. In the message area, type list global marketing.

e. Send the message. The mailing list server will return mailing list names that include the word marketing.

f. When you receive an answer from the mailing list server, scan the list of mailing list names and note which ones related to marketing look interesting.

Advanced Challenge Exercise

- Send a message to listserv@listserv.net using the info command requesting information about the list you think looks interesting.
- Retrieve your messages.
- If the message containing information about the list contained a link to a Web page, click it and examine the information on the Web page.

g. Print a copy of all messages received.

h. Exit your e-mail program and browser, if necessary.

▼ INDEPENDENT CHALLENGE 2

A colleague, in a recent conversation, listed many of the benefits of subscribing to a mailing list. Based on this colleague's recommendation, you decide to join a mailing list.

a. Start your Web browser, go to www.course.com/illustrated/internet4, click the Unit F link, then click the L-Soft link under Independent Challenge 2. The L-Soft International organization's Web page appears. L-Soft produces and licenses the LISTSERV mailing list software.

b. Click the CataList link, then scroll down the Web page until you see the List information section. Click the View lists with 10,000 subscribers or more link. A Web page appears that lists hundreds of mailing lists. Each mailing list is accessible via a link.

c. Scroll down the list of mailing lists and locate one that interests you. Click the link of a list you want to join. A new Web page appears displaying information about the list.

d. Scroll down until you can see a line describing how to subscribe to the list or a link to subscription information. The line will read, in part, "To subscribe, send mail to …" Make a note of the list's name and the administrative address.

e. Click the e-mail link to the administrative address. If the address does not appear as a link, start your e-mail program, then create a new message addressed to the list's administrative address.

f. Compose the message to subscribe to the list, then send the message.

g. If the mailing list server has any specific instructions, follow its requests.

h. When the mailing list server sends you a welcome message, forward it to your instructor.

▼ INDEPENDENT CHALLENGE 2 (CONTINUED)

Advanced Challenge Exercise

- Send a request for information to the list. (*Hint*: Refer to Table F-1.)
- Send a request to retrieve the names and e-mail address of list members.
- Use another command listed in the info message you receive from the list server.

i. Read the messages on the list for a few days. After you have read several messages, unsubscribe from the list.

j. When you receive the confirmation of your removal from the list, forward it to your instructor.

k. Exit your Web browser and e-mail program.

▼ INDEPENDENT CHALLENGE 3

Laura Jensen is president of Rockin' Tees, a small manufacturer of printed t-shirts that specializes in creating designs using images of famous rock bands. Rockin' Tees must either purchase the rights to use band names and likenesses or agree to pay negotiated per-shirt royalties to the bands. Laura needs to estimate the demand for t-shirt designs before she negotiates with the bands' agents and agrees to payment terms. She wants you to check out chat rooms related to rock music to find out which rock bands are mentioned most frequently.

a. Start your Web browser, go to **www.course.com/illustrated/internet4**, click the **Unit F link**, then click the **Yahoo! Chat link** under Independent Challenge 3.

b. Examine the chat topics on the Yahoo! Chat Web page and explore some of the chat rooms to which they lead. Remember that you are collecting information for Laura, so stay focused on her research question: Which rock bands are mentioned most frequently in the chats?

c. Send an e-mail message to your instructor that lists three of the most frequently mentioned bands.

d. Exit your Web browser.

▼ INDEPENDENT CHALLENGE 4

Dan Rivetti is the director of Triangle Research, a small laboratory that tests metal parts and assemblies using physical and computer models. Usually, Dan knows enough about the general design of the parts and assemblies to be able to develop the testing procedures. Sometimes, however, he wants to conduct background research and contact experts in the field before designing his testing procedures. Dan heard that newsgroups offer such information and the opportunity to post inquiries, but he has also heard that some newsgroups are more reliable than others. Dan asks you to help him evaluate the quality of some newsgroups.

a. Start your Web browser, go to **www.course.com/illustrated/internet4**, click the **Unit F link**, then click the **Google Groups link** under Independent Challenge 4.

b. Type **sci.** in the Search text box, then click **Search Groups**.

c. Examine and follow some of the links on the results page. Look for two newsgroups in a similar topic area, one moderated and one unmoderated.

d. Examine a sample of messages from each type of newsgroup devoted to the same topic.

e. Describe the differences you found between the postings in the moderated and unmoderated newsgroups. Explain which type of newsgroup would best serve Dan's needs.

f. Exit your Web browser.

▼ VISUAL WORKSHOP

Go to **www.course.com/illustrated/internet4**, click the **Unit F link**, then click the **Topica link** under Visual Workshop. Conduct a search on this Web site to display information similar to the information shown in Figure F-26.

FIGURE F-26

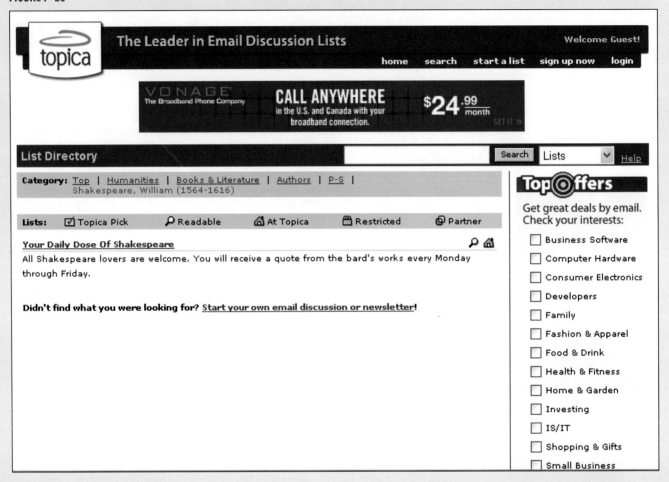

Downloading Programs and Sharing Files

OBJECTIVES

Investigate freely downloadable programs
Understand downloading programs and file sharing
Locate a program using a download site
Download a program using Internet Explorer
Download a program using Firefox
Install a downloaded program
Establish an FTP session
Use FTP to download a file
Open a compressed file
Compress files

When you use the Internet, you sometimes need to transfer files between your computer and other computers on the Internet. To **download** a file means to receive the file on your computer from another computer. To **upload** a file means to send it from your computer to another computer. After the transfer is complete, you must know how to install and use the program files that you downloaded. To speed up downloading and uploading you can compress files to make them smaller. DigiComm produces and installs digital wireless communications products and technologies worldwide. Nancy Moore, the director of international sales and installations, has asked you, the computer support specialist, to equip staff members with an Internet file transfer program and a program that compresses files.

Investigating Freely Downloadable Programs

Internet users are often pleasantly surprised to discover that many programs are available for download at no cost. A large selection of programs is available online, from anti-virus software to interactive games. Before you start downloading programs and files over the Internet, you investigate the types of files and programs that are available.

DETAILS

Freely downloadable software falls into the categories listed below:

• Freeware

Software that is available fully functional, at no cost to users, and with no restrictions is called **freeware**. Figure G-1 shows Freeware4u, a Web site that allows Internet users to download freeware.

• Shareware

Shareware is similar to freeware, but it is usually available for free during a short evaluation period. After that evaluation period expires—usually after a specified number of days or a specific number of uses—shareware stops functioning. Shareware users are expected to stop using the shareware after the specified initial trial period and uninstall it from their computers. Otherwise, anyone who likes the program and wants to continue using it, is requested to **license** it, which means to pay a fee for its use. Figure G-2 shows the screen that appears when you try to start WS_FTP Home after the 30-day trial period. Shareware is usually more reliable than freeware because the shareware developer is sometimes willing to accept responsibility for the program's operation. Usually, shareware developers have an established way for users to report any bugs and receive free or low-cost software upgrades and patches.

• Limited Edition (LE) Software

Limited edition (LE) software is a free, but restricted version of shareware that provides most of the functionality of the full version of the program with one or more useful features of the full version omitted. If you like the limited edition, you can purchase the full version of the program. Because the complete versions of limited edition software are inexpensive, most users of the limited edition will purchase the upgraded, comprehensive version so they can use its additional capabilities.

• Licensed (or Full) Version Software

Regardless of which type of software you use to evaluate a product, most developers provide you with a means of contacting them to purchase a license to use the full version of the evaluation copy. Purchasing a license involves paying a fee to get a code to unlock the software and render it fully functional. Usually this means that you click a button or link somewhere in the program interface that says "Buy Now" or "Register Now." When you click this button or link, you are connected to the programmer's Web site and you are asked to pay a fee to license the software. After you pay the fee, you usually receive the license in the form of a registration or serial number that you are then requested to enter the next time you start the program. Once you type in the license code, the software should work with no restrictions.

Clues to Use

Understanding the risks of freeware

Freeware users must accept the implicit or explicit warning that the software might contain errors, called **bugs**, which could cause the program to halt, malfunction, or even damage the user's computer. The main risk associated with using freeware is that its limited testing sometimes results in a program that contains multiple bugs, and the software's developer is rarely liable for any damage that the freeware program might cause. On the other hand, a lot of good-quality commercial software started as freeware. Before you use freeware, you should use a Web search engine to locate reviews before you download, install, virus check, and use any freeware program to see what kinds of successes and problems its users have reported.

FIGURE G-1: Freeware4u Web site

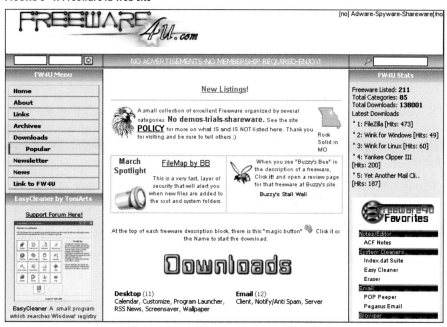

FIGURE G-2: Screen that appears in WS_FTP Home at the end of the trial period

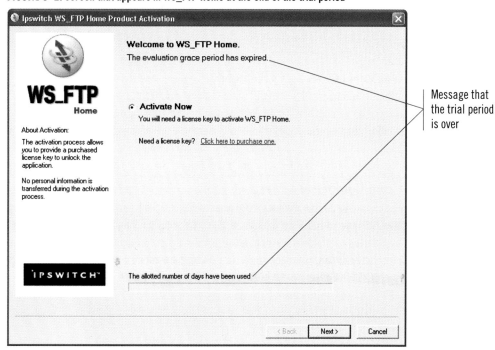

Message that
the trial period
is over

Understanding Downloading Programs and File Sharing

UNIT G
Internet

You can download shareware and freeware from Web sites on which they are stored. To download programs, you can use HTTP or FTP. You can also transfer files over the Internet with **peer-to-peer (PTP)** file sharing, which is the process of transferring files directly from one computer to another. With PTP, users install a PTP program and then make files in certain folders on their computers available to other users of the PTP program. Before you download any programs for DigiComm, you decide to investigate the various methods of downloading programs and sharing files over the Internet.

DETAILS

Some of the methods for downloading programs and sharing files are listed below:

- **Downloading Programs Using HTTP**

  Many Web sites are devoted to making programs available for downloading. You can use HTTP and your browser to download a program directly from the Web site of the company or programmer that developed the program or from a download site. A **download site** is a Web site that contains freeware and shareware programs organized in categories.

- **Downloading Programs Using FTP**

  You can also use FTP to download software from an **FTP server**, which is a server that uses FTP to transfer files rather than HTTP. An **FTP server program** runs on an FTP server, allows file transfer to and from the server by FTP, and manages FTP access to the server's files. You can use FTP with your browser by typing ftp:// and then the URL for the FTP site, or you can use an **FTP client program**, which is a program that resides on your computer and allows you to transfer files between your computer and another computer connected to it using the rules for FTP. Figure G-3 shows a popular FTP client program, WS_FTP Home. The left pane lists the files and folders on the local computer (that is, your computer) and the right pane lists the files and folders on the remote computer.

- **Sharing Files Using PTP File Sharing**

  When you transfer files using PTP file sharing, you transfer files directly from one computer to another without going through a Web site, Web server, or FTP server. Computers on a LAN or WAN are usually configured to allow users to share files stored in certain folders; in other words, if a user on one computer stores a file in a shared folder on that computer, users on other computers in the network can open that folder and use the file. With PTP file sharing software, users can do the same thing over the Internet.

- **Using Compressed Files**

  QUICK TIP
  The most common file extension for a compressed file is .zip, which is why some people refer to compressed files as **.zip files** or **zipped files**.

  You use a **file compression program** to reduce a file to a fraction of its original size, creating a **compressed file** (sometimes called an **archived file**). The smaller file size of compressed files allows you to transfer files over a network more quickly than full-size files. Compressed files can save you significant time downloading, especially over an Internet connection with a slow modem. In order to access the compressed files, you need to use a file compression program to decompress the files.

FIGURE G-3: FTP client program

Open folder on
local computer

Contents of
folder on local
computer

Open folder
on remote
computer

Contents of
folder on
remote
computer

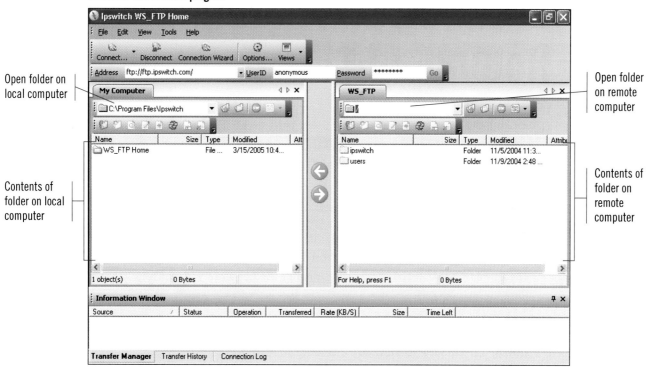

Clues to Use

Transferring music and photo files

Internet users can also download digital music and share photos online. To download music files, Internet users can register with a Web site such as Napster, iTunes, Rhapsody, and MusicMatch; these sites have obtained the legal right to distribute the musical works they offer for sale. Some of these sites allow users to purchase and download songs that they can then store on a CD or a portable music player. Other sites charge a monthly subscription fee so that users can listen to an unlimited number of songs stored on the company's Web server via a streaming transmission. In a streaming transmission, the Web server sends the first part of the file to the Web browser, which begins playing the file; and while the browser is playing the first part of the file, the server is sending the next segment of the file. This file is not stored permanently on the subscriber's computer. To share photos online, Internet users can sign up for an account with companies such as Snapfish, Ofoto, and Shutterfly, which allow users to create online photo albums. Users upload digital photos to the company's Web server, then give other people a password so that they can see the uploaded photos. If people want, they can pay a fee to the company and request a printed photo be mailed to them.

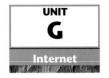
Locating a Program Using a Download Site

You can use your Web browser to download a program from the Web. You can download programs from a download site or you can often download a program directly from the Web site of the company or programmer that developed the program. To download and install some of the programs that DigiComm staff members need, you need an FTP client program. You conduct a search for FTP client programs on a download site and download a popular program.

STEPS

1. **Go to www.course.com/illustrated/internet4, click the Unit G link, then click one of the links to a download site under Lesson 3**
    The download site that you chose opens. You can select a category in which to search, such as Games or Internet. Each category contains subcategories that allow you to narrow your search. You can also type a search expression.

2. **If necessary, scroll down, click the Utilities link or the Utilities & Drivers link, then scroll down, if necessary, to view the available subcategories**
    Figure G-4 shows the subcategories listed on the Utilities Web page at ZDNet Downloads.

QUICK TIP

Sometimes the download count is a good resource for discovering popular and useful programs because these programs usually have larger download counts.

3. **Click the FTP link**
    A list of FTP programs appears, similar to the list on Download.com shown in Figure G-5. The results page includes links to Web sites with more information about each program listed and a link from which you can download each program. It also might show the date when each file was uploaded, the number of times each file has been downloaded, user reviews of the program, and the size of the downloadable file. After reading the reviews of several programs, you decide that you want to investigate the FTP client program, CuteFTP Home.

4. **Type cuteftp in the search expression text box, click Go or something similar to start the search, then scroll down the list until you see CuteFTP Home with a number after it**
    The number next to the program name is the version number; this number will change as the program is updated.

TROUBLE

The steps in this book use CuteFTP 7 Home. Your version number might differ.

5. **Click the CuteFTP Home 7.0 link**
    The download page for CuteFTP Home opens. Note that it is a very popular program that has been downloaded many times. Most download sites include user ratings and reviews that you can read to help determine if you want to download the particular program. Figure G-6 shows the download page for Cute FTP Home on Download.com.

6. **Click the GlobalSCAPE link next to Publisher**
    The GlobalSCAPE home page opens in a new browser window. You can read more about a program at the publisher's Web site. You can also check to be sure that the version of the program on the download site is up-to-date.

7. **Click the Products link on the GlobalSCAPE site, click the CuteFTP Home link, then read about the CuteFTP Home program**
    The version of CuteFTP Home on the GlobalSCAPE site might be a later version than the one on the download site. Usually, it is a good idea to download and use the latest version. However, many publisher's Web sites require you to enter personal information before you can download the program, so for the purposes of this lesson, you will download the version available on the download site.

8. **Click the Close button in the browser window title bar to close the window with GlobalSCAPE page in it**
    You see the download page for CUTEFTP Home on the download site you chose.It's a good idea to check user reviews if any are available.

9. **Scroll down to see if there are any user reviews or ratings, click the See all user reviews and ratings link if it appears on the page, then read the user reviews**

FIGURE G-4: Subcategories in Utilities on ZDNet Downloads

Search expression text box

Current category

Subcategories

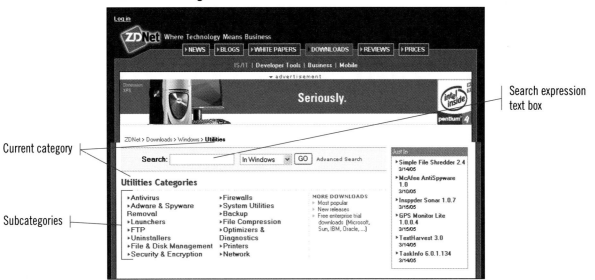

FIGURE G-5: List of FTP programs at Download.com

Click to sort list by program name

Link to Web page describing program in detail

File size

Date program was uploaded to this Web site

Search expression text box

Click to see next page of programs

Click to download program

Number of times this program has been downloaded

Click to read reviews and ratings

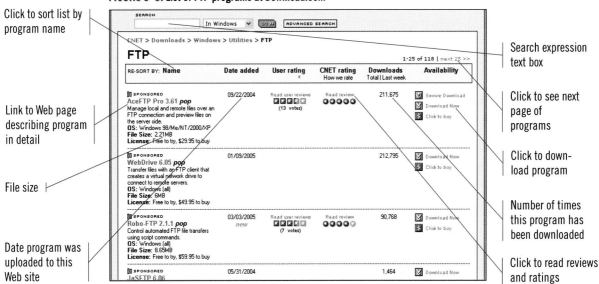

FIGURE G-6: Download page for CuteFTP Home on Download.com

Version number on your screen might differ

Link to download file

Link to publisher

Description of license

Trial period

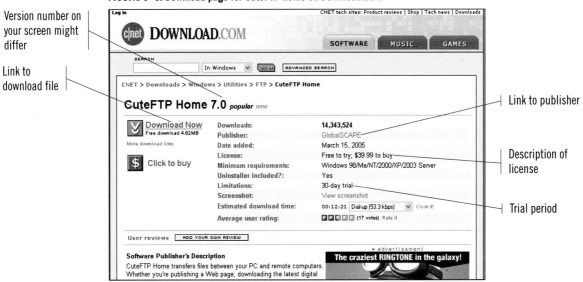

Internet

Downloading a Program Using Internet Explorer

After evaluating a shareware program to determine if it meets your needs and is a reliable program, you can download the trial version of the program so that you can decide if you like the program and want to license it. After you specify the program that you want to download, whether from a download site or a publisher's Web site, you will be prompted to save the program on your computer. It is a good idea to designate one folder on your computer for storing downloaded files so that you can easily find them later. When the download is complete, you can access the program file in Windows Explorer. ▰▰▰▰▰ You decide to download the CuteFTP Home program to install on DigiComm computers. You will use it for the trial period and then decide whether to license it.

STEPS

TROUBLE

If you are using Firefox, skip to the next lesson.

TROUBLE

If the File Download–Security Warning dialog box does not open after 15 seconds, click the "here" link to start the download.

TROUBLE

If the dialog box already closed, a previous user selected the Close this dialog box when download completes check box. Skip Step 5.

1. **If necessary, locate the download page for CuteFTP Home on the download site you chose**

2. **Click the** Download Now link **or something similar to start downloading the file**

   The Download in Progress window appears, telling you to click the "here" link if your download does not start. See Figure G-7. Next, the File Download – Security Warning dialog box opens asking if you want to run or save the file.

   If the Information Bar dialog box or only the yellow Information Bar appears, see the Clues to Use box titled "Working with the Information Bar" in this lesson.

3. **Click** Save **in the File Download – Security Warning dialog box**

   The Save As dialog box opens enabling you to specify the location where the file is saved.

4. **Click the** Save in list arrow**, navigate to the drive and folder where your Solution Files are stored, then click** Save

   A dialog box that shows the progress of the download appears as the file downloads to your computer. See Figure G-8. When it has finished downloading, the dialog box changes to the Download Complete dialog box.

5. **Click** Close

   The dialog box closes and you are returned to the browser window.

6. **Exit your browser**

FIGURE G-7: Download in Progress window

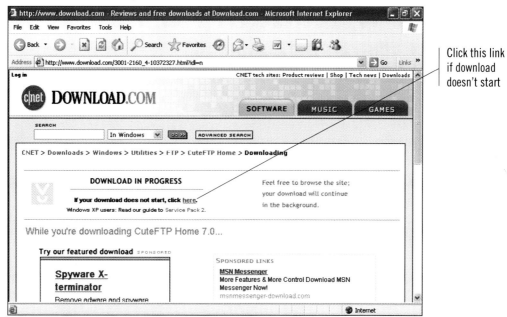

Click this link
if download
doesn't start

FIGURE G-8: Dialog box showing progress of download

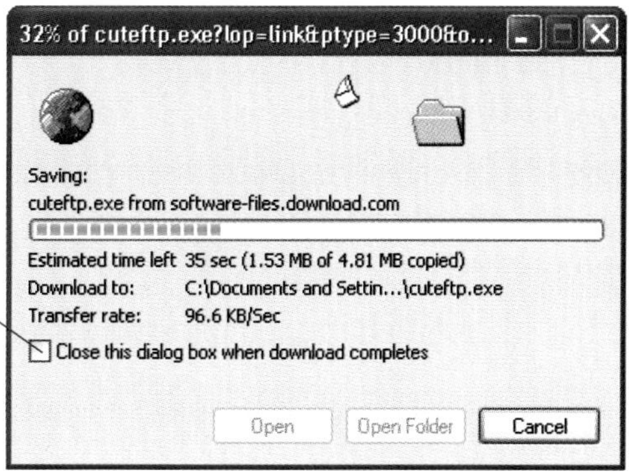

Click to check
this option for
closing the
dialog box
automatically
when download
is complete

Clues to Use

Working with the Information Bar

The Information Bar might appear below the Address bar in the Internet Explorer window, telling you that the site was blocked from downloading files to your computer. In addition, the Information Bar dialog box might appear telling you that the Information Bar appeared near the top of the browser window. See Figure G-9. If the Information Bar dialog box appears, click OK in the dialog box. (If the Information Bar dialog box does not open but the Information Bar appears, a previous user clicked the Do not show this message again check box in the Information Bar dialog box.) To download the file, you need to override the security setting. Click the Information Bar. On the menu that appears, click Download File. The Information Bar disappears and the File Download dialog box appears. Continue with Step 3 in the lesson.

FIGURE G-9: Information Bar and Information Bar dialog box

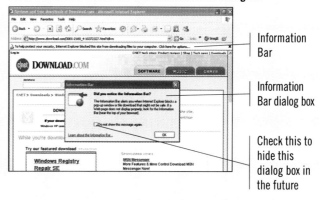

Information
Bar

Information
Bar dialog box

Check this to
hide this
dialog box in
the future

Internet

UNIT G
Internet

Downloading a Program Using Firefox

After evaluating a shareware program to determine if it meets your needs and is a reliable program, you can download the trial version of the program so that you can decide if you like the program and want to license it. After you specify the program that you want to download, whether from a download site or a publisher's Web site, you will be prompted to save the program on your computer. In Firefox, the **Download Manager** that opens when you download a file keeps track of your downloads. This is helpful if you need to find a list of recently downloaded files. Once the download is complete, you can access the program file in Windows Explorer. **••** You decide to download the CuteFTP Home program to install on DigiComm computers. You will use it for the trial period and then decide whether to license it.

STEPS

TROUBLE
If you are using Internet Explorer, skip to the next lesson.

1. **If necessary, locate the download page for CuteFTP Home on the download site you chose**

2. **Click** Tools **on the menu bar, click** Options**, then click** Downloads
   The Downloads tab in the Options dialog box opens.

3. **If necessary, click the** Ask me where to save every file option button, **click the** Show Download Manager window when a download begins check box **to insert a check mark, then click the** Close the Download Manager when all downloads are complete check box **to remove the check mark**
   Compare your screen to Figure G-10.

TROUBLE
If no dialog box opens after 15 seconds, click the "here" link to start the download.

4. **Click** OK **to close the Options dialog box, then click the** Download Now link **or something similar to begin downloading the file**
   The Opening cuteftp.exe dialog box opens.

5. **Click the** Save to Disk option button**, if necessary, then click** OK
   The Enter name of file to save to dialog box opens enabling you to specify the location where the file is saved.

6. **Click the** Save in list arrow**, then navigate to the drive and folder where your Solution Files are stored, then click** Save
   The Download Manager appears and shows the progress of the download as the file downloads to your computer. See Figure G-11. When it has finished downloading, the dialog box changes so it is titled Downloads and the file is listed as "Done" with links to Open and Remove the file next to the filename. See Figure G-12. You can leave the file listing in the Download Manager, or you can remove it.

QUICK TIP
If there were more than one file listed in the Download Manager and you wanted to remove them all from the list, you could click Clean Up in the Download Manager or click Tools on the menu bar, click Options, click Privacy, then click Clear next to Download Manager History.

7. **Click the** Remove link **next to cuteftp.exe in the Download Manager**
   The file you downloaded is still on your computer, but it is removed from the list in the Download Manager.

8. **Click the** Close button **in the Download Manager title bar**
   The dialog box closes and you are returned to the browser window.

9. **Exit your browser**

FIGURE G-10: Downloads page in the Options dialog box

Click to set a default folder for all downloads

Click to see Downloads page in this dialog box

Options to configure Download Manager

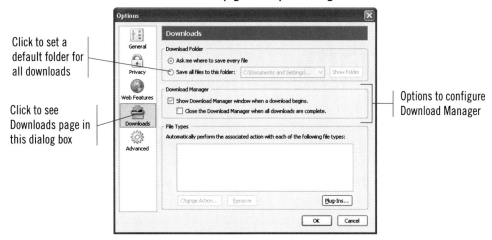

FIGURE G-11: Download Manager showing progress of download

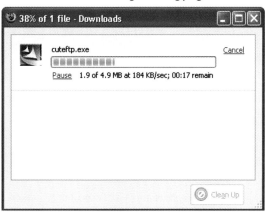

FIGURE G-12: Download Manager when download is complete

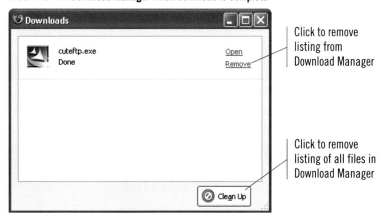

Click to remove listing from Download Manager

Click to remove listing of all files in Download Manager

Designating a folder for downloaded programs

It is a good idea to create or designate a folder on your computer to where you download all files from the Internet, so that you can easily find them when you need to install them. In Firefox, you can set the Downloads options so that files are automatically saved to a specific folder. To do this, click Tools on the menu bar, click Options, then click Downloads. In the Download Folder section at the top of the dialog box, click the Save all files to this folder option button, click the list arrow next to that option, then click Other to open the Browse for Folder dialog box. In this dialog box, you can click the plus sign next to a folder to see subfolders in that folder, and then you can click the folder to which you want to download all of your program files.

Internet

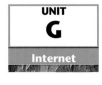

Installing a Downloaded Program

After you download a program from the Internet, you must install the program on your computer to use it. Usually, you can double-click a program file to install the program. The program file often facilitates installation by including an **installation wizard**, which is a series of dialog boxes that help you complete the installation process step-by-step. When you install a program, you must agree to the program's license agreement before the program will install. The **license agreement** is a contract between the publisher of the software and the person who is installing the software; it usually states that the software cannot be copied and resold, and it details restrictions for the software's use. ▓▓▓▓▓ You checked with Savan Chen, manager of technical services at DigiComm, to verify that it's okay to install CuteFTP on the computers in your office. You install the program on your computer.

STEPS

 Before completing the steps in this lesson, ask your instructor if you may install the program.

1. **Exit any programs that are running**
   You should always exit all programs before installing a new program.

2. **Click the Start button on the taskbar, point to All Programs, point to Accessories, then click Windows Explorer**
   Your screen should look similar to Figure G-13.

   > **TROUBLE**
   > If your computer is not set to display filename extensions, the file will appear as cuteftp instead.

3. **Navigate to the drive and folder where your Solution Files are stored, then double-click cuteftp.exe**
   The .exe file extension is an abbreviation for "executable," which means that the file is a program that you can run. The Open File - Security Warning dialog box opens.

4. **Click Run**
   The InstallShield Wizard dialog box opens. After a moment, it tells you that the InstallShield Wizard will install CuteFTP 7 Home and the Next button appears.

5. **Click Next**
   The License Agreement appears, as shown in Figure G-14.

6. **Read the License Agreement, then click Yes**
   The Install Shield Wizard dialog box prompts you to choose a destination location. The default folder for both is C:\Program Files\GlobalSCAPE\CuteFTP Home.

   > **TROUBLE**
   > If a dialog box opens indicating that you have an "ini" file that will be erased, click No so the installing program does not destroy an important file.

7. **Click Next to accept the default destination folder in which the program files will be stored**
   The next dialog box in the InstallShield Wizard opens with the Typical option button selected.

8. **Click Next to accept the Typical setup**
   After a moment, the InstallShield Wizard dialog box tells you that CuteFTP 7 Home has been installed.

9. **Click the Launch CuteFTP 7 Home check box to deselect it, then click Finish**

FIGURE G-13: Windows Explorer window

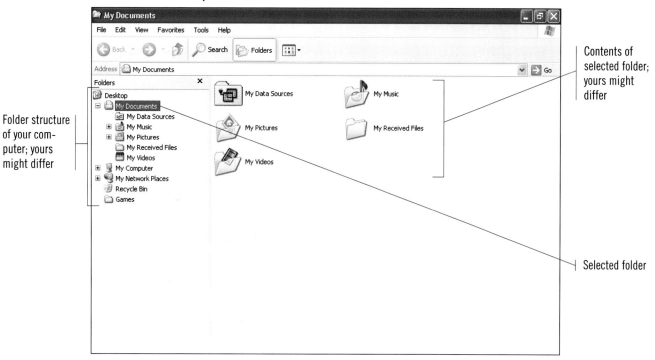

Folder structure of your computer; yours might differ

Contents of selected folder; yours might differ

Selected folder

FIGURE G-14: License Agreement

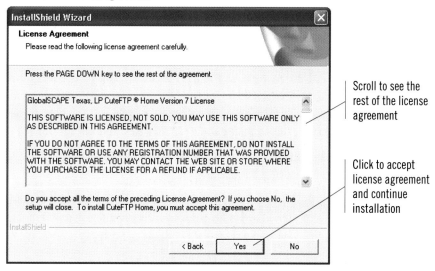

Scroll to see the rest of the license agreement

Click to accept license agreement and continue installation

Clues to Use

Checking files for viruses

After downloading anything from the Internet—even files from reputable sources—your first priority is to scan the file for viruses. Although you can configure anti-virus software to regularly scan the files on your hard disk to find infected files, the most popular anti-virus programs don't scan files while you're downloading them. However, you can set up anti-virus software to scan programs and documents before you open them. To ensure the safety of your computer when you download files, you should use a combination of these methods. You can download many high quality anti-virus programs from the Internet and install and use them for a limited time to determine their appropriateness for your own security needs.

Internet

Establishing an FTP Session

To use an FTP client to download programs and files from another computer connected to the Internet, you need to create and save an **FTP session profile**, which is a collection of information about the FTP server. The FTP session profile includes the URL of the server you want to access as well as a user name and password that the client will use to log in to the FTP server. An **FTP session** is the interaction between your computer and the remote computer after you connect to the FTP server. Publicly accessible FTP servers allow you to use **anonymous FTP** to log in and use FTP without having a personal account. When you use anonymous FTP to connect to a publicly accessible FTP site, you are restricted to particular files and directories on the public server. The method of logging in to a computer on which you have an account (with a user name and password) and using that account to send and receive files is called **named FTP** or **full-privilege FTP**. Nancy has asked you to investigate file compression programs for use at DigiComm. A popular file compression program is WinZip. To download WinZip using CuteFTP Home, you first need to create an FTP session profile for the FTP server where the WinZip program is stored.

STEPS

TROUBLE

If you do not see CuteFTP Home on the All Programs menu, make sure that you downloaded and installed the CuteFTP Home program correctly. Ask your instructor or system administrator for help, if necessary.

1. **Click the** Start button, **point to** All Programs, **point to** GlobalSCAPE, **point to** CuteFTP Home, **then click** CuteFTP 7 Home

   The CuteFTP Home program starts and the Welcome to CuteFTP 7 Home dialog box opens. This box appears until you license the program by purchasing it and entering the serial number.

2. **Click** Continue

   The CuteFTP Connection Wizard dialog box opens. You will close this.

3. **Click** Cancel, **click** Yes **in the dialog box that opens asking if you are sure you want to exit the Connection Wizard, click** Close **in the Tip of the Day dialog box, click** Exit **in the Site Manager dialog box, then click the** Maximize button **in the CuteFTP 7.0 title bar**

   The main CuteFTP Home window opens.

4. **Click the** list arrow **next to the list box at the top of the left pane, then click** My Computer

   See Figure G-15. The pane on the left shows the contents of the current folder on the local computer (the computer you are working on). The pane on the right will show the contents of the current folder on the remote computer (the computer at the FTP site). Now you will add a site to the site list in CuteFTP.

5. **Click** Tools **on the menu bar, point to** Site Manager, **then click** Display Site Manager

   The Site Manager dialog box opens.

6. **Click** New **in the Site Manager dialog box, then click** FTP Site **on the menu that appears**

   A new, untitled site is added to the site list on the left and tabs appear on the right.

7. **Type** WinZip **in the Label text box, then press** [Tab]

8. **Type** ftp.winzip.com **in the Host address text box**

   Many FTP sites on the Internet use the prefix "ftp" followed by the domain name. For example, the FTP site for Mozilla is ftp.mozilla.org.

9. **Click the** Anonymous option button, **if necessary**

   When you select the Anonymous option button, you do not need to type any information in the Username or Password text boxes. See Figure G-16. If you had full-privilege access, you would click the Normal option button, then type your username and password in the appropriate text boxes.

TROUBLE

If you receive an "access denied" message, the WinZip FTP site is busy. You can try again later.

10. **Click** Connect, **then in the Prompt dialog box that appears, click** OK

    The Site Manager dialog box closes and CuteFTP connects to the WinZip FTP site.

CKnow.com to know about computers

FIGURE G-15: CuteFTP Home program window

Click to open a different folder on local computer

Contents of open folder on local computer; yours might differ

Currently disconnected from remote computer

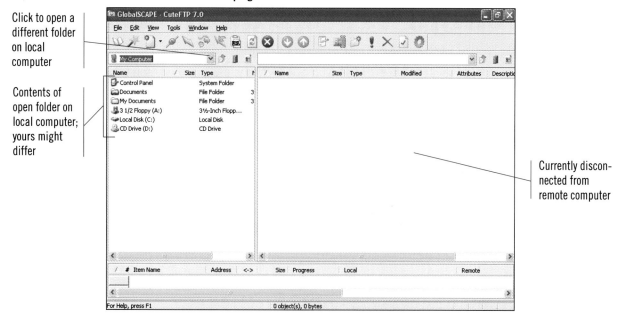

FIGURE G-16: Site Manager in CuteFTP Home

Name you give site

Site address

Select for anonymous login

Click to connect to selected FTP site

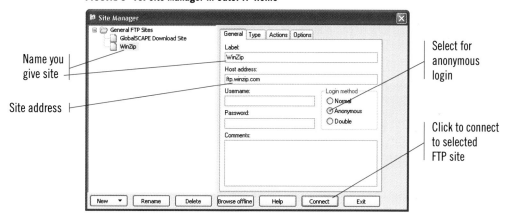

Clues to Use

Using your browser to navigate an FTP site

You can use a browser to navigate an FTP site and to upload and download files to and from the site. For example, you can connect to the WinZip FTP site using your browser by typing **ftp.winzip.com** in the Address or Location bar. After you access the site, the URL in the Address or Location bar changes to ftp://ftp.winzip.com. This is because the protocol that FTP sites use is FTP instead of HTTP. If you have full-privilege access to an FTP site and have a user name and password, you can log in by typing the protocol, **ftp://**, followed by your user name, a colon, your password followed by the @ symbol, then the URL of the FTP site. For example, if you had full-privilege access to the WinZip site with UserName and Password, you would

type **ftp://UserName:Password@winzip.com** in the Address or Location bar. When you access an FTP site using a browser, you will see the organization of the folders (also called directories) and files on the FTP site, similar to the organization of folders and files on a computer's hard drive. Double-clicking a folder opens the folder and displays its contents. Double-clicking a file opens the file in a new browser window, starts the program associated with the file and opens the file, or begins downloading the file to your computer. If you log in anonymously, you may be prevented from opening certain files and folders that require full-privilege access. To move up (or back) one folder, you click the Up to higher directory link.

STEPS

Using FTP to Download a File

After you create a session profile and connect to an FTP site, you can download available files from the FTP server. You can use the WinZip FTP site you logged in to in the previous lesson to download the WinZip file compression program. ░▒▓ Now that you are connected to the WinZip FTP site, you use your FTP client to download the WinZip program.

> 🛑 *Before completing the steps in this lesson, ask your instructor if you may complete Steps 5-10 and install the WinZip program.*

TROUBLE

If you don't see the filename winzip90.exe listed, go to *www.course.com/illustrated/internet4*, click the Unit G link, read the notes for Lesson 8, return to the CuteFTP window, then click the correct filename.

QUICK TIP

You can also drag the selected file from one pane to the other to download or upload it.

1. **Click the** list arrow **next to the list box at the top of the left pane, then navigate to the drive and folder where your Solution Files are stored**
   The left pane displays your Solution Files.

2. **In the right pane, click** winzip90.exe
   Figure G-17 shows the file winzip90.exe selected.

3. **Click the** Download button 🔽 **on the toolbar**
   CuteFTP begins to download the selected file (winzip90.exe) from the FTP server shown in the right pane to the selected folder on your computer shown in the left pane. A Progress bar appears at the bottom of the window, as shown in Figure G-18. When the Progress bar disappears, the file transfer is complete and the winzip90.exe program is saved on your computer. The time required to transfer the program file varies according to your computer's connection type and speed.

4. **After the file has finished downloading, click the** Close button **in the CuteFTP 7.0 title bar**
   You disconnect from the WinZip FTP site and the CuteFTP Home program closes.

5. **Click the button on the taskbar that identifies the folder containing your Solution Files, if necessary, then double-click the file** winzip90.exe **in the right pane**
   The WinZip 9.0 SR-1 Setup dialog box opens.

6. **Click** Setup
   The WinZip Setup dialog box opens. See Figure G-19.

7. **Click** OK **to accept the default location for the installation**
   WinZip starts installing and another WinZip Setup dialog box opens.

8. **Click** Next**, click** View License Agreement**, read the license agreement that appears in a WinZip Installation window, click the** Close button **in the WinZip Installation window title bar, click** Yes**, then click** Next
   Here you can choose to use WinZip in the classic mode or with a wizard.

9. **Click the** Start with WinZip Classic option button**, if necessary, click** Next **three times, then click** Finish
   The WinZip (Evaluation Version) program window opens.

10. **Click the** Close button **in the WinZip program window**

FIGURE G-17: WinZip program file name selected

Click to download selected file

Path to current folder on local computer; yours might differ

Current folder is empty on local computer

winzip90.exe selected

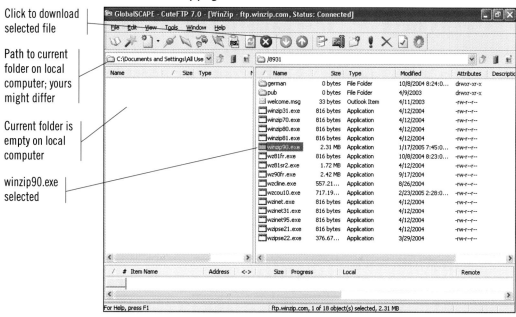

FIGURE G-18: Downloading a file using CuteFTP Home

File partially downloaded

Progress bar

Name of file being downloaded

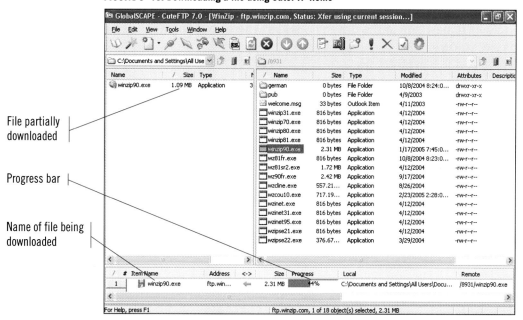

FIGURE G-19: WinZip Setup dialog box

Folder in which WinZip will be installed

Internet

Opening a Compressed File

After you download a compressed file, you must restore the file to its original size before you can open or run it. The process of restoring a compressed file to its original form is called **file decompression**, **file extraction**, or **file expansion**. To open a compressed file, you need a file compression program, such as WinZip. Nancy wrote a memo for the DigiComm sales staff instructing them to learn more about DigiComm's new wireless router, DigiMAXX. She used WinZip to compress her memo and a sales information sheet into one file. She asked you to open the compressed file and look over the information.

STEPS

1. **In the open Windows Explorer window, navigate to the drive and folder where your Data Files are stored, then double-click** DigiMAXX.zip

   The WinZip dialog box opens, as shown in Figure G-20.

2. **Click** Use Evaluation Version

   The .zip file opens and the files in the DigiMAXX.zip file are listed in the WinZip (Evaluation Version) window, as shown in Figure G-21.

   <table>
   <tr><td>

   QUICK TIP

   To extract a specific file in a zip file, click the file that you want to extract, then click the Extract button on the toolbar.

   </td></tr>
   </table>

3. **Click the** Extract button **on the toolbar**

   The Extract dialog box opens.

4. **In the list of drives and folders, click the** plus signs **next to the appropriate drive and folders to navigate to the drive and folder where your Solution Files are stored**

   Your screen should look similar to Figure G-22.

5. **Click** Extract

   The two files are extracted to your computer. You could open the documents in any word processor that reads rtf files (rich text files).

Willcom
Compressed

-rar
-winzip
-7zip

FIGURE G-20: WinZip dialog box

Click to use
evaluation
version of
WinZip

These buttons might be arranged
in a different order

FIGURE G-21: Contents of DigiComm.zip

Files contained in the
zipped file

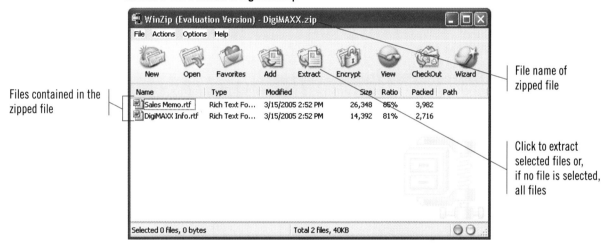

File name of
zipped file

Click to extract
selected files or,
if no file is selected,
all files

FIGURE G-22: Extract dialog box

Location of Solution
Files selected (your
location might differ)

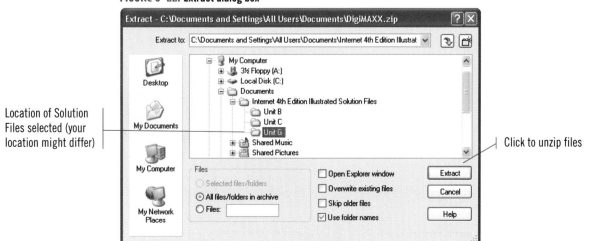

Click to unzip files

Compressing Files

If you need to transfer large files over the Internet, you should compress them to make the upload and download times shorter. To compress files, you need a file compression program, such as WinZip. When you add a file to a compressed file, you do not remove the original file from its location; rather you add a copy of the file to the compressed file. ▰▰▰ Nancy wants you to re-compress the two files she sent to you and make them available for the sales representatives to download from DigiComm's network server.

STEPS

1. **Click the** New button **on the WinZip toolbar**

   The New Archive dialog box opens. Compressed files are referred to as **archives** in WinZip.

2. **Click the** Save in list arrow, **then navigate to the drive and folder where your Solution Files are stored**

3. **Click in the** File name text box, **if necessary, type** Info from Nancy, **then click** OK

   The New Archive dialog box closes, and the Add dialog box opens.

4. **Click the** Look in list arrow, **navigate to the drive and folder where your Solution Files are stored, then click** Sales Memo.rtf

   See Figure G-23.

5. **Click** Add

   The Add dialog box closes and Sales Memo.rtf is listed in the WinZip (Evaluation Version) – Info from Nancy.zip window.

<table>
<tr><td>

QUICK TIP

To add more than one file to a WinZip archive at a time, press and hold the Ctrl key while you click the files you want to add in the Add dialog box.

</td><td>

6. **Click the** Add button **on the toolbar, click** DigiMAXX Info.rtf **in the Add dialog box, then click** Add

   DigiMAXX Info.rtf is added to the list of files in the Info from Nancy compressed file.
   See Figure G-24.

7. **Click the** Close button **in the WinZip title bar**

   The WinZip program closes.

</td></tr>
</table>

FIGURE G-23: File to add to archive in Add dialog box

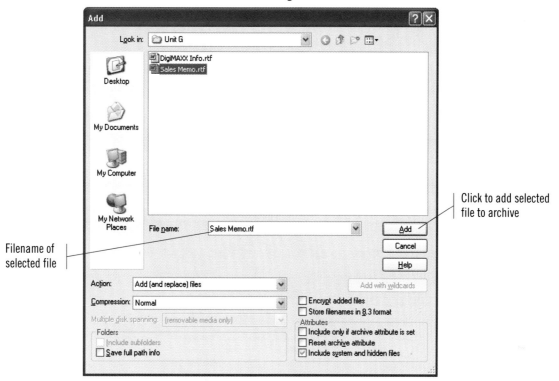

Filename of selected file

Click to add selected file to archive

FIGURE G-24: Files in Info from Nancy archive

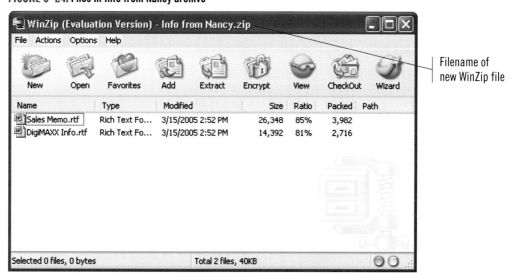

Filename of new WinZip file

Practice

▼ CONCEPTS REVIEW

Identify each element of the FTP client program window shown in Figure G-25.

FIGURE G-25

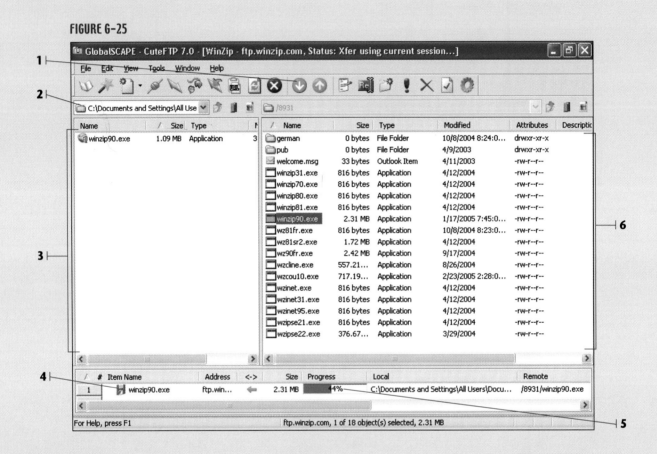

Match each term with the statement that best describes it.

7. PTP

8. Anonymous FTP

9. Upload

10. Download

11. Freeware

12. Shareware

13. Download site

14. FTP client program

a. A method used to log in to public FTP sites

b. Software that you can download for free to use for a short evaluation period

c. To transfer files from a remote computer to your computer

d. A type of software that you can download for free with no restrictions on its use

e. Acronym for peer-to-peer file sharing

f. To transfer files from your computer to a remote computer

g. A program that allows transfer of files between computers using FTP

h. A Web site that contains freeware and shareware programs organized in categories

Select the best answer from the list of choices.

15. To use full-privilege FTP, you must:
    a. log in with the user name "anonymous."
    b. enter your e-mail address as your password.
    c. have an account on the FTP server to which you're connecting.
    d. use a specific FTP client program.

16. What is the name of the process you use to log in to a publicly accessible remote FTP server when you don't have a personal account?
    a. Anonymous FTP
    b. Unknown FTP
    c. Guest FTP
    d. FTP.COM

17. Limited edition software is:
    a. fully functional software that is available to anyone at no cost and with no restrictions attached to its use.
    b. the commercial version of a software program.
    c. a free, restricted version of shareware that provides most of the functionality of the full commercial version.
    d. usually available at no cost for a short evaluation period, after which users are requested to pay for its use.

18. To use an FTP client program to download files and programs from a given server, you need to:
    a. view the server's contents in a Web browser.
    b. start WinZip.
    c. start Internet Explorer.
    d. create an FTP session profile for the server.

19. FTP works:
    a. between any connected computers.
    b. only between computers connected via the Internet.
    c. only between computers connected via a local network.
    d. only between connected computers that are near one another.

20. Which of the following program types do you use to reduce a file to a smaller size?
    a. Downloaded program
    b. FTP client program
    c. PTP program
    d. File compression program

21. Which of the following types of software allows you to use the program for an unlimited amount of time with no program restrictions for free?
    a. Freeware
    b. Shareware
    c. Limited Edition software
    d. Licensed software

1. **Locate a program using a download site.**
   a. Go to www.course.com/illustrated/internet4, click the Unit G link, then click the Tucows link under Skills Review 1.
   b. Search on the term zip.
   c. Examine the search results, and read the reviews for at least three file compression programs.

2. **Download a program using a browser.**
   a. Go to www.course.com/illustrated/internet4, click the Unit G link, then click the one of the links under Skills Review 2.
   b. Click the Internet link, click the Tools and Utilities link, then click the Bookmark Managers link.
   c. Click the Name link (the column head) to sort the list in alphabetical order, then scroll down and click the FavoriteSync 3.0 (or another number higher than 3.0) link. This program synchronizes the Internet Explorer Favorites on several computers.
   d. Download the FavoriteSync software and save the file to the drive and folder where your Solution Files are stored.
   e. If necessary, close any open dialog boxes when the download is complete.

3. **Install a downloaded program.**
   a. Check with your instructor or system administrator for permission to install FavoriteSync.
   b. Exit all open programs.
   c. If you have permission, open Windows Explorer, then navigate to the drive and folder where your Solution Files are stored.
   d. Double-click FavoriteSyncInstall.exe. Check with your instructor, then click Run in the dialog box that opens warning you that the publisher could not be verified. (*Hint*: You will learn more about this type of security issue in Unit I.)
   e. Follow the installation directions.
   f. If you don't want FavoriteSync to start every time you start Windows, click the Start button, point to All Programs, then point to Startup to display the programs that will start every time you start Windows. Right-click FavoriteSync, then click Delete on the shortcut menu.

4. **Establish an FTP session**
   a. Start CuteFTP Home.
   b. Display the Site Manager dialog box.
   c. Add a new site with the following information:
      Label: Mozilla
      Host address: ftp.mozilla.org
      Login method: Anonymous
   d. Connect to the Mozilla FTP site.

5. **Use FTP to download a file.**
   a. In the Mozilla FTP site, double-click the pub folder.
   b. Double-click the mozilla.org folder.
   c. In the left pane, navigate to the drive and folder where your Solution Files are stored.

    d. Scroll down in the right pane, then download the README file to your computer. This is a text file that explains the purpose of the Mozilla.org FTP site.

    e. When the program has downloaded, close CuteFTP.

6. Open a compressed file.

    a. Open the artist.zip file from the drive and folder where your Data Files are stored.

    b. Press and hold the Ctrl key, click path.JPG and birth.JPG file, then release the Ctrl key.

    c. Extract the two selected files to the drive and folder where your Solution Files are stored.

7. Compress files.

    a. Create a new WinZip archive named Images stored in the drive and folder where your Solution Files are stored.

    b. Add path.JPG and birth.JPG from the location where your Solution Files are stored to the Images.zip archive file.

    c. Exit WinZip.

▼ INDEPENDENT CHALLENGE 1

A friend of yours owns an Apple Macintosh computer. The Macintosh runs the Mac OS operating system rather than Windows. The most prevalent type of compressed files for Macintosh users is the .sit file, rather than .zip. .sit is an abbreviation for the name of the program that creates these files, StuffIt. Your friend has downloaded a .sit file, but she doesn't have a program to open it. She asks you to help her locate a program that can open a .sit file.

    a. Go to www.course.com/illustrated/internet4, click the Unit G link, then click one of the links under Independent Challenge 1.

    b. Click the list arrow next to the search expression text box, then click In Downloads.

    c. Search for "stuffit."

    d. In the search results list, identify the most recent version of StuffIt for the MacOS (this is the program name with the highest number and with MacOS listed next to OS under the program name), then click the link.

    e. Read the information about the program.

    f. Send an e-mail message to your instructor that includes the URL for the Web page on the download site where you can download the program.

Advanced Challenge Exercise

    ■ Your friend wants to download a program that will help her create lists. Go to www.course.com/illustrated/internet4, click the Unit G link, click the Tucows link under Advanced Challenge Exercise in Independent Challenge 1, then search for a To-do list manager program for the Macintosh operating system.

    ■ Click the link for a file that you find, then click the link to go to the developer's Web site.

    ■ Explore the developer's Web site and see if that developer has any other programs that your friend might find useful.

    ■ Send an e-mail message to your instructor that includes the URL for the developer's Web site and a sentence explaining the to-do list manager program you found, as well as a sentence identifying any other programs on the developer's Web site that your friend might find useful.

    g. Exit your Web browser.

▼ INDEPENDENT CHALLENGE 2

You own Internet Adventures, a one-person consulting company that provides a variety of consulting services to small and medium-size companies. You charge an hourly rate to help companies find and download information on the Internet. You are working for a large CPA firm that wants you to create bookmarks and favorites for Web sites that are of interest to tax preparers. Some members of the tax-preparation team use Microsoft Internet Explorer, whereas others use Netscape Navigator. When team members find interesting Web sites, they use their Web browser to create either an Internet Explorer favorite or a Navigator bookmark. The team members don't always have time to create a bookmark for the Web site in the other Web browser, so they end up losing some of the URLs. You remember reading a review about several shareware products that might be able to maintain a library of common bookmarks that Internet Explorer and Navigator can share.

    a. Start your Web browser.

    b. Go to **www.course.com/illustrated/internet4**, click the **Unit G link**, then click the one of the links under Independent Challenge 2.

    c. Type **convert bookmarks** in the search expression text box, then click **Go** (or something similar) to start the search.

    d. Scroll down the list of results and click **Bookmark Converter 2.9**. If you cannot find that bookmark program in the list, then scroll down the list and look for a bookmark program whose description indicates that it can convert bookmarks between Internet Explorer and Netscape.

    e. Download the Bookmark Converter program, and save it to the drive and folder where your Solution Files are stored.

    f. Start WinZip, then create a new archive named **Bookmark Converter Installation File** stored in the drive and folder where your Solution Files are stored.

    g. Add the file you just downloaded to the archive, then exit WinZip.

    h. Open Windows Explorer, navigate to the drive and folder where your Solution Files are stored, install the Bookmark Converter program, then open it and examine its features.

    i. Close all open programs.

▼ INDEPENDENT CHALLENGE 3

As the director of computing at Baseline High School, you and a staff of three people ensure that the school's computer lab of 45 PCs functions properly. Last week, a virus infected every computer in the lab, and you had to close the lab to prevent the virus from spreading to students' disks and other computers. Each lab computer has McAfee Virus Scan software installed, but the installed version does not recognize and cannot eradicate the new virus pattern. You need to download the latest virus data file from McAfee.

    a. Start CuteFTP Home.

    b. Create a new session profile using the profile name **McAfee**, the host address **ftp.mcafee.com**, and the anonymous login method.

    c. Connect to McAfee's FTP site.

    d. To see the antivirus data files on the remote computer, use the following pathname: **/pub/antivirus/datfiles/4.x**.

    e. Change the local folder in Cute FTP Home to display the location of your Solution Files.

    f. On the remote computer, select the filename that begins with **dat** and ends with the filename extension **.zip**.

    g. Download the file.

Advanced Challenge Exercise

    ■ Open CuteFTP Home help, then search for information about protecting the Site Manager with a password.

    ■ Open the Site Manager Encryption dialog box and assign a password for opening the Site Manager. (*Note*: Passwords are case-sensitive; that is, "password" is different than "PASSWORD" or "Password.")

    ■ Click **OK**, exit CuteFTP Home, then restart CuteFTP Home.

    ■ Type the password you assigned in the Password text box in the Site Manager Access Password dialog box, then click **OK**.

    ■ Remove the password you assigned.

    h. Exit all open programs.

▼ INDEPENDENT CHALLENGE 4

You work for PCD Resources, an company that supplies human resources services to other companies. They recently added a new computer system to the office, and you have been hired to help the staff find and download programs they might find useful. Your manager told you that several people have complained that they are confused about the difference between downloading files using a browser and downloading files using an FTP client program. He asked you to create a short report on the similarities and differences between FTP and HTTP.

a. Use a search engine and find information describing what each protocol was originally designed for.

b. Find information describing each protocol's most common uses today.

c. Find information describing any overlapping uses between the two protocols.

d. Write at least two paragraphs summarizing your findings.

e. Use WinZip or another file compression program and compress the file you created in Step D.

f. Use e-mail to send your compressed file to your instructor as an attachment.

g. Exit all open programs.

Internet

▼ VISUAL WORKSHOP

Open CuteFTP Home, then complete the Site Manager dialog box shown in Figure G-26. Log in to the Netscape FTP site, and then explore the contents of the pub folder.

FIGURE G-26

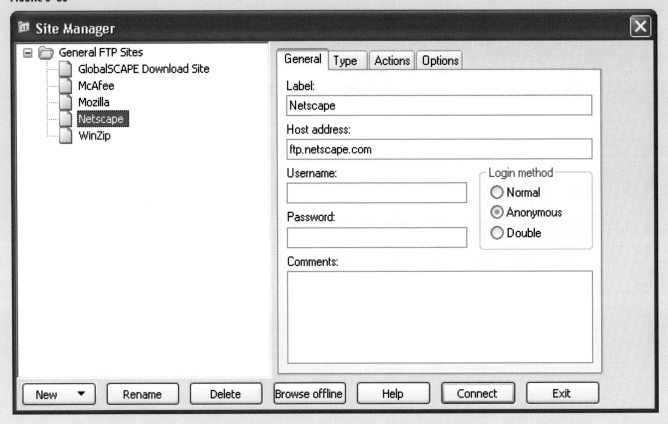

UNIT
H
Internet

Extending Browser Capabilities

OBJECTIVES

Understand graphics
Understand multimedia
Understand browser extensions
Locate browser extensions
Download and install extensions with Internet Explorer
Download and install extensions with Firefox
Use browser extensions

Many Web sites include files in file formats that Web browsers cannot display by default. These file formats are used primarily for elaborate graphics and multimedia content. Most browsers can display graphics on Web sites, but in order to properly display audio and video files, you need another program. You can enable a Web browser to interpret almost any file format on the Web by installing programs for the Web browser. These programs are often small and can be downloaded for free. In this unit, you will download, install, and use these programs. Remes Video Productions (RVP) is a video production company that specializes in producing training and safety videos. Mark Remes, the company's founder, wants to expand his business outside the Minneapolis/St. Paul area and he has hired you to market the company on the Web. He wants you to create a Web site that includes samples of the company's video work.

Understanding Graphics

In addition to basic text, most Web sites incorporate images or art, known as **graphics**, into their designs. Graphics can help Web site users find information more easily, and they can strongly influence the Web site's look and feel. 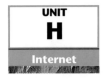 Before you research the best way to incorporate graphics into the RVP Web site, you ask Franco, the company's Webmaster, to give you an overview of common graphic file formats used in Web pages.

DETAILS

Common file formats used in Web pages are described below:

- GIF

    GIF, an acronym for Graphics Interchange Format, is a file format that can contain up to 256 colors. GIF is a popular file format because it is compressed, which means that the browser downloads the images quickly. GIF uses **lossless compression** technology, which reduces the file size without any loss of data. The algorithm that compresses GIF files is owned by Unisys, and programs that create GIF files must pay a licensing fee to Unisys to use this file format. An **animated GIF** file combines several images into a single GIF file so that the images can be displayed one after the other to simulate movement.

- JPEG

    JPEG, an acronym for Joint Photographic Experts Group, is a file format that can store over 16 million colors, which is particularly useful for photographs. JPEG is also a compressed file format, but it uses **lossy compression** technology, which eliminates redundant and unnecessary data in an image to reduce the file size. The discarded data isn't usually noticeable to the human eye. The greater the level of compression, the more data is lost and the smaller the file size gets. Figure H-1 shows the page for Vincent van Gogh's self-portraits on the WebMuseum site. The images of the paintings are in JEPG file format to preserve the colors of the painting and to reduce the file size to a manageable size for viewing on the Web. Most graphics on the Web are saved in the GIF or JPEG file formats.

- PNG

    The PNG format is a license-free compressed format that is similar to GIF, but it cannot be used to create animations. Although its promoters hope that it will become the prevailing Web standard, it is not yet widely used because some browsers cannot display PNG files.

- Uncompressed File Formats

    Other file formats used on the Web are Windows bitmap file format (.bmp), Tagged Image File Format (or TIFF) format (.tif), and PC Paintbrush format (.pcx). These formats are all uncompressed graphics formats. Web page designers usually avoid these formats because a Web browser takes too long to download them.

Self-Portrait Dedicated to Paul Gauguin
1888 (130 Kb); Oil on canvas, 60.5 x 49.4 cm (23 3/4 x 19 1/2 in); Fogg Art Museum, Harvard University, Cambridge, MA

JPEG images

Self-Portrait in front of the Easel
1888 (200 Kb); 65 x 50.5 cm

Self-Portrait with Bandaged Ear
1889 (250 Kb); Oil on canvas, 60 x 49 cm; Courtauld Institute Galleries, London

Self-Portrait
1889 (250 Kb); Oil on canvas, 65 x 54 cm (25 1/2 x 21 1/4 in); Musee d'Orsay, Paris

Self-Portrait

Clues to Use

Using clip art

A collection of individual icons, shapes, and other graphics is known as **clip art**. Clip art is available for free use or for purchase on many Web sites. Some Web sites offer clip art or tools for helping you find clip art. Often you can browse clip art by subject category or search for images associated with a keyword you specify. Clip art files are often GIF or BMP files. Figure H-2 shows the Concepts category in the Microsoft Office Clip Art and Media collection of clip art. When you use graphics that you download from a Web site, you must be careful not to violate the image owner's rights. Check the Web site copyright notices and conditions-of-use statements for information about using the images.

FIGURE H-2: Microsoft Office Clip Art and Media Concepts category

Clip art images

Understanding Multimedia

In addition to graphics some Web sites incorporate sound, animation, and video, known collectively as **multimedia**. Web pages can communicate information by playing music or showing a video. A popular technique for transferring both sound and video files on the Web is called streaming transmission. In a **streaming transmission**, the Web server sends the first part of the file to the Web browser, which begins playing the file. While the browser is playing the first part of the file, the server is then sending the next segment of the file. You know that Mark wants to add multimedia elements to the RVP Web site. You ask Franco to give you an overview of multimedia file formats used on Web pages.

DETAILS

Common multimedia formats are described below:

QUICK TIP

In order for your computer to play sounds, it must also be equipped with a sound card and either speakers or earphones.

- **Audio File Formats**

  - The **Wave (WAV) format** digitizes audio waveform information at a user specified sampling rate and can be played on any Windows computer that supports sound. WAV files can be very large; a WAV file that stores one minute of CD-quality sound can be more than 1 megabyte in size.

  - The **MIDI (Musical Instrument Digital Interface) format** does not digitize the sound waveform; instead, it digitally records information about each element of the sound, including its pitch, length, and volume. MIDI files are much smaller than WAV files and are therefore often used on the Web. Figure H-3 shows a Web page that offers many MIDI files to listen to.

  - The **AU format** is the audio file format used by the UNIX operating system. Browsers need to be able to recognize this file format because many of the pages available on the Web were originally created on computers running the UNIX operating system. These files are approximately the same size as WAV files.

  - The **MPEG Audio Layer 3 (MP3) format** is the audio portion of a compressed video format developed by the International Standards Organization's **Moving Picture Experts Group** (MPEG). Files in the MP3 format are somewhat lower in quality than WAV files, but they are 90 percent smaller.

- **Video File Formats**

  AVI and **MPEG** are common formats used for video on the Web, and they can be played using the same software that plays many other multimedia file types, including the player that comes with Windows. AVI files are uncompressed files and can be very large. MPEG files use lossy compression.

- **Proprietary File Formats**

  - **RealAudio format** for audio files and the **RealVideo format** for video files are file formats developed by RealNetworks, Inc. These files have filename extensions of .ra, .ram, or .rmj. To play these files, you must download and install one of the Real file players from Real.com.

  - Proprietary Windows Media Player file formats include **Windows Media Audio (wma)**, **Windows Media Video (wmv)**, and **Advanced Systems Format (asf)**. These files will play only in Windows Media Player. Figure H-4 shows a list of music clips on Barnes & Noble.com that can be played with Windows Media Player.

  - **QuickTime** is a proprietary video format developed by Apple Computer. It works equally well on Windows and Macintosh computers. You need to download the QuickTime player to play a QuickTime video.

FIGURE H-3: Web site with MIDI files

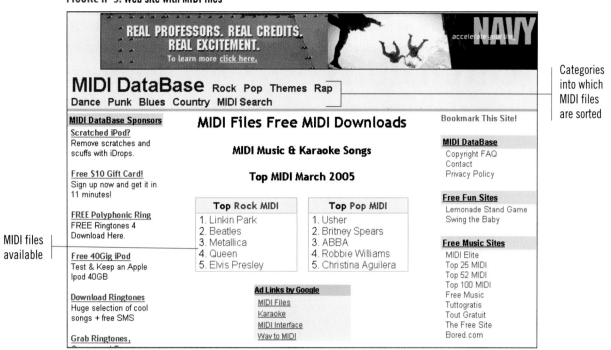

Categories into which MIDI files are sorted

MIDI files available

FIGURE H-4: Windows Media Player audio clips on Barnes & Noble.com

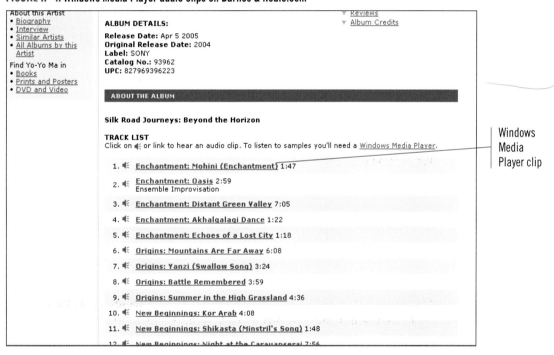

Windows Media Player clip

Clues to Use

Sharing MP3 files

MP3 files became wildly popular just as disk storage on personal computers dropped in price and CD writers (also called CD burners) became affordable for home use. Their smaller size made MP3 files easy to send from one person to another over the Internet, and file sharing software, such as Napster and Kazaa, became very popular. Companies in the recording industry and the recording artists themselves were not happy. Recording companies and artists filed suits against Napster and other file-sharing sponsors for violating copyright laws. The recording companies were generally successful in obtaining court orders or out-of-court settlements to prevent further copyright violations in many cases. Some companies still provide MP3 files but charge fees that are returned to recording companies and artists to pay for their use. Many individuals, however, still violate the law and share MP3 files that contain copyrighted works.

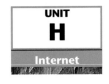

Understanding Browser Extensions

Browser extensions enhance the capabilities of Web browsers by allowing a Web browser to perform tasks that it was not originally designed to do. There are three categories of browser extensions. **Plug-in** browser extensions are programs that a Web browser starts to display or play a specific file type. Plug-ins can start only from within a Web browser. **Helper application** or **helper app** browser extensions are separate programs, such as a spreadsheet program, that are launched to display or play some files, such as a spreadsheet, that can start independently of Web browsers. **Add-ons** are browser extensions that enhance your browsing experience, such as toolbars that let you access a search engine without opening its Web site. ▰▰▰ You want to include video clips on the RVP Web site, and you need to decide on a format that potential users can easily view with a Web browser. You begin the process by reviewing some of the types of browser extensions that are available.

DETAILS

Categories of browser extensions are discussed below:

- **Document and Productivity**

  Document and productivity browser extensions let you use a Web browser to read documents, such as documents saved in **PDF format**, a format that allows documents to maintain a consistent layout and format on different computers when viewed using Adobe Reader.

QUICK TIP

Real estate agents use iPIX to display a 360-degree view of the rooms in a house they have listed for sale.

- **Image Viewer**

  Image viewer browser extensions let the Web browser display graphics, such as interactive road maps or file formats other than the standard GIF and JPEG formats. For example, the iPIX plug-in lets you view a specially created digital image from all angles by panning an image left, right, up, or down to see it from the sky, ground, or to turn it in a circle. See Figure H-5 for an example of an iPIX image.

- **Animation**

  Animation browser extensions allow you to play interactive games, view animated interfaces, listen to streaming CD-quality audio music and speech, and view instructional presentations. One of the most popular animation extensions is Macromedia's **Shockwave Player**. Figure H-6 shows an example of a Shockwave-enhanced game. Macromedia's **Flash Player**, another popular animation plug-in, has become so popular that it is installed automatically with some browsers.

- **Sound Player**

  Sound player browser extensions let your Web browser play non-standard audio file formats. Many sound player extensions are available, including Beatnik and RealPlayer.

QUICK TIP

QuickTime was one of the first video players developed.

- **Video Player**

  Video player browser extensions deliver movies to Web browsers over the Internet. When you click a movie link, the movie downloads and begins playing in its own window. Popular video players include QuickTime, RealPlayer, and Windows Media Player.

- **3-D**

  Virtual Reality Modeling Language or **VRML** (pronounced "ver-mal") is a programming language used to create three-dimensional environments in which users can navigate and interact with a three dimensional scene. Popular applications for VRML plug-ins are games in which players can interact with the objects they encounter and location tours, such as one that a university might provide to allow a virtual campus tour by enabling the observer to turn any direction and seem to walk around and through buildings. **Extensible 3D (X3D),** the next generation for 3D on the Web, will be supported by new browser extensions. There are also other 3D Web technologies available as plug-ins for your browser. Figure H-6 shows an example of a Shockwave-enhanced game that also uses 3D Groove, a 3D plug-in.

FIGURE H-5: Web page containing iPIX image

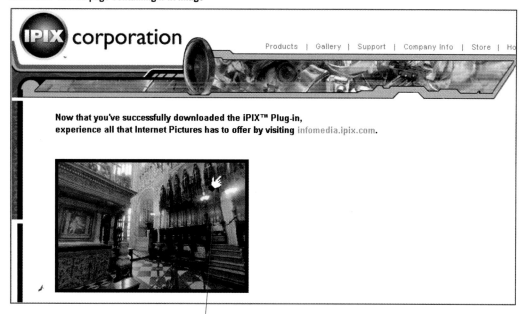

Drag pointer around image
to change view of scene

FIGURE H-6: Browser-based video game using Shockwave MX and 3D Groove

Locating Browser Extensions

You can find and download browser extensions from different Web sites. Some download sites include a list of links to browser extensions, which are grouped by category or function.  Before deciding on a video format for displaying samples of RVP's work on the Web site, you want to see which file formats are handled by the most popular and highest-rated browser extensions. You review the audio and video plug-ins listed on a couple of plug-in download sites.

STEPS

1. **Go to** www.course.com/illustrated/internet4, **click the** Unit H link, **then click one of the links to a download site under Lesson 4**

2. **Type** plug-ins **in the search expression text box, then click** Go

   A search results page opens with various plug-ins listed in descending order by the date the software was added to the list.

3. **Click the** Downloads link **(the column head)**

   Clicking a column heading sorts the list based on the contents of the column. The list is sorted in descending order based on the number of times each item has been downloaded. For each plug-in, the download site lists the title and version number, release date, type of license, rating, and file size. See Figure H-7 for a list of popular plug-ins available at Download.com.

TROUBLE

Your results page might look different because the plug-ins and their statistics change over time.

4. **Scroll down to view the most popular downloads**

   Notice all of the different plug-ins that you can download.

5. **Type** shockwave player **in the search expression dialog box, then click** Go

   The search results page that opens displays a Shockwave Player link followed by a version number at the top of the list.

6. **Click the** Shockwave Player link

   The download page for Shockwave Player opens with a description of the plug-in, similar to Figure H-8. Shockwave is a very popular plug-in; according to Macromedia (the publisher of Shockwave), over 200 million Internet users enhance their Internet experience using Shockwave Player to play games and view animated content.

Clues to Use

How do you know when you need a plug-in?

When you are browsing the Web, you might encounter Web pages that indicate you need a specific plug-in to view or hear the Web page's content. If you do not have the required plug-in to play the content, nothing happens; you see only what your Web browser can activate without hearing a sound, for example, or seeing a video. The Web page might also display an icon or empty frame, indicating that you are missing a plug-in. Most Web pages that require a plug-in to display or play their content contain a link to the Web site where you can download the required plug-in or display a dialog box that provides information about the missing plug-in and where to obtain it. When you click the link, the developer's Web site opens so you can download the plug-in. You can often allow the Web browser to automatically install the plug-in right then and there, after which the full Web page content will be available through your Web browser.

FIGURE H-7: Popular plug-ins available at Download.com

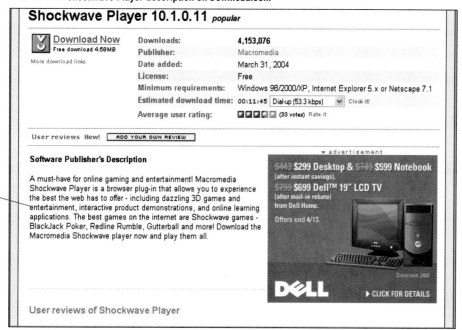

CNET > Downloads > Windows > **Search results for plug-ins**

Search results   1-25 of 175 | next 25 >>

RE-SORT BY: **Name**	**Date added**	**User rating**	**CNET rating** How we rate	**Downloads** Total	Last week	**Availability**
Winamp 2.91 *pop* Play MP3, MP2, CD, MOD, and WAV audio files. **OS:** Windows 95/98/NT/2000 **File Size:** 1.62MB **License:** Free	04/21/2003	Read user reviews (86 votes)	Read review	25,161,984	Download Now
Sonique 1.96 Enjoy your MP3, CD, WAV, MOD, and WMA tracks with superior audio quality and impressive visual effects. **OS:** Windows (all) **File Size:** 2.66MB **License:** Free	04/19/2002	Read user reviews (117 votes)	Read review	10,954,302	Download Now
Winamp Full 2.91 *pop* Play MP3, MP2, MOD, M-Juice, and WAV audio files with this popular program. **OS:** Windows 95/98/NT/2000 **File Size:** 2.21MB **License:** Free	04/21/2003	Read user reviews (92 votes)	Read review	5,110,649	Download Now
JetAudio Basic 6.1.4.63 *pop* Play audio and video files, convert to other file formats, and burn CDs. **OS:** Windows 98/Me/2000/XP **File Size:** 12.37MB **License:** Free	03/21/2005 *new*	Read user reviews (118 votes)	Read review	4,767,905	Download Now

Click to sort plug-in software in order of popularity

FIGURE H-8: Shockwave Player description on Download.com

Shockwave Player 10.1.0.11 *popular*

☑ **Download Now**
Free download 4.58MB
More download links

Downloads:	**4,153,076**
Publisher:	Macromedia
Date added:	March 31, 2004
License:	Free
Minimum requirements:	Windows 98/2000/XP, Internet Explorer 5.x or Netscape 7.1
Estimated download time:	00:11:45 Dial-up (53.3 kbps) ▾ Clock it!
Average user rating:	(33 votes) Rate it

User reviews New!   [ADD YOUR OWN REVIEW]

Software Publisher's Description

Description of Shockwave Player

A must-have for online gaming and entertainment! Macromedia Shockwave Player is a browser plug-in that allows you to experience the best the web has to offer - including dazzling 3D games and entertainment, interactive product demonstrations, and online learning applications. The best games on the internet are Shockwave games - BlackJack Poker, Redline Rumble, Gutterball and more! Download the Macromedia Shockwave player now and play them all.

User reviews of Shockwave Player

Downloading and Installing Extensions with Internet Explorer

You download and install browser extensions just as you would other software for your computer. Internet Explorer allows you to automatically download and install some browser extensions by simply clicking a link on a Web page. Plug-ins are generally small programs that don't require a lot of system resources. Although many plug-ins are available, you should limit yourself to installing only plug-ins that you will use often. You investigate how easy it would be for potential Web site users to install a required plug-in by adding the Shockwave plug-in to your Web browser.

STEPS

Check with your instructor or technical support person before installing this plug-in. If you do not get approval to install it, read the instructions without performing the steps.

1. **Go to** www.course.com/illustrated/internet4, **click the** Unit H link, **then click the** Macromedia Downloads link **under Lesson 5**

    You want to make sure you download the most recent version of Shockwave Player, so you go to Macromedia's site rather than using a download site. The Macromedia download page opens.

2. **Click the** Macromedia Shockwave Player link

3. **Click** Install Now

    The Internet Explorer - Security Warning dialog box opens asking if you want to install this software.

4. **If the Information Bar dialog box opens, click** OK **in the dialog box**

5. **If the yellow Information Bar appears at the top of the browser window, click it, then click** Install ActiveX control **on the menu that appears**

6. **Click** Install

    The Installing Shockwave Player dialog box opens and shows the progress of the download and installation, as shown in Figure H-9. When the installation is complete, another dialog box opens asking if you want to install the Yahoo! Toolbar for Internet Explorer.

7. **Click the** Install Yahoo! Toolbar for Internet Explorer check box **to deselect it, then click** Next

    The installation of Shockwave continues. Internet Explorer closes and restarts, and you are returned to the Shockwave Download page on Macromedia's Web site. When the installation is complete, a message informing you of this briefly appears as shown in Figure H-10, then the message is replaced with a Shockwave animation. If your computer has speakers, you might also hear accompanying music.

FIGURE H-9: Installing Shockwave Player dialog box

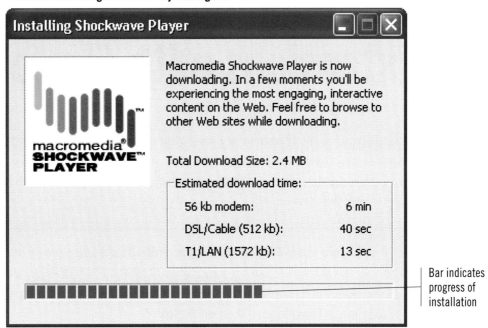

Bar indicates progress of installation

FIGURE H-10: Shockwave Download page after Shockwave is installed

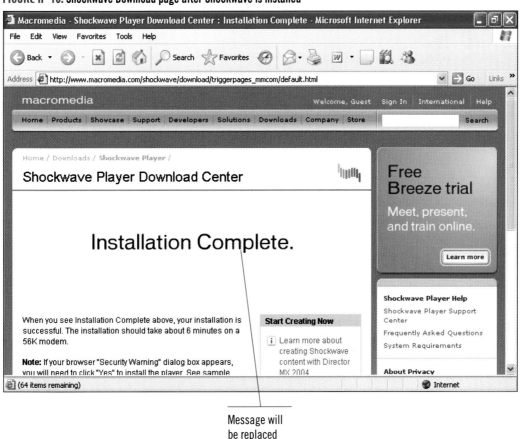

Message will be replaced with animation

Downloading and Installing Extensions with Firefox

You download and install browser extensions just as you would other software for your computer. You first download the browser extension to your computer, then double-click it to run the installation wizard. Plug-ins are generally small programs that don't require a lot of system resources. Although many plug-ins are available, you should limit yourself to installing only plug-ins that you will use often. ░░░░ You investigate how easy it would be for potential Web site users to install a required plug-in by adding the Shockwave plug-in to your Web browser.

STEPS

 Check with your instructor or technical support person before installing this plug-in. If you do not get approval to install it, read the instructions without performing the steps.

1. **Go to** www.course.com/illustrated/internet4, **click the** Unit H link, **then click the** Macromedia Downloads link **under Lesson 6**

   The Macromedia download page opens.

2. **Click the** Macromedia Shockwave Player link

3. **Click** Download Now

   The Opening Shockwave_Installer_Slim.exe dialog box opens. The only option available is the Save to Disk option.

4. **With the Save to Disk option button selected, click** OK

   The Enter name of file to save to dialog box opens.

5. **Click the** Save in list arrow, **navigate to the drive and folder where your Solution Files are stored, then click** Save

   The file downloads and a Download Complete alert box briefly appears in the lower-right corner of the screen.

> **TROUBLE**
> If your computer is not set to display filename extensions, the file will appear as Shockwave_Installer_Slim instead.

6. **If the Downloads dialog box is still open, click its** Close button **to close it, exit Firefox, open Windows Explorer and display the contents of your Solution Files folder, then double-click the** Shockwave_Installer_Slim.exe file

   The Installing Shockwave Player dialog box opens, as shown in Figure H-11.

7. **Click** Install

   A dialog box opens asking if you want to install the Yahoo! Toolbar for Internet Explorer.

8. **Click the** Install Yahoo! Toolbar for Internet Explorer check box **to deselect it, then click** Next

   A dialog box displays the progress of the installation. When the installation is complete, another dialog box opens telling you that the installation was successful.

9. **Click** Finish

   The dialog box closes, then Firefox starts automatically and opens the Shockwave Download page on Macromedia's Web site. When the installation is complete, a message informing you of this briefly appears as shown in Figure H-12, then the message is replaced with a Shockwave animation. If your computer has speakers, you might also hear accompanying music.

FIGURE H-11: Installing Shockwave Player dialog box

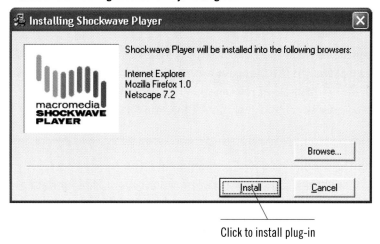

Click to install plug-in

FIGURE H-12: Shockwave Download page after Shockwave is installed

Message will be replaced with animation

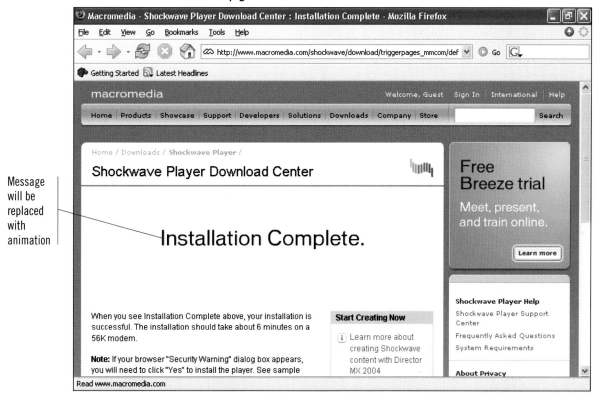

Clues to Use

Firefox extensions from Mozilla Update

Firefox was designed to give programmers an easy way to write program extensions. Anyone who writes a Firefox extension can submit it to the site administrator of the Mozilla Update Web site. After the site administrator tests it and accepts it, it will be added to the list of extensions available on this site. To install an extension from this site, you click Tools on the menu bar, click Extensions to open the Extensions window, then click the Get More Extensions link. The Extensions page on the Mozilla Updates Web site opens in a page tab. After you find the extension you want to install, click its link to open its installation page, then click the Install Now link on that page. The Software Installation dialog box opens. Click Install Now in that dialog box. The dialog box closes and the Extensions window appears again, displaying the progress of the extension as it is installed. After the installation is complete, the new extension is added to the bottom of the list in the Extensions window. Read the description of the extension. Many extensions will not be completely installed until you restart Firefox.

Internet

Using Browser Extensions

If the required browser extension is installed, you do not have to do anything special to view content on a Web page that requires that particular browser extension; the Web page will display the content as it was designed. Mark asks if you can show him some Web sites that use the Shockwave and Flash Players so he can get a sense of the kind of content they can display.

STEPS

> **TROUBLE**
> You must have the Shockwave player installed to complete Steps 1 through 3.

1. **Go to the Student Online Companion at** www.course.com/illustrated/internet4, **click the** Unit H link, **then click the** Timex Shockwave Demo link **under Lesson 7**
   The browser loads the page and displays the content, similar to Figure H-13.

2. **Click one of the buttons on the watch**
   Something on the watch changes each time you click a button.

3. **Click one of the program buttons on the right side of the Shockwave window**
   Depending on the button you click, the image or the text in the window changes.

4. **When you are finished viewing the Shockwave demonstration, return to the Student Online Companion at** www.course.com/illustrated/internet4

> **TROUBLE**
> If a dialog box opens telling you that you need to install or update the Flash Player, or if you do not see any content on the page, follow the on-screen instructions to install it. If you are working in a lab, check with your instructor or technical support person first.

5. **Click the** Coca-Cola Flash Demo link **under Lesson 7**
   The browser loads the page and displays the Flash animation, similar to Figure H-14.

6. **Move the mouse pointer over the buttons and watch the content change**

7. **Exit your browser and close any open windows**
   After viewing the animation, Mark decides that any multimedia content developed for RVP will require the Shockwave or Flash Player plug-ins because it is safe to assume that most users of the site will have them installed already.

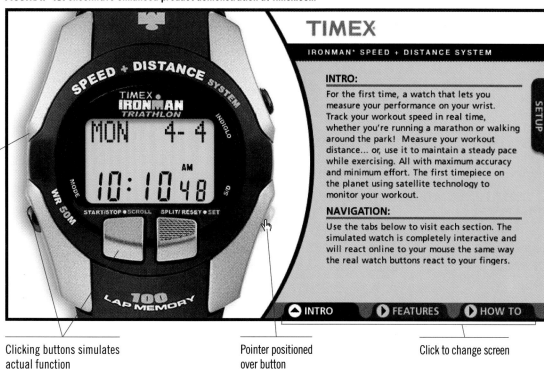

The watch you see might be different from this watch, but you should still be able to "click" buttons

Clicking buttons simulates actual function

Pointer positioned over button

Click to change screen

FIGURE H-14: Flash animation on Coca-Cola Web site

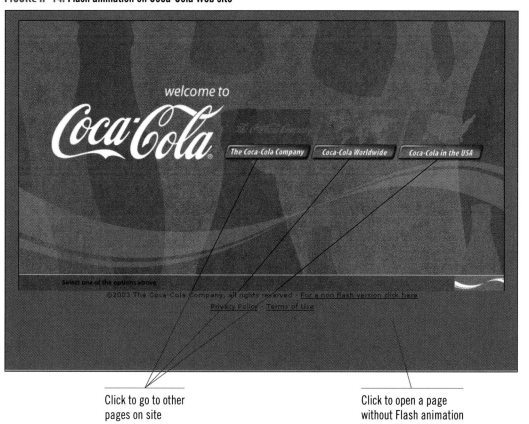

Click to go to other pages on site

Click to open a page without Flash animation

Internet

Practice

▼ CONCEPTS REVIEW

Match each term with the statement that best describes it.

1. Graphics
2. Multimedia
3. Browser extension
4. Lossy compression
5. Animated GIF
6. MIDI format
7. Plug-in
8. JPEG
9. MP3
10. QuickTime

a. A browser extension that starts from within a browser
b. Graphic file format that is good for photographs
c. Proprietary file format that works on both Windows and Macintosh systems
d. Several images combined into a single GIF file displayed one after the other to simulate movement
e. A program you install to expand your Web browser's capabilities
f. Images or art used in Web pages
g. File compression technique that deletes unnecessary information from a file to reduce its size
h. Sound, animation, and video on a Web page
i. Audio file format that digitally records information about each element of the sound
j. Audio files that are 90% smaller than WAV files

Select the best answer from the list of choices.

11. A browser extension:
    a. is a program that you can only open from your Web browser.
    b. enhances the capabilities of a Web browser by allowing the browser to perform tasks that it was not originally designed to do.
    c. is an executable file that causes harm to a computer.
    d. expands the width of the browser window.

12. The technique for transferring sound and video on the Web in which the server sends part of the file to the browser to begin playing it while the server sends the next part of the file is called _____.
    a. multimedia transmission
    b. plugging in
    c. streaming transmission
    d. extensibility

13. Which of the following is such a popular plug-in that it is now included in many browsers?
    a. Flash
    b. Shockwave
    c. QuickTime
    d. RealPlayer

14. Which of the following is a separate program that launches independently of the Web browser to display or play some files?
    a. Flash
    b. Shockwave
    c. Plug-in
    d. Helper application

15. Which of the following file formats uses lossy compression?
    a. AU format
    b. WAV

c. JPEG

d. GIF

16. **Which of the following file formats uses lossless compression?**

    a. AU format

    b. WAV

    c. JPEG

    d. GIF

17. **A programming language used to create three-dimensional environments in which users can navigate and interact with a three-dimensional scene is:**

    a. HTML.

    b. VRML.

    c. iPIX.

    d. Shockwave.

18. **Which of the following is a file format that allows documents to maintain a consistent layout and format on different computers?**

    a. WAV

    b. PDF

    c. MPEG

    d. AU format

19. **Which of the following is an uncompressed video file format?**

    a. MPEG

    b. AVI

    c. MP3

    d. AU format

▼ SKILLS REVIEW

1. **Locate browser extensions.**

    a. Go to the Student Online Companion at www.course.com/illustrated/internet4, click the Unit H link, then click one of the links under Download Sites in Skills Review 1.

    b. Click the Internet link, click the Browsers link, then click the Plug-ins link.

    c. Scroll through the list to view the available downloads.

    d. Return to the Student Online Companion at www.course.com/illustrated/internet4, click the Unit H link, then click the Google Downloads link under Skills Review 1.

    e. Read the descriptions of the various downloads available from Google.

    f. Click the More info link under Google Toolbar, then click the link that will provide you with more information about the Google Toolbar for your browser.

2. **Download and install a browser extension with Internet Explorer.**

    a. Go to the Student Online Companion at www.course.com/illustrated/internet4, click the Unit H link, then click the iPIX link under Skills Review 2.

    b. Click the more link next to IPIX Immersive Plug-In.

    c. Make sure that the description of the plug-in is correct for your browser, then click Download. (If the description of the plug-in indicates that it is not the correct version for your browser, click the Alternative plug-ins link, select your operating system and your browser, click Proceed, then click the Download the iPIX Plug-in link. If you see a message telling you that you need an ActiveX Control, check with your instructor or technical support person, then follow the instructions for downloading the Control.)

    c. If the Information Bar dialog box opens, click OK in the dialog box.

    d. If the Information Bar appears, click it, then click Install ActiveX Control on the shortcut menu.

    e. If the Internet Explorer - Security Warning dialog box opens, click Install.

    f. After the installation is complete, an image appears at the bottom of the Web page displaying "You have successfully downloaded the iPIX Plug-in." Double-click the image, then click the new image to rotate it.

Internet

3. **Download and install a browser extension with Firefox.**

    a. Go to the Student Online Companion at www.course.com/illustrated/internet4, click the Unit H link, then click the iPIX link under Skills Review 3.

    b. Click the more link next to IPIX Immersive Plug-In.

    c. Click the Alternative plug-ins link, select Windows 95/98/Me/2000/NT/XP as your operating system, select Firefox/Mozilla as your browser, then click Proceed.

    d. In the Manual Plug-in Install Instructions window, click the Download the iPIX Plug-in link.

    e. In the Opening ipix_win_plugin.zip dialog box, click the Save to Disk option button, if necessary, then click OK.

    f. In the Enter name of file to save to dialog box, navigate to the drive and folder where your Solution Files are stored, then click Save.

    g. When the download is complete, exit your browser, use Windows Explorer to locate the ipix_win_plugin.zip file, then double-click it to start WinZip and display the compressed files.

    h. Extract the AppSub32.dll and NpIpx32.dll files to the drive and folder where the Firefox extensions are stored. (*Hint*: This is usually C:\Program Files\Mozilla\plugins or C:\Program Files\Mozilla Firefox\plugins.)

    i. Restart Firefox, return to the Student Online Companion at www.course.com/illustrated/internet4, click the Unit H link, click the iPIX link under Skills Review 3, click the Gallery link, click the first image under IPIX Visual Documentation, click the IPIX Plug-in link, then click on the image to rotate it.

4. **Use browser extensions.**

    a. Go to the Student Online Companion at www.course.com/Illustrated/Internet4, click the Unit H link, then click one of the links under Shockwave Demos in Skills Review 4.

    b. Interact with the site.

    c. Return to the Student Online Companion at www.course.com/illustrated/internet4, click the Unit H link, then click one of the links under Flash Demos in Skills Review 4.

    d. Watch the Flash animation.

    e. Exit your browser.

▼ INDEPENDENT CHALLENGE 1

You work as a technology consultant specializing in helping small businesses and independent contractors take full advantage of the Internet in their work. You generally install a couple of useful browser extensions for your clients. You want to identify other useful extensions that your clients might find helpful in their work.

    a. Start your Web browser.

    b. Go to www.course.com/illustrated/internet4, click the Unit H link, then click one of the links under Independent Challenge 1 to locate and research a browser extension not already used in this unit.

    c. Write a paragraph describing how the browser extension extends a Web browser's capabilities (what it does that a Web browser can't do alone).

    d. Include the URL of the Web page on the publisher's Web site from where you can download this browser extension. Also include the URL of a Web page that makes use of this browser extension. (*Hint*: Such Web pages are often listed on the Web site of the company that makes the browser extension.)

Advanced Challenge Exercise

    ■ If you use Internet Explorer, locate IESpell, which checks your spelling as you type in text boxes on Web pages, on the download site you chose; if you use Firefox, locate FoxyTunes, which allows you to control media players without leaving the browser.

    ■ Visit the publisher's Web page and make sure you are downloading the most current version of the program.

    ■ Download and install the program you found for your browser.

    e. Exit your Web browser and close any open windows.

▼ INDEPENDENT CHALLENGE 2

A friend of yours is a third-grade language skills teacher at Midland Elementary School. The school had to close its music program because the state has cut its budget severely over the past several years. Your friend believes that it is important to expose your third-graders to the music of the great composers, such as Beethoven and Mozart. She does not have a budget for buying CDs, so she asked you to help her find some music files to play on the computer. You have heard that single musical instruments, particularly pianos, sound realistic in the MIDI format.

a. Go to the Student Online Companion page at www.course.com/illustrated/internet4, click the Unit H link, and then click one of the links under Independent Challenge 2.

b. Examine the MIDI files available on the site you chose.

c. Return to the Student Online Companion at www.course.com/illustrated/internet4, click the Unit H link, and then examine the MIDI files available on two other sites.

d. Evaluate the files offered on these Web pages or the pages to which they lead, then note the URLs of the two best sites to give to your friend.

e. Exit your Web browser.

▼ INDEPENDENT CHALLENGE 3

Jon Sagami is the manager of the Ski-Town Ski and Snowboarding School at Arrowhead Mountain in the Colorado Rocky Mountains. Jon wants to expand the school's marketing efforts with a Web site that lets visitors to Arrowhead Mountain learn more about the school and its merchandise. To make the Web site more fun to use, Jon wants to use virtual reality, motion, and sound to create a virtual reality ski slope on the Web site for entertainment purposes.

a. Go to the Student Online Companion at www.course.com/illustrated/internet4, click the Unit H link, and then click one of the links under Independent Challenge 3.

b. Search for 3D plug-ins on the download site you chose.

c. Click several of the links to programs on the results pages and read their descriptions to see if one might be appropriate for an on-screen simulated race. Print the description of each plug-in you think might work (make sure you find at least three).

d. Visit the Web site of at least one of the publishers and see if you can view a demonstration of the plug-in.

e. Write a brief description of the plug-ins you chose and explain why you chose them.

f. Exit your browser.

▼ INDEPENDENT CHALLENGE 4

Les Bolton is a real estate broker in upstate New York. He wants to expand his Web site to include virtual tours of homes he is listing for sale. He asked you to research this and find some Web sites that offer tours.

a. Go to www.course.com/illustrated/internet4, click the Unit H link, then click one of the links under Independent Challenge 4.

b. On the Web site you chose, find the link to view a sample virtual tour.

c. Return to the Student Online Companion Web page for Unit H, then view the sample tours on two other Web sites listed under Independent Challenge 4.

d. Write a brief description of each of the products you found, including the cost.

Advanced Challenge Exercise

- Go to a download site of your choice, then search for software you can buy to create virtual tours. (*Hint*: Include "real estate" in your search expression.)
- Research the programs you found and find out whether users will need a plug-in to view tours created using that software.
- Compare the products you found in Steps b and c with the products you found in this Advanced Challenge Exercise, and decide what product you will recommend to Les.

e. Exit your Web browser.

▼ VISUAL WORKSHOP

Go to **www.course.com/illustrated/internet4**, click the **Unit H link**, then click the **Shockwave Games link** under Visual Workshop. Find the page for the Daily Jigsaw, similar to Figure H-15. Click the **play free online link** and play the game.

FIGURE H-15

Increasing Web Security

OBJECTIVES

Understand security threats on the Internet
Minimize security risks on the Internet
Strengthen security in Internet Explorer
Strengthen security in Firefox
Check security features on a Web Site
Understand cookies
Manage cookies in Internet Explorer
Manage cookies in Firefox
Protect e-mail from viruses and interception

When an individual or organization creates a Web site and publishes it on the Internet, the Web site becomes vulnerable to security threats. **Security** is broadly defined as the protection of assets from unauthorized access, use, alteration, or destruction. Individuals and organizations must secure their Web servers so that the data stored on them is protected from being stolen or altered and that the connections to them are protected from being intercepted. Individuals and organizations must also secure their own computers with adequate safeguards against potential security and privacy threats that occur when they use them to access the Internet using a Web browser and an e-mail program. ▨▨▨ Riverview Rowing Club in Victoria, British Columbia, has experienced a tremendous growth in membership over the past two years. The members have been asking the board of directors to provide t-shirts, jackets, and memorabilia, such as coffee mugs and pens, with the club's logo on it. The board decided to make these items available via their Web site in the hopes that they will sell to the general public as well. Because you have some experience with Web site design, the board has asked you to set up the site so that they can accept payments via the Web. You decide to research how to make transactions secure and how to maintain customers' privacy over the Internet.

UNIT
I
Internet

Understanding Security Threats on the Internet

Internet sites and users are vulnerable to security threats, such as stealing users' identities, files, and hard drive space; misdirecting or intercepting e-mail messages; or illegally obtaining and using passwords to access private accounts, such as online bank services. If you understand how security on the Internet can be compromised, you can then take steps to minimize your risks when you're online. You begin your research by investigating basic security concerns for Internet users.

DETAILS

Some of the security risks Internet users are exposed to are described below:

Data Confidentiality

Many Web sites include forms in which users can efficiently supply information, such as their names and addresses, to an organization. If security features are not deliberately put into place by a Web site administrator, submitting information over the Web is about as secure as sending the same information on a postcard. Figure I-1 shows an alert box in Internet Explorer that reminds users of this fact.

Sniffer Programs

At any point along a data packet's trip from source to destination, anyone can use a tool known as a **packet sniffer** or **sniffer program** to monitor and analyze it. Used illegally, a packet sniffer can capture user names, passwords, and other personal information.

Phishing

Phishing occurs when an individual tries to obtain confidential information from people via e-mail by pretending to be a familiar organization or institution, such as a bank. The e-mail message might ask the recipients to click a link in the message and use the form that opens to "confirm" personal information, such as names, account numbers, and Social Security numbers, or to reset their passwords by supplying their current passwords and new passwords. Any information provided by users is then stolen by the phisher.

> **QUICK TIP**
>
> Another form of phishing is pharming, in which users are redirected to a spoofed site without their knowledge or consent and without clicking a link in an e-mail message.

Spoofing

Web sites that look like they belong to one organization but actually belong to someone else are **spoofed**. Phishers use spoofed Web sites to make their victims believe that they are visiting the organization's real Web site. The site looks like the organization's real Web site, and the URL in the Address or Location bar starts with the name of the company (such as www.ebay.com). The underlying IP address, however, will not match the real one that belongs to the company being spoofed.

> **QUICK TIP**
>
> When a computer is connected to the Internet, it receives traffic through a port from other computers without its user even realizing it.

Port Scan

A **port** on a computer is like a door; it permits traffic to enter and leave a computer. A computer has over 65,000 ports for different processes, such as HTTP/World Wide Web traffic (port 80) and FTP traffic (port 21). A **port scan** occurs when one computer tests all or some of the ports on another computer to determine whether its ports are open, closed, or stealth (the user has hidden its state). Someone could use open ports on your computer to access data on your computer.

Viruses, Worms, and Trojan Horses

A **virus** is a program that runs on your computer without your permission and performs undesired tasks, such as deleting the contents of your hard disk. Worms and Trojan horses are variants of viruses. Many Web sites, such as the one in Figure I-2, provide news and information about viruses.

> **QUICK TIP**
>
> Many browser plug-ins, such as Shockwave, are ActiveX controls or applets.

Web Page Programs

Programs that Web pages can download to your computer and run are called **scripts**, **ActiveX controls**, or **Java applets**. These programs are used by Web page designers to enrich and personalize a user's interaction with a Web page. Such programs can also be written with malicious intent, however, destabilizing programs and even risking data loss on a user's computer.

FIGUREI-1: Security alert box in Internet Explorer

FIGUREI-1: Security alert box in Internet Explorer

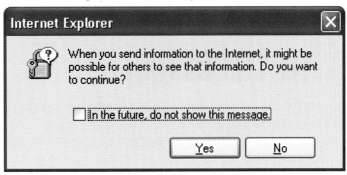

FIGURE I-2: Web page on Computer Associates' Web site containing information about viruses

Latest and most critical virus threat

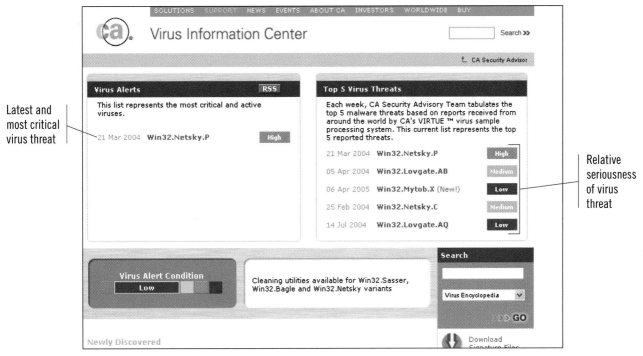

Relative seriousness of virus threat

Clues to Use

Brute force attacks

A **brute force attack** occurs when someone uses a program to enter character combinations until the system accepts a user name and password, thereby gaining access to the system. Some systems will send a warning to the computer's operator or lock out a user name when someone attempts to log in to a system a predetermined number of times without succeeding. Depending on the system to which the person gains access, the damage can range anywhere from reading a person's e-mail messages to gaining access to accounts at financial institutions. Another example of a brute force attack is when someone submits combinations of numbers to a Web site that accepts credit card payments until the site accepts a valid credit card number. In this case, the person can then charge goods and services using the credit card number that he has discovered and stolen. People who create and use strong passwords and avoid using the same password for multiple logins are less likely to have their accounts threatened in this manner.

Internet

Minimizing Security Risks on the Internet

As you have seen, the Internet can expose users to many types of security risks. Fortunately, informed users can take simple **countermeasures**, which are procedures, programs, and hardware that detect and prevent each type of computer security threats. You continue your research for the club's Web site by researching popular countermeasures to common security threats.

DETAILS

Some common countermeasures are described below:

Encryption

When you submit personal data, such as credit card numbers or other identifying information, to a Web site, you should ensure that the data you send and receive is encrypted. **Encryption** is the process of scrambling and encoding data transmissions using a mathematically-based program. Encryption produces a string of characters that is unreadable except by the person with the key. A **key** is the mathematical code used to **decrypt**, or reverse the encryption of, the data. Without the key, anyone using a sniffer program or other program won't be able to read the data they are intercepting.

Digital Certificates

- A **digital certificate** is an encrypted and password-protected file that contains information to authenticate and prove a person's or organization's identity. Usually, a digital certificate contains the certificate holder's name, address, and e-mail address; a key; the certificate's expiration date or validity period; and a **certificate authority** (CA), an organization that verifies the certificate holder's identity and issues the digital certificate.

- A **server certificate** is a digital certificate that authenticates a Web site for its users so the user can be confident that the Web site is not spoofed. A server certificate also ensures that the transfer of data between a user's computer and the server with the certificate is encrypted so that it is both tamper-proof and free from being intercepted. Figure I-3 shows a basic representation of how digital certificates work.

User Identification

Many Web sites let returning customers log on to an account that they have created on the server to make it easy for them to schedule services and check on their account status. **User identification** is the process of identifying a user to a computer. Most computer systems implement user identification with user names and passwords; the combination of a user name and password is sometimes called a **login**.

User Authentication

User authentication is the process of associating a person and his identification with a very high level of assurance. One method of user authentication is asking one or more questions to which only the authentic user could know the correct answers.

Secure Sockets Layer (SSL)

Many Web sites that process financial transactions use the **Secure Sockets Layer (SSL) protocol** to protect sensitive information as it travels over the Internet. Web pages that use SSL are encrypted, and the site has a server certificate that users can access to authenticate its validity. Web pages secured by SSL also have URLs that begin with https://; the "s" indicates a secure connection. When a connection between a computer and a server is secure, the Web browser displays an icon (usually a closed padlock) on the status bar to indicate a secure site. Figure I-4 shows a secure page in Internet Explorer, and Figure I-5 shows a secure page in Firefox.

Firewalls

A **firewall** is a software program or hardware device that controls access between two networks, such as a local area network and the Internet or the Internet and a computer. A firewall can control port scans and other incoming traffic by rejecting it unless you have configured it to accept the traffic.

QUICK TIP

A strong password contains many characters consisting of random strings of letters not found in a dictionary, including numbers and special characters, and combinations of uppercase and lowercase letters; for example, using your first name or birthdate is not a strong password, but Rfp*^h90 is.

QUICK TIP

A new protocol, the **Secure Electronic Transaction (SET)** protocol, is more complex and more secure than the SSL protocol.

FIGURE I-3: Processing a certificate

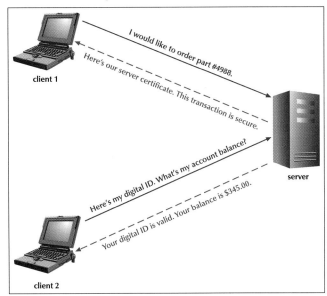

FIGURE I-4: Internet Explorer encryption indicator

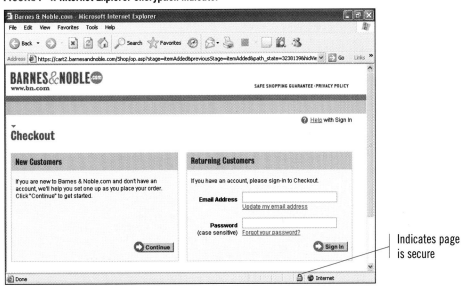

Indicates page is secure

FIGURE I-5: Firefox encryption indicator

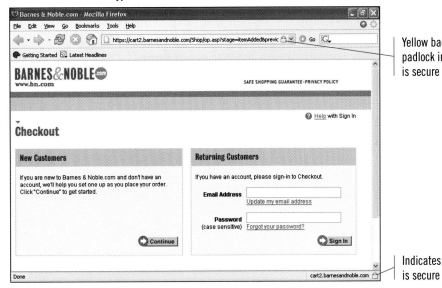

Yellow background and padlock indicate page is secure

Indicates page is secure

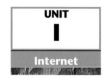

Strengthening Security in Internet Explorer

Programs that travel with applications to a browser and execute on the user's computer are security risks. A **Java applet** is a program written in the Java programming language that can execute and consume a computer's resources. A **JavaScript program**, instructions (**scripts**) written in the JavaScript programming language, can send information to another computer over the Internet. For example, a cleverly written JavaScript program could examine your computer's programs and e-mail a file from your computer back to a Web server. **ActiveX controls** are Microsoft's technology for writing small applications that perform some action in Web pages, but these components have full access to a computer's file system. For example, a hidden ActiveX control in a Web page could scan a hard drive for PCX and JPEG files and print them on any network printer. Most Java applets, JavaScript programs, and ActiveX controls are beneficial, but you should take steps to protect your computer from potential attacks that use them. Perhaps the simplest strategy is to prevent these programs from running. ▚▚▚▞ You want to be sure that the club's Web site will be compatible with users' security settings. You decide to investigate how to disable your Web browser from running Java and JavaScript programs and ActiveX controls.

STEPS

> **TROUBLE**
> If you are using Firefox, skip to the next lesson.

1. **Click** Tools **on the menu bar in your browser, click** Internet Options, **then click the** Security tab

   The Security tab of the Internet Options dialog box opens with Internet selected as the Web content zone. See Figure I-6. The Local intranet zone contains any computers on your LAN. The security settings for this zone are minimal. Unless you add sites to the Trusted sites and Restricted sites zones, all Web sites are in the Internet zone.

> **TROUBLE**
> If the Default Level command is grayed out and not available, your security level is already set to the default level of Medium. Skip Step 2.

2. **Click** Default Level

   The default security level is Medium, and a description of the security level appears next to the slider.

3. **Drag the slider up to change the level to** High

   This provides the highest level of security as you are using the Internet; Java applets, JavaScript programs, and ActiveX controls are not allowed to run. However, this means that some Web sites that use these Web programs will no longer work properly.

4. **Click** Custom Level

   The Security Settings dialog box opens, similar to the one shown in Figure I-7.

5. **Scroll down the Settings list box to view the available options**

   The list box allows you to specify how to deal with many different types of Web page contents and programs, including ActiveX controls, Java applets, and scripts.

6. **Click** Cancel

   The Security Settings dialog box closes.

7. **Click** Cancel

   The Internet Options dialog box closes without changing your security settings.

FIGURE I-6: Security tab in Internet Options dialog box

Zone includes computers on LAN

Selected Web content zone

Drag slider to change security level

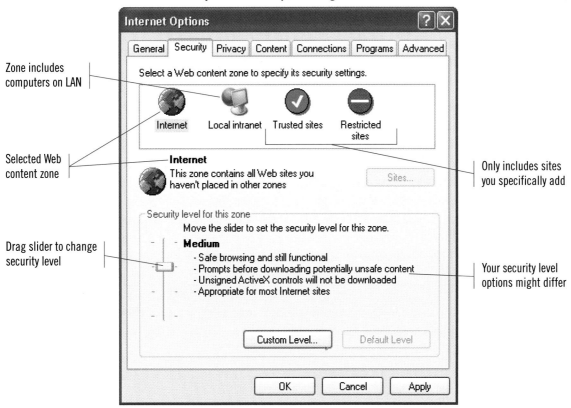

Only includes sites you specifically add

Your security level options might differ

FIGURE I-7: Security Settings dialog box

Options for ActiveX components

Scroll to see more options

Internet

Strengthening Security in Firefox

Programs that travel with applications to a browser and execute on the user's computer are security risks. A **Java applet**, a program written in the Java programming language, can execute and consume a computer's resources. A **JavaScript program**, instructions (**script**) written in the JavaScript programming language, can send information to another computer over the Internet. For example, a cleverly written JavaScript program could examine your computer's programs and e-mail a file from your computer back to a Web server. Most Java applets and JavaScript programs are beneficial, but you should take steps to protect your computer from potential attacks that use them. Perhaps the simplest strategy is to prevent these programs from running. 🔲🔲🔲 You want to be sure that the club's Web site will be compatible with users' security settings. You decide to investigate how to disable your Web browser from running Java and JavaScript programs.

STEPS

TROUBLE

If you are using Internet Explorer, skip to the next lesson.

1. **Click** Tools **on the menu bar in your browser, click** Options, **then click** Web Features

   The Web Features panel of the Options dialog box opens. See Figure I-8.

2. **Click the** Enable JavaScript check box **to select it, if necessary, then click** Advanced

   The Advanced JavaScript Options dialog box opens, as shown in Figure I-9. These options allow you to decide what scripts are allowed to do when you view Web pages.

3. **Click** Cancel

   The Advanced JavaScript Options dialog box closes.

QUICK TIP

Firefox does not support **ActiveX controls**, which are Microsoft's technology for writing small applications that perform some action in Web pages, but you can add a browser extension to run ActiveX controls if you wish.

4. **Click the** Enable Java **and** Enable JavaScript check boxes **to clear them**

   Now as you are using the Internet, Java applets, and JavaScript programs are not allowed to run. However, this means that some Web sites that use these Web programs will no longer work properly.

5. **Click** Cancel

   The Options dialog box closes without changing your security settings.

FIGURE I-8: Web Features panel in Options dialog box

Click to display Web Features panel

Java and JavaScript options

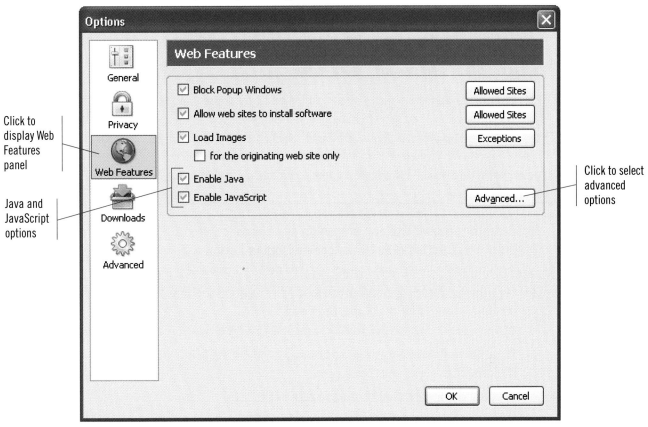

FIGURE I-9: Advanced JavaScript Options dialog box

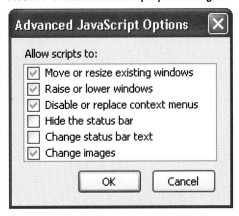

Checking Security Features on a Web Site

Before you send information such as credit card numbers, addresses, and phone numbers over the Internet, you should check the Web page to determine if it will be encrypted during its transmission from the Web server. ▰▰▰▰ You know that you will have to use encryption and set up a secure page so that people will feel safe providing their credit card numbers on the club's Web site. You want to learn more about how other sites do this, so you investigate another secure site on the Web.

STEPS

1. **Go to the Student Online Companion at** www.course.com/illustrated/internet4, **click the Unit I link, then click the** Hotels.com link **under Lesson 5**

   The home page for Hotels.com appears. First you need to choose a destination.

2. **Click the** New York option button **in the find a hotel section, accept the default values for the dates or number of rooms, then click** Go!

   After a moment, a Web page on which you can select a hotel in New York appears.

3. **Scroll down if necessary, then click the link for the first hotel in the list**

   The information page for that hotel appears.

4. **Click** Book It **for the first room and rate in the list**

   The page changes to collect booking information from you. This page is secure, as indicated by the padlock on the right side of the status bar in the browser window. Before you send your credit card number over the Internet, you should check the Web page's security features.

5. **Double-click the** padlock **in the status bar**

   If you are using Internet Explorer, the Certificate dialog box opens with the General tab selected. See Figure I-10. If you are using Firefox, the Page Info dialog box opens with the Security tab selected. See Figure I-11. These dialog boxes indicate that the Web site is verified, which means that a digital certificate is on file and valid. The Firefox Page Info dialog box also specifically mentions that the page is encrypted.

6. **If you are using Internet Explorer, click the** Details tab**; if you are using Firefox, click** View

   If you are using Internet Explorer, you can scroll down the list on the Details tab to see information about the Web site's digital certificate. See Figure I-12. If you are using Firefox, the Certificate Viewer dialog box opens with information about the Web site's digital certificate. See Figure I-13.

7. **If you are using Internet Explorer, click** OK**; if you are using Firefox, click** Close**, then click the** Close button **in the Page Info dialog box title bar**

FIGURE I-10: General tab in the Certificate dialog box in Internet Explorer

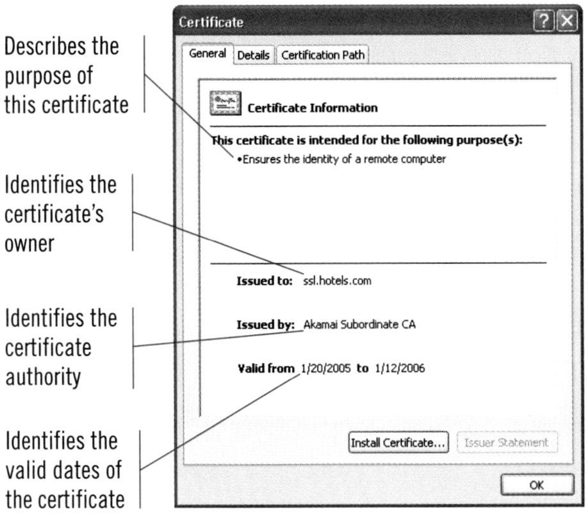

FIGURE I-11: Security tab in the Page Info dialog box in Firefox

Describes the purpose of this certificate

Identifies the certificate's owner

Identifies the certificate authority

Identifies the valid dates of the certificate

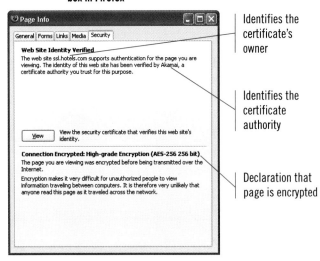

Identifies the certificate's owner

Identifies the certificate authority

Declaration that page is encrypted

FIGURE I-12: Details tab for Hotels.com in the Certificate dialog box in Internet Explorer

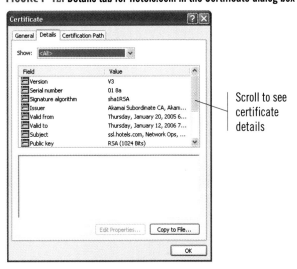

Scroll to see certificate details

FIGURE I-13: Certificate Viewer for Hotels.com in Firefox

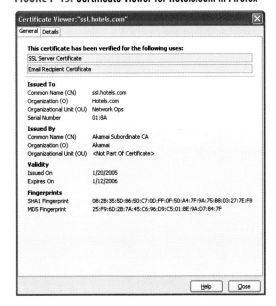

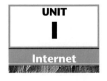

Understanding Cookies

A **cookie** is a small text file that a Web site stores on your computer. Cookies contain information that makes your Web-browsing experience simpler and more personalized by storing information about your **clickstream**, the sequence of links you click while visiting a Web site. For example, an online bookstore might store your book preferences in a cookie. When you revisit the bookstore, the Web site might inform you of new books available by the same author as the one whose book you purchased previously. Sometimes, however, cookies are intrusive and are created without your consent. For example, some Web sites might use cookies to collect information about your interests and then use this information to try to market products or services to you. ▰▰▰▰ You are considering using cookies on the club's site. Before you make this decision, you decide to learn more about cookies that are helpful and cookies that could be considered intrusive.

DETAILS

Types of cookies are described below:

- **Cookies that Enhance Browsing**

  A cookie is not a program and it can only store information that you provide to the Web site that creates it. Sometimes you provide this data openly, such as when you enter a value in a field on a form. Other times, the cookie might silently record your behavior at a Web site. Only the Web site that stored the cookie on your hard drive can read it, and it cannot read other cookies on your hard drive or any other file on your computer.

QUICK TIP

To avoid Web bugs in e-mail messages, make sure your e-mail program prevents pictures from downloading unless you specifically permit them to; if your e-mail program does not have this option, use Plain Text instead of HTML formatting for your messages.

- **Web Bugs**

  A **Web bug**, sometimes called a **clear GIF** or a **transparent GIF**, is a small, hidden graphic on a Web page or in an e-mail message that is designed to work in conjunction with a cookie to obtain information about the person viewing the page or e-mail message and then send that information to a third party. The hidden graphic is usually a GIF file with a size of one pixel, which is approximately the same size as the period at the end of this sentence. The process of downloading the clear GIF file can identify your IP address, the Web site you last visited, and other information about your use of the site in which the clear GIF has been embedded, and then record this information in the cookie file. Figure I-14 shows a section of an HTML document that creates a Web bug in a Web page, and Figure I-15 shows part of the Web page that contains the Web bug shown in Figure I-14. Clearly, you would need to examine the HTML document that created this Web page to find the Web bug.

QUICK TIP

Usually, if you do not want to see the ads in adware, you can pay a fee to the software publisher, which will provide you with a code to unlock the software and disable the ads.

- **Adware**

  Adware is a general category of software that includes advertisements to help pay for the product in which they appear. Some freeware is actually adware. Your free use of the software is supported in part by the revenue the software publisher generates from the adware. As a whole, adware does not cause any security threats because the user is aware of the ads and the parties responsible for including them are clearly identified in the programs.

- **Spyware**

  Spyware is a category of adware in which the user has little control over or knowledge of the ads and other monitoring features it contains. A Web bug is an example of spyware because the clear GIF and its actions are hidden from the user. Some programs you install, especially freeware and shareware programs, might include spyware to track your use of the program and the Internet or to collect data about you. Some companies provide information to users about spyware, but many do not.

FIGURE I-14: HTML document containing a Web bug

File location of Web bug

```
<FRAMESET ROWS="*,20" BORDER=0 FRAMEBORDER=0 FRAMESPACING=0>
<!-- Start of Doubleclick Tracking Code: Please do not remove -->
<SCRIPT language="JavaScript">
var axel = Math.random()+"";
var a = axel * 10000000000000;
document.write('<IMG
SRC="http://ad.doubleclick.net/activity;src=585966;type=counter;cat=oran;ord=1;num=' + a + '?"
WIDTH=1 HEIGHT=1 BORDER=0>');
</SCRIPT>
<NOSCRIPT>
<img src='http://127.0.0.1:3388/bug.cgi'>

</NOSCRIPT>
<!-- End of Doubleclick Tracking Code: Please do not remove -->
```

Cookie identification number generated for the current user

FIGURE I-15: Web page containing a Web bug

Location of Web bug

Clues to Use

Addressing privacy concerns

Potential customers of Web-based businesses are also concerned about their privacy. Web sites can collect a great deal of information about customers' preferences, even before they place an order. No general standards currently exist for maintaining confidentiality regarding such information. Although many business Web sites include statements of their customer privacy policies, no laws exist requiring such statements or policies. Web site owners can purchase assurance certifications that certify the Web site as meeting some criteria for conducting business in a secure and privacy-preserving manner.

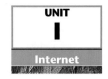
Managing Cookies in Internet Explorer

One way to minimize risks associated with cookies is to manage the cookies that are stored on your computer. You can prevent cookies from being saved on your computer. Although this choice totally eliminates problems with cookie misuse, it also blocks your access to some Web sites that rely on cookies for basic information about your preferences. For example, if you visit a Web site that requires a membership, without a cookie, you might need to sign in every time you open a new Web page on the Web site. Fortunately, Web browsers can also distinguish between different types of cookies, and you can block more intrusive cookies while allowing harmless ones. You can also set your Web browser to warn you when a Web site is attempting to create a cookie file, or you can block your computer from storing cookie files altogether. As you continue your investigation, you remember a friend told you that he blocks all cookies from being stored on his computer. You decide to investigate how to change your Web browser preferences relating to cookies.

STEPS

TROUBLE

If you are using Firefox, skip to the next lesson.

1. **Click** Tools **on the menu bar, click** Internet Options, **then click the** Privacy tab **in the Internet Options dialog box**

   The Privacy tab in the Internet Options dialog box opens. The Privacy tab contains a slider bar, which allows you to adjust your Web browser's privacy level to one of six preset specifications. The description of the cookies allowed on your computer appears next to the slider. Figure I-16 shows the slider set to Medium.

2. **Click** Sites

   The Per Site Privacy Actions dialog box opens. You can set rules for cookies from specific Web sites.

3. **Type** www.course.com **in the Address of Web site text box, then click** Allow

   Course.com is added to the list of Managed Web sites with a setting of Always Allow. See Figure I-17. You can also remove a Web site from the list of sites from which cookies are allowed.

4. **Click** www.course.com **in the Managed Web sites list, click** Remove, **then click** OK

   The Per Site Privacy Actions dialog box closes.

5. **Click the** General tab **in the Internet Options dialog box**

   You can delete cookies from this tab.

6. **Click** Settings **to open the Settings dialog box, then click** View Files

   After a moment, the list of files in the Temporary Internet Files folder opens in a Windows Explorer window.

7. **Click the** Name column heading **to sort the list alphabetically by filename, then scroll to find the files that start with "Cookie:"**

   You will see a list of cookies stored on your computer. You can delete one or all of the cookies in this window.

8. **Click the** Close button **in the Temporary Internet Files title bar, then click** Cancel **in the Settings dialog box**

9. **Click** Delete Cookies **on the General tab in the Internet Options dialog box**

   The Delete Cookies warning box opens. You decide not to delete all of your cookies for now.

10. **Click** Cancel **in the Delete Cookies warning box, then click** Cancel **in the Internet Options dialog box**

FIGURE I-16: Privacy tab in the Internet Options dialog box

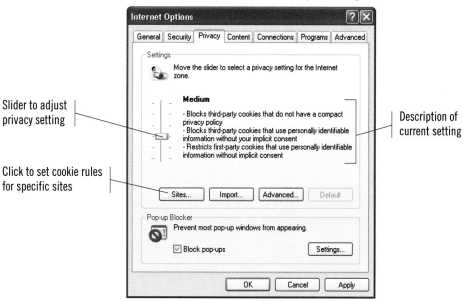

Slider to adjust privacy setting

Description of current setting

Click to set cookie rules for specific sites

FIGURE I-17: Web site added to list of Managed Web sites in Per Site Privacy Actions dialog box

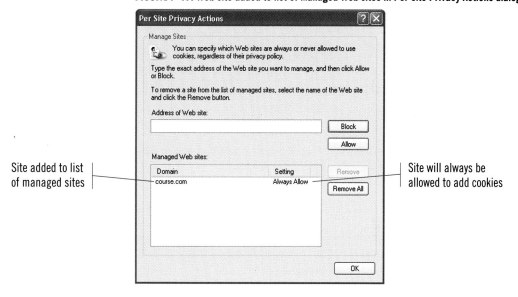

Site added to list of managed sites

Site will always be allowed to add cookies

Clues to Use

Customizing the Internet Explorer Pop-up Blocker

Pop-ups are usually advertisements that appear in small windows that appear in front of the current window. (Pop-ups that appear behind the current window are sometimes called **pop-unders**.) By default, Internet Explorer blocks pop-ups. You can customize the Pop-up Blocker in Internet Explorer. Click Tools on the menu bar, click Internet Options, then click the Privacy tab. To turn the Pop-up Blocker on or off, click the Block pop-ups check box in the Pop-up Blocker section. To specify on which sites pop-ups are allowed to appear, click Settings to open the Pop-up Blocker Settings dialog box, type the URL in the Address of Web site to allow text box, then click Add.

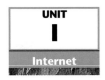

Managing Cookies in Firefox

One way to minimize risks associated with cookies is to manage the cookies that are stored on your computer. You can prevent cookies from being saved on your computer. Although this choice totally eliminates problems with cookie misuse, it also blocks your access to some Web sites that rely on cookies for basic information about your preferences. For example, if you visit a Web site that requires a membership, without a cookie, you might need to sign in every time you open a new Web page on the Web site. Fortunately, Web browsers can also distinguish between different types of cookies, and you can block more intrusive cookies while allowing harmless ones. You can also set your Web browser to warn you when a Web site is attempting to create a cookie file, or you can block your computer from storing cookie files altogether. As you continue your investigation, you remember a friend told you that he blocks all cookies from being set on his computer. You decide to investigate how to change your Web browser preferences relating to cookies.

STEPS

TROUBLE
If you are using Internet Explorer, skip to the next lesson.

1. **Click Tools on the menu bar, click Options, then click Privacy in the Options dialog box**

   The Privacy panel in the Options dialog box lists various settings you can change.

2. **Click the plus sign next to Cookies, if necessary**

   The options for dealing with cookies appear. Your screen should look similar to Figure I-18. You can choose to accept all cookies, only cookies from the originating site, or no cookies. You can also choose to delete all cookies by clicking Clear in the Cookies section.

3. **Click the Keep Cookies list arrow**

   The options in this list allow you to choose whether to keep cookies until they expire, only for the current session, or for a dialog box to be displayed every time a Web site tries to add a cookie, giving you the option to choose whether to allow the cookie, allow it only for this session, or deny the cookie.

4. **Click the Keep Cookies list arrow again to close the list without changing the setting, then click Exceptions**

   The Exceptions dialog box opens. You can set rules for cookies from specific Web sites.

5. **Type www.course.com in the Address of web site text box, then click Allow**

   Course.com is added to the list of Web sites with a setting of Allow. See Figure I-19. You can also choose to allow the cookie only for the current browser session. You decide not to make this change to the cookie rules at this time.

6. **Click Cancel**

   The Exceptions dialog box closes.

7. **Click View Cookies**

   The Stored Cookies dialog box opens displaying a list of cookies stored on your computer. You can delete one or all of the cookies in this window.

QUICK TIP
You can also click Clear next to Cookies in the Privacy panel in the Options dialog box to delete all stored cookies.

8. **Click a cookie in the list**

   Information about the cookie appears in the section of the dialog box below the list. Figure I-20 shows a cookie stored by midlandpet.com. You decide not to delete all of your cookies for now.

9. **Click Cancel in the Stored Cookies dialog box, then click OK in the Options dialog box**

Clues to Use

Customizing how Firefox handles pop-ups

Pop-ups are usually advertisements that appear in small windows that appear in front of the current window. (Pop-ups that appear behind the current window are sometimes called **pop-unders**.) By default, Firefox blocks pop-ups. You can customize how Firefox blocks them. Click Tools on the menu bar, click Options, then click Web Features. To turn the pop-up blocker option on or off, click the Block Popup Windows check box. To specify on which sites pop-ups are allowed to appear, click Allowed Sites to open the Allowed Sites dialog box, type the URL in the Address of web site text box, then click Allow.

FIGURE I-18: Privacy page in the Options dialog box

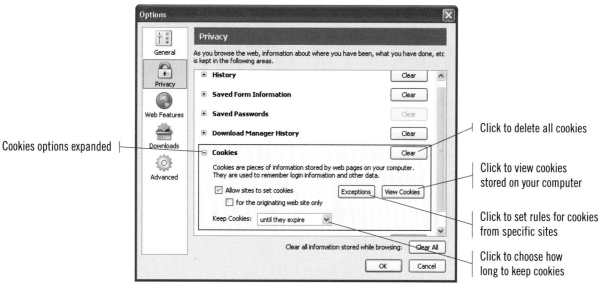

Cookies options expanded

Click to delete all cookies

Click to view cookies stored on your computer

Click to set rules for cookies from specific sites

Click to choose how long to keep cookies

FIGURE I-19: Web site added to list of allowed Web sites in Exceptions dialog box

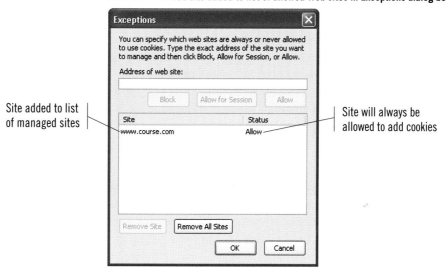

Site added to list of managed sites

Site will always be allowed to add cookies

FIGURE I-20: Cookie for Midlandpet.com in Stored Cookies dialog box

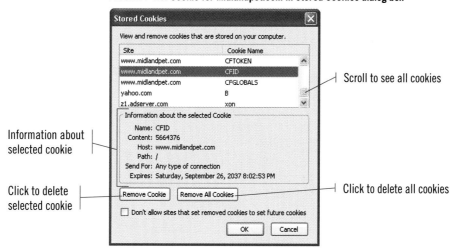

Scroll to see all cookies

Information about selected cookie

Click to delete selected cookie

Click to delete all cookies

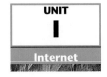

UNIT
I
Internet

Protecting E-Mail from Viruses and Interception

Although the Web is an important area to focus on for understanding Internet security, it's not the only area of concern. Protecting your computer when using e-mail must go hand in hand with Web protection to eliminate the most common Internet-based threats to your computer. Fortunately, you can greatly limit your exposure to destructive programs carried by e-mail by taking a few simple precautions, such as installing programs that protect your computer or verifying that your attachments are safe before you open them. ▄▄▄▄▄ As you conclude your preparatory research for the club's Web site, you want to understand how e-mail risks might affect the company's online strategy. You know that you will have a Contact link on the site, and you want to review the steps you and others at the club will need to take to limit their exposure to problems via e-mail.

DETAILS

Some tools for protecting your computer from e-mail threats are:

QUICK TIP

Some Webmail systems, such as Hotmail, automatically check their users' e-mail messages for viruses.

- **Anti-virus Software**

  As explained earlier in this unit, viruses, worms, and Trojan horses are destructive programs that can wreak havoc on your computer. **Anti-virus software** is available, however, which can block damage from any viruses, worms, or Trojan horses that you might receive by e-mail and keep such programs from using your e-mail program to reproduce. Figure I-21 shows a comparison chart on AntiVirusEbook.com of some popular anti-virus programs. Because anti-virus software is often available for free at colleges and universities, you should check with your instructor or system administrator to see if this software is available to protect your computer. After you install anti-virus software, you must run regular updates to keep the anti-virus protection up-to-date since new viruses are constantly being written.

- **Handling E-Mail Attachments**

  You can increase your e-mail security by modifying your e-mail practices. Don't save or open attachments from anyone—even people you know well—without scrutinizing the e-mail message first. An attachment ending with .exe is a program file; opening it runs the program on your computer with unknown consequences. Always be sure you know what a program will do and that you're certain of the sender's identity before opening it. Additionally, because worms replicate by sending nonsense messages to people listed in the victim's address book, make sure the accompanying e-mail message makes sense and is specific to you. If the message is short and general, even if it's from a friend, it might simply be a worm's trick to get you to open the attachment. If you get a lot of e-mail every day, using anti-virus software can be a worthwhile investment because it can find and delete any viruses, worms, or Trojan horses attached to e-mail messages before they are even visible in your e-mail program.

- **Encryption Software**

  If you use e-mail to send sensitive information, such as sensitive business information or financial data, it's good practice to use encryption software for e-mail. Like Web browser encryption, e-mail encryption scrambles a message's contents in a way that can only be decoded by the intended recipient; therefore, a packet sniffer can not be used to illegally intercept the contents of e-mail messages.

FIGURE I-21: Anti-virus comparison chart on AntiVirusEbook.com

AntiVirus Software Comparison Chart
AntiVirusEbook.com

● Email this page to a friend!

Product	Scans inbound and/or outbound email	Protects you from malicious scripts	Built in Firewall	Scans Zip (compressed) files	Technical support is available by	Average retail price
Kaspersky Anti-Virus Professional Pro 4.0	Scans **both** inbound and outbound!	Yes	No	Yes, it even scans Linux TAR, GZ, and RAR files!	Email	$49
Norton AntiVirus 2002	Scans both inbound and outbound!	Yes	No	No	Email and phone	$49
PC-cillin 2002	Inbound only	Yes	Yes	Yes	Email and limited phone	$39
F-Secure Anti-Virus Personal Edition	Inbound only	No	Yes	Only if manually set	Email and phone	$80
Norman Virus Control 5.0	Inbound only	No	No	No	Email	$60
Panda Platinum	Inbound only	No	No	Yes	Email	$30
McAfee VirusScan 6.0	Inbound only	Yes	No	No	Email	$40
Vexira Antivirus				Yes, it also scans Linux	Email and	

Clues to Use

Dealing with spam

As spam has grown to become a serious problem for all e-mail users and providers, new approaches have been devised or proposed to combat it. Some of these approaches require new laws to be passed, and some require technical changes in the mail handling systems of the Internet. In January, 2004, the U.S. CAN-SPAM (Controlling the Assault of Non-Solicited Pornography and Marketing) law went into effect. Researchers who track the amount of spam noted a drop in the percentage of spam messages in February and March, 2004. However, by April the rate was back up. It appeared that spammers slowed down their activities after the CAN-SPAM law was passed to see if they would actually be prosecuted. For the most part, they were not, and the spammers went right back to work. Unfortunately, CAN-SPAM and similar laws are ineffective at preventing spam because many spammers use e-mail servers located in countries that do not have (and that are unlikely to adopt) anti-spam laws, and spammers can move their operations from one server to another in minutes. For now, the best way to make spammers easier to find and ban or prosecute is to make changes in the way e-mail is sent over the Internet.

Internet

Practice

▼ CONCEPTS REVIEW

Identify the dialog boxes shown in Figures I-22 and 1-23 if you are using Internet Explorer and in Figures I-24 and I-25 if you are using Firefox.

FIGURE I-22

1.
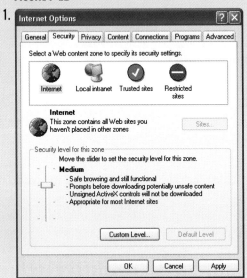

FIGURE I-23

2.
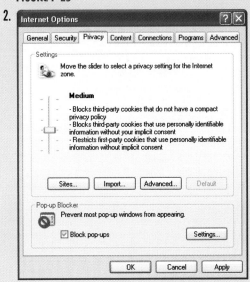

FIGURE I-24

3.
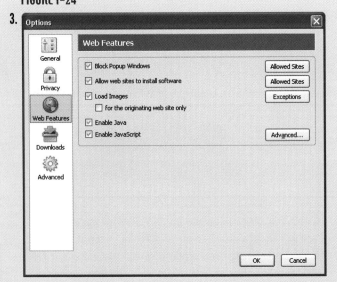

FIGURE I-25

4.

Match each term with the statement that best describes it.

5. ActiveX control *e*
6. Cookie *f*
7. Security *g*
8. Encrypt *d*
9. Phishing *a*
10. Sniffer program *c*
11. Digital certificate *b*
12. Clickstream *h*

a. Trying to obtain confidential information from people via e-mail
b. An encrypted and password-protected file that contains information to authenticate and prove a person's or organization's identity
c. A program that monitors and analyzes data packets as they travel over the Internet
d. Scrambling and encoding data transmissions
e. Microsoft's technology for writing small applications that perform some action in Web pages
f. A text file that Web sites can use to track your browsing habits
g. The protection of assets from unauthorized access, use, alteration, or destruction
h. The sequence of links you click while visiting a Web site

Select the best answer from the list of choices.

13. Web sites that look like they belong to one business but actually belong to someone else are:
    a. phished.
    b. spoofed.
    c. encrypted.
    d. authenticated.

14. The best way to protect your computer against worms is to:
    a. prevent Web sites from storing cookies on your computer.
    b. use encryption software, such as PGP.
    c. disable Web page programs in your Web browser.
    d. install anti-virus software.

15. A small, hidden graphic on a Web page or in an e-mail message that is designed to work in conjunction with a cookie to obtain information about the person viewing the page or e-mail message and to send that information to a third party is:
    a. a Web bug.
    b. spyware.
    c. adware.
    d. virus.

16. A _____ is when one computer tests all or some of the ports of another computer to determine whether its ports are open, closed, or stealth.
    a. phishing program
    b. virus
    c. port scan
    d. sniffer program

17. The process of identifying a user to a computer is called:
    a. user identification.
    b. user authentication.
    c. digital certification.
    d. SSL protocol.

18. A software program or hardware device that controls access between two networks is a(n):

    a. ActiveX control.

    b. Java applet.

    c. firewall.

    d. cookie.

19. Which of the following stores information about your clickstream?

    a. ActiveX control

    b. Spyware

    c. Web bug

    d. Cookie

▼ SKILLS REVIEW

1. Strengthen security in Internet Explorer.

    a. If you are using Internet Explorer, open the Internet Options dialog box; if you are using Firefox, skip to Skills Review 2.

    b. Switch to the Security tab, if necessary.

    c. Click Default Level if it is not grayed out, then drag the slider to High and read the description of the settings.

    d. Try to drag the slider down below Medium, then click OK in the notification dialog box that opens telling you that you must set this zone to Medium or higher.

    e. Open the Security Settings dialog box.

    f. Scroll down and examine the settings for ActiveX controls, then click Cancel.

    g. Click Cancel in the Security Settings dialog box.

2. Strengthen security in Firefox.

    a. If you are using Firefox, open the Options dialog box; if you are using Internet Explorer, skip to Skills Review 3.

    b. Switch to the Web Features page in the Options dialog box, if necessary.

    c. Select the Enable JavaScript check box, if necessary, then open the Advanced JavaScript Options dialog box.

    d. Examine the options in the dialog box, then click Cancel.

    e. Clear the Enable Java and Enable JavaScript check boxes, if necessary.

    f. Click Cancel in the Options dialog box.

3. Check security features on a Web Site.

    a. Go to the Student Online Companion at www.course.com/illustrated/internet4, click the Unit I link, then click the Amazon.com link under Skills Review 3.

    b. Perform a search or follow links to find a book that you want to purchase.

    c. After you have selected a book that you like, click the Add to Shopping Cart link.

    d. Click the Proceed to Checkout link.

    e. Click the Sign in using our secure server link.

    f. Double-click the padlock.

    g. List three ways you know this Web page is a secure Web site.

4. Manage cookies in Internet Explorer.

    a. If you are using Internet Explorer, open the Internet Options dialog box; if you are using Firefox, skip to Skills Review 5.

    b. Switch to the Privacy tab, if necessary.

    c. Drag the slider down to Low, if necessary, and read the description of the types of cookies that would be blocked with this setting.

    d. Drag the slider up to High and read the description of the types of cookies that would be blocked with this setting.

    e. Open the Per Site Privacy Actions dialog box.

    f. Add www.microsoft.com as a site that is always allowed to leave cookies on your computer.

    g. Remove www.microsoft.com from the list of Managed Web sites, then switch to the General tab in the Internet Options dialog box.

    h. View the files in the Temporary Internet Files folder.

    i. Click the Last Modified column heading twice to sort the files in descending order by date modified (most recently modified file first).

    j. Examine the filename of the first file in the list that starts with "Cookie" and see if you can determine which site deposited that cookie.

    k. Close the Temporary Internet Files folder window, click Cancel in the Settings dialog box, then click OK in the Internet Options dialog box.

    l. Exit your browser.

5. Manage cookies in Firefox.

    a. If you are using Firefox, open the Options dialog box; if you are using Internet Explorer, skip this Skills Review exercise.

    b. Switch to the Privacy page in the Options dialog box, if necessary.

    c. Expand the Cookies section.

    d. Open the Exceptions dialog box.

    e. Add www.microsoft.com as a site that is always allowed to leave cookies on your computer.

    f. Click Cancel in the Exceptions dialog box, then open the Stored Cookies dialog box.

    g. Scroll down to find the cookies deposited by Hotels.com, then click one and examine the information about the cookie you selected.

    h. Click Cancel in the Stored Cookies dialog box, then click OK in the Options dialog box.

    i. Exit your browser

▼ INDEPENDENT CHALLENGE 1

Now that you understand more about Internet security and potential risks associated with using the Internet, you want to take steps to secure your Internet use. Start by finding out about your school's or employer's anti-virus and anti-spyware resources.

a. Ask your instructor or system administrator if your school makes anti-virus software available to students and staff.

b. If your school does not make anti-virus software available, ask your instructor or system administrator about the school's plan for safe computing. Find out if other safeguards are in place to limit exposure to viruses for users of the school's computers. Summarize your research in a paragraph, then write another paragraph analyzing what you've found. State whether you think students and staff at your school are adequately protected against viruses, and why.

c. If your school does make anti-virus software available, download it to your computer and install it. Use information on your school's Web site along with the software's help section to understand and enable its main features. Also download the most recent virus definitions from the software company's Web site. Then write a paragraph describing the steps you took to download and install the software, and another paragraph summarizing the software's features.

d. Find out how your school protects computers from spyware.

Advanced Challenge Exercise

- Go to **www.course.com/illustrated/internet4**, click the **Unit I link**, click one of the links to a download site under Independent Challenge 1, then search for Ad-aware, a free software program that detects and removes adware.
- Read the description of Ad-aware, then download and install the program. (**STOP:** If you are working on a public computer or in a lab, make sure you have permission to install software before installing Ad-aware.)
- Click **Scan Now**, then click the option to perform a smart system-scan.
- One the scan is complete, click **Next** to examine the list of programs found.
- Click the **Close button** in the Ad-aware title bar to quit without taking any action on the list of programs found.

e. Close your Web browser.

▼ INDEPENDENT CHALLENGE 2

You're interning in a lawyer's office for a summer. Because you understand some of the technical aspects of Internet security, your manager has asked you to evaluate PGP, a security program that she's considering using for sensitive communications.

a. Go to the Student Online Companion at **www.course.com/illustrated/internet4**, click the **Unit I link**, click one of the links to a download site under Independent Challenge 2, then search for a program that will let you encrypt e-mail messages.

b. Find at least two programs that you think will work.

c. Click the links to the publishers' Web sites and read more detailed information on the sites explaining how the programs work.

d. Write at least three paragraphs summarizing your findings. Include a description of the basic features of each program, minimum computer system requirements, and the differences between them.

e. Close your Web browser.

▼ INDEPENDENT CHALLENGE 3

In a class, you're discussing how to balance Web use with privacy concerns. You've been assigned to write a paper on whether all cookies are intrusive.

a. Use your favorite search engine to research different kinds of cookies.

b. Write at least two paragraphs about a type of cookie that you might not want saved on your computer. Explain why you wouldn't want it saved on your computer, and include an example of how this type of cookie might be used by Web sites you interact with.

c. Write at least two more paragraphs about a type of cookie that some Web users might find useful, including an explanation of why, and an example of how it might be used. Be sure to include the terms "third-party cookie" and "first-party cookie" in your descriptions, and explain what the terms mean.

d. Close your Web browser.

▼ INDEPENDENT CHALLENGE 4

Three times in the last six months, someone has successfully penetrated the computer system at Bolton Brokerage Services and defaced the home page in the same way that a person might use spray paint to add graffiti to a highway underpass or public restroom. The owner has hired you to look into the security measures he should take to prevent the break-ins his business is experiencing.

a. Go to the Student Online Companion at **www.course.com/illustrated/internet4**, click the **Unit I link**, and then click the **SecurityMetrics Free Port Scan link** under Independent Challenge 4.

b. Click the option to run a free port scan on your computer. It might take several minutes for the port scan results to appear. (**STOP:** Do not run a port scan on a public computer unless you have permission to do so from your lab's administrator.)

c. Use your browser's Print button to print the results page. In a report addressed to the owner, answer the following questions.

- How secure is your computer?
- What actions can you take to protect any open ports?
- If you do not have any open ports, what actions have you already taken to protect your computer? (If you are in a public computer lab and do not have access to security information, explain the countermeasures that you believe are in place to secure open ports.)

d. Return to the Student Online Companion page at **www.course.com/illustrated/internet4**, click the **Unit I link**, and then click the **VeriSign link** under Independent Challenge 4.

e. Use the VeriSign Web site to determine the cost of Secure Sockets Layer certificates. When you find this information, use your browser to print it.

Advanced Challenge Exercise

- Use your favorite search engine to find information on how firewalls work.
- Go to **www.course.com/illustrated/internet4**, click the **Unit I link**, click one of the links to a download site under Independent Challenge 4, then search for ZoneAlarm.
- Download the free version of ZoneAlarm and install it on your computer. (**STOP:** If you are working on a public computer or in a lab, make sure you have permission to install software before installing ZoneAlarm.)
- Run ZoneAlarm, then try to return to the Student Online Companion at **www.course.com/illustrated/internet4**. Describe what happens, then give permission for your browser to access the Internet.
- If you don't want to run ZoneAlarm every time you start your computer, click the Preferences tab in the ZoneAlarm program window, click the Load ZoneAlarm at startup check box to remove the check mark, then click Yes in the warning box that appears.

f. Close your Web browser.

▼ VISUAL WORKSHOP

Go to www.course.com/illustrated/internet4, click the Unit I link, then click the New York Times link under Visual Workshop to go to that newspaper's Web site. Find the list of cookies shown in Figure I-26 if you are using Internet Explorer and in Figure I-27 if you are using Firefox. (If you are using Internet Explorer and you can't find the cookies shown in the figure, scroll to the right, then click the Last Accessed column heading twice to sort the list in order by date, and look for the most recent cookies.) If you are using Internet Explorer, write down the filename and the Expires date for each of the four cookies called out in the figure. If you are using Firefox, write down the site name (the URL in the list) and the Expires date for the five cookies shown in the figure.

FIGURE I-26

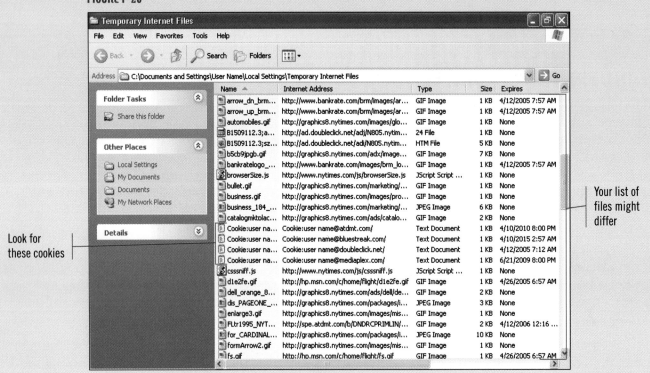

FIGURE I-27

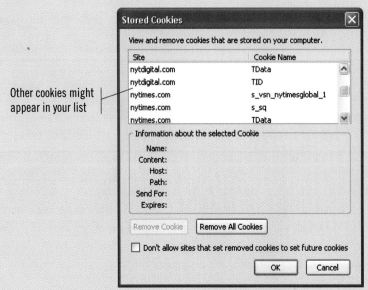

Using Other Browser and E-Mail Programs

OBJECTIVES

Use Netscape 7.2
Use Opera
Use iRider
Use Netscape 7.2 Mail
Use Eudora
Use Thunderbird
Use Gmail

There are many browsers, e-mail client programs, and Webmail services that you can use. Internet Explorer, one of the browsers covered in this book, is the most popular browser in use today. Firefox, the other browser discussed in this book, is another choice that more and more people are using. Some other popular browsers are Netscape, Opera, and iRider. Outlook Express is a very popular e-mail client program, and Hotmail is a popular Webmail service; these are covered in the lessons in this book. Other e-mail client programs you can use are Netscape Mail, Eudora, and Mozilla's Thunderbird, and Gmail is a relatively new free Webmail service. This appendix covers some of the significant differences between each of these programs and the ones discussed in the units.

Using Netscape 7.2

Netscape 7.2 is sometimes referred to as Netscape and sometimes as Navigator. The look and feel, as well as many of the commands in Netscape 7.2, are similar to Firefox, so start by reading the Firefox lessons throughout the book and then refer to this lesson in the appendix when you need additional information.

DETAILS

- **Starting Netscape 7.2**

  To start Netscape 7.2, click **Start** on the taskbar, point to **All Programs**, point to **Netscape 7.2**, then click **Navigator**.

- **Examining the Browser Window**

  To examine the Netscape 7.2 window, click the **New Tab button** just above the content in the browser window on the left, and then click the **Netscape.com tab**. Figure 1 shows the Netscape 7.2 browser window. Netscape 7.2 has the same components discussed in Lesson 4, "Starting a Web Browser," in Unit B, *Understanding Browser Basics*, and it has the following differences:

  - **Personal Toolbar**: Allows you to add buttons to it to make your browsing easier and more efficient.
  - **Netscape Toolbar**: Contains the Netscape button, which contains common commands in a menu, the Search text box, and other buttons.
  - **Close toolbar button**: Allows you to close the menu bar or a toolbar, and then re-open it by clicking the same button.
  - **Component bar**: Allows you to quickly switch from one task to another; for example, you can switch from using the Netscape browser to using the Netscape e-mail program.

- **Creating Bookmarks**

  To save a Web page as a bookmark, click **Bookmarks** on the menu bar, then click **Bookmark This Page.**

- **Strengthening Security**

  To change security options, click **Edit** on the menu bar, click **Preferences**, then click **Advanced.** See Figure 2.

- **Managing Cookies**

  Click **Edit** on the menu bar, click **Preferences**, click **Privacy & Security**, click the **Expand arrow** next to Privacy & Security to view the list of options, if necessary, then click **Cookies**. See Figure 3. To manage cookies for a specific site, you can click **Cookie Manager** in the Cookies panel in the Preferences dialog box, or you can click **Tools** on the menu bar, click **Cookie Manager**, then select the option you want for handling cookies on that site.

Clues to Use

Netscape 8.0

At the time this book was published, Netscape 8.0 was available only in beta test version (a pre-release version of the software). Netscape 8.0 is similar to Netscape 7.2, but there are several differences. Netscape 8.0 has a **search field**, in which you can type a term and then search the Web for pages that contain that term.

Netscape 8.0 also introduces the **multibar**, a toolbar in which up to 10 open toolbars are represented by numbered buttons. When you click one of the numbered buttons, the toolbar to the right of the multibar changes to the toolbar you chose.

FIGURE 1: Netscape 7.2 Web browser window

Title bar
Menu bar
Back button
Close Toolbar button
Netscape toolbar
Click to open a new tab
Home button
Component bar

Stop button
Location bar
Reload button
Personal toolbar
Scroll bar
Status bar

FIGURE 2: Advanced options in Preferences dialog box in Netscape 7.2

JavaScript options

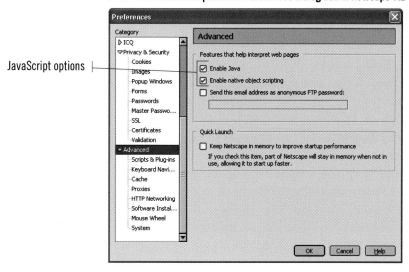

FIGURE 3: Cookies options in Preferences dialog box in Netscape 7.2

Options for setting rules for cookies

Options for length of time to keep cookies

Click to delete individual cookies

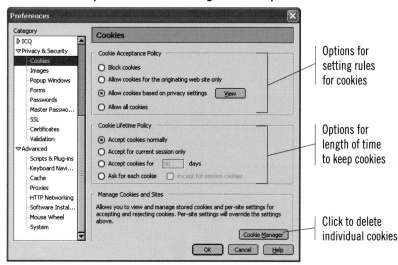

Using Opera

Opera is a powerful browser that is available in a free version and a registered version. If you choose to use the free version, an ad banner appears in the upper-right of the browser window. The look and feel of Opera is unique, but it is closer to that of Firefox than Internet Explorer. Start by reading the Firefox lessons throughout the book and then refer to this lesson in the appendix when you need additional information.

DETAILS

- **Starting Opera**

  To start Opera, click **Start** on the taskbar, point to **All Programs**, point to **Opera**, click **Opera**, click the **Start with home page option button**, then click **Start**. If this is the first time you are using Opera, the Welcome to Opera dialog box opens when you start Opera. It contains options for choosing the type of ads you want to see. Click the option button next to the option you want, then click **OK**.

QUICK TIP

At the time this book was published, Opera 8.0 was available only in beta test version; it should not vary substantially from the description of Opera 7.5 presented in this lesson.

- **Examining the Browser Window**

  Figure 4 shows the Opera 7.5 browser window. To make your screen match the figure, click **View** on the menu bar, point to **Toolbars**, click **Main bar** if there is no check mark next to it, or click a blank area of the window if there is a check mark next to it, click the **Panels button** on the toolbar to select it, if necessary, click the **New page button** just above the content in the browser window on the left, and then click the **Opera Search tab**. Opera 7.5 has the title bar, menu bar, page tabs, scroll bar, and the Back, Reload, and Home buttons discussed in Lesson 4, "Starting a Web Browser," in Unit B, *Understanding Browser Basics*, and it has the following differences:

  - **Main bar**: Contains the Print and Home buttons and other buttons that make navigating the Web easier.
  - **Address field**: Is the same as the Location or Address bar.
  - **Search field**: Allows you to search for Web pages on the Web that contain the term you type in the field.
  - **Zoom field**: Allows you to enlarge or shrink the page you are viewing.
  - **Padlock icon**: Appears on the Address bar instead of on the status bar as in most browsers; it indicates the security status of the currently displayed Web site.
  - **Panel bar**: Allows you to open panels to perform tasks related to the panel name.

QUICK TIP

To view the Panel bar in Opera 8.0, click View on the menu bar, point to Toolbars, then click Panels, if it is not already selected.

  - **Status bar**: Is not open in Opera by default. To open it, click **View** on the menu bar, point to **Toolbars**, then click **Status bar**. It appears between the toolbar and the page tabs.
  - **Rewind button**: Allows you to jump to the home page on the current Web site, or if you are already on a site's home page, allows you to jump to the last page you visited on the previous Web site.
  - **Fast forward button**: Analyzes the current page and then jumps to the next most likely page.
  - **Stop button**: Appears only while a page is loading, then it changes to the Reload button.

- **Creating Bookmarks**

  To save a Web page as a bookmark, click **Bookmarks** on the menu bar, click **Add page here** or **Add to bookmarks** to open the Bookmark properties dialog box as shown in Figure 5, then click **OK**.

- **Managing Bookmarks**

  To manage bookmarks, click **Bookmarks** on the menu bar, then click **Manage Bookmarks**. See Figure 6.

- **Strengthening Security**

  To change security options, click **Tools** on the menu bar, click **Preferences**, then click **Security**.

- **Managing Cookies**

  To manage cookies, click **Tools** on the menu bar, click **Preferences**, then click **Privacy**.

FIGURE 4: Opera Web browser window

Title bar
Menu bar
Main bar
Home button
New page button
Rewind button
Back button
Fast forward button
Reload button
Zoom field

Panel bar (might appear in a different position on your screen)

Address field
Advertising banner
Search field
Padlock icon

Scroll bar

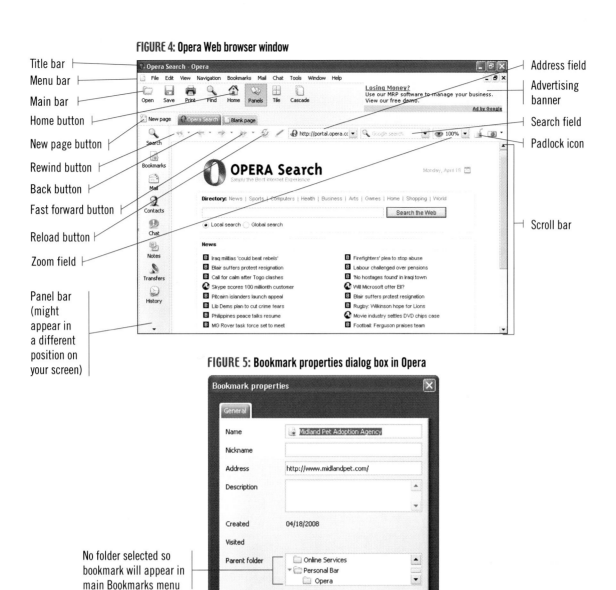

FIGURE 5: Bookmark properties dialog box in Opera

No folder selected so bookmark will appear in main Bookmarks menu

FIGURE 6: Bookmarks window in Opera

Bookmarks page open in new page tab

New bookmark

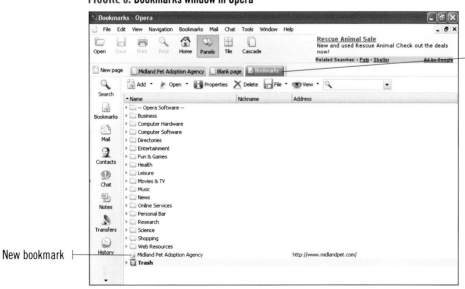

Internet

Using iRider

iRider is a one of the few browsers that is not available in a free version. You may use it for a short time, but after the trial period, you must pay to register it. It has many powerful features that make it attractive to some users. Although the look and feel of iRider is unique, the steps for using it are similar to those for using Internet Explorer. Start by reading the Internet Explorer lessons throughout the book and then refer to this lesson in the appendix when you need additional information.

DETAILS

- **Starting iRider**

  Click **Start** on the taskbar, point to **All Programs**, then click **iRider**.

- **Examining the iRider Window**

  Figure 7 shows the iRider Web browser window. iRider has the same components discussed in Lesson 4, "Starting a Web Browser," in Unit B, *Understanding Browser Basics*, and it has the following differences:

  - **Links bar**: Contains frequently-used favorites.
  - **Pages list**: Allows you to quickly navigate between open pages.
  - **Page pin**: Allows you to specify that a page will always be listed in the Pages list. A page that is always listed in the Pages list is called a **pinned page**.
  - **Next Page button**: Allows you to jump to the page that was opened next in the Pages list. Note that this is not always the next page in the list.
  - **Parent button**: Allows you to jump to the page that contains the link to the current page. This button is grayed out (not available) if you did not arrive at the current page by clicking a link.

- **Right-Clicking Links**

  Right-click any link on a Web page. The linked page opens in the Pages list. This is called Surf-Ahead. You can click several links in a row, then click them in the Pages list to view them, instead of clicking each one and waiting for it to load or continually returning to the start page to click another link.

- **Copying from a Web Site**

  Go to **www.midlandpet.com**, click the **Directions & Contact link**, point to the **map image**, then press and hold the right mouse button for one second. After a second, the shortcut menu appears. In iRider you must hold the right-mouse button to make shortcut menus appear to override the Surf-Ahead option.

- **Creating Bookmarks**

  - To save a Web page as a bookmark, click **Favorites** on the menu bar, click **Add Page(s)** to open the Add Page(s) to Favorites dialog box, then click the **Selected option button** to add the current page to the Favorites list as shown in Figure 8.
  - In the Add Page(s) to Favorites dialog box, click the **Site option button** to add all the pages in the site to the favorite; click the **All option button** to add all the open pages in the Pages list to the favorite; and click the **Pinned only check box** to add only pinned pages in the selected option to the favorite.
  - To create a new favorites folder, click **New Folder** to open the New Favorites Folder dialog box, type the name of the new folder in the Folder name text box, click **OK**, then click **OK**.

FIGURE 7: iRider Web browser window

Title bar

Menu bar

Back button

Next Page button

Links bar

Address bar

Pages list

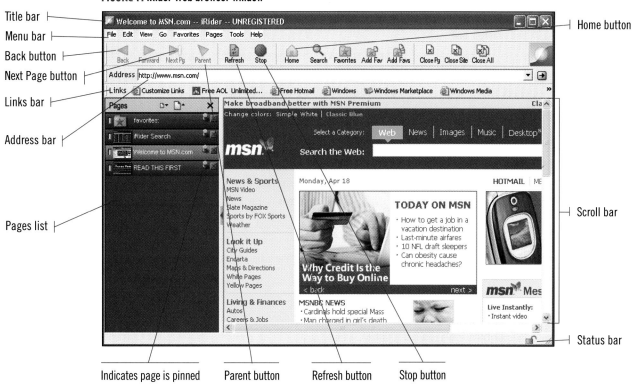

Home button

Scroll bar

Status bar

Indicates page is pinned   Parent button   Refresh button   Stop button

FIGURE 8: Add Page(s) to Favorites dialog box in iRider

Select option for adding pages to favorites list

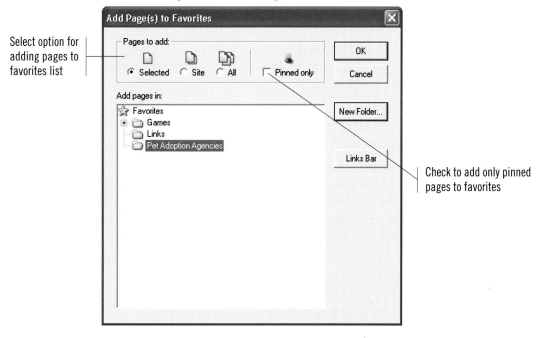

Check to add only pinned pages to favorites

Internet

Using Netscape 7.2 Mail

Netscape 7.2 Mail is an e-mail client program, so the steps are similar to those for Outlook Express. Start by reading the Outlook Express lessons and steps throughout the book and then refer to this lesson in the appendix when you need additional information. (*Note*: Netscape 8.0 does not come with an integrated e-mail client program.)

DETAILS

- **Starting Netscape 7.2 Mail**

  To start Netscape Mail, click **Start** on the taskbar, point to **All Programs**, point to **Netscape 7.2**, click **Mail and Newsgroups**, click the **Expand arrow** next to your account name in the pane on the left, if necessary, then click **Inbox** under your account name.

- **Examining the Mail Window**

  Figure 9 shows the Netscape 7.2 Mail window. Netscape 7.2 Mail has the same components in Lesson 2, "Starting Outlook Express and Exploring the Mail Window," in Unit C, *Using E-Mail*, and it has the following differences:

  - **Get Msgs button**: Functions the same as the Send/Recv button in Outlook Express.
  - **Compose button**: Functions the same as the Create Mail button in Outlook Express.
  - **Search bar**: Allows you to filter the messages you see in the message list by preset categories in the View list, and also allows you to filter the message list for messages that contain only the search text you specify in the Search text box.
  - **Trash folder**: Holds deleted messages.
  - **Templates folder**: Holds formatted messages that you can double-click to create a new message based on that format.
  - There is no Outbox folder; messages are sent immediately after you click Send.

- **Sending a Message**

  To add a Cc e-mail address, you must click in the box below the To box, click the **To arrow**, then click **Cc**. See Figure 10.

- **Saving an Attachment**

  To save an attachment, click the message in the message list, right-click the attachment filename in the Preview pane, then click **Save As** on the shortcut menu. See Figure 11.

- **Creating a Folder**

  To create a new folder, right-click the folder in which you want the folder to appear, then click **New Folder** on the shortcut menu.

- **Maintaining the Address Book**

  To open the Address Book window, click the **Address Book button** at the bottom of the Folders list, then click **Personal Address Book** in the Address Books list on the left. If you use AOL instant messaging service (AIM), your contacts from your AIM buddy list appear in the list of contacts on the right.

- **Creating Contacts and Groups**

  To create a new contact card, click **New Card** on the Address Book toolbar; to create a new group, click **New List** on the Address Book toolbar. To address a message using the Address Book, type the first few letters of a contact name or e-mail address in the To or Cc boxes in the Compose window, and then select the desired e-mail address from the list of choices that appears.

FIGURE 9: Netscape 7.2 Mail window

Compose button

Get Msgs button

Folders list (you might have additional folders in your list)

Address Book button

Toolbar

Inbox folder

Message list (you might have messages listed)

Preview pane

FIGURE 10: Compose window in Netscape 7.2 Mail

Text entered in Subject text box also appears in title bar

Send button

Click to change to Cc

Subject is hidden

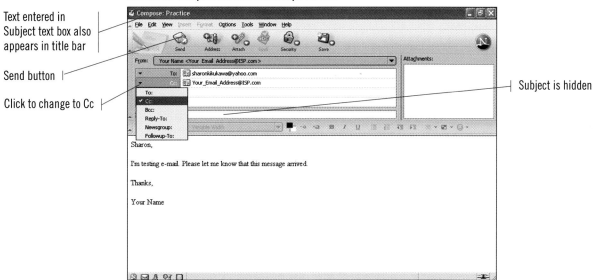

FIGURE 11: Saving an attachment in Netscape 7.2 Mail

Indicates an attachment

Messages received today show only the time

Right-click for commands to handle attachment

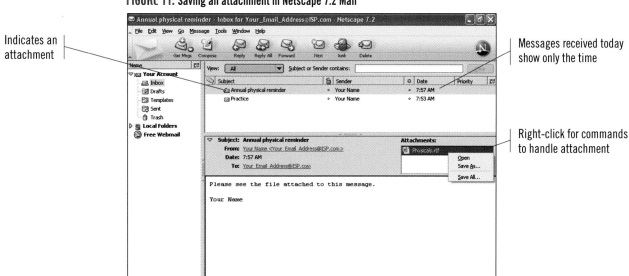

Internet

Using Eudora

Eudora is an e-mail client program. The steps for using Eudora are similar to those for Outlook Express. Start by reading the Outlook Express lessons and steps throughout the book, and then refer to this lesson in the appendix when you need additional information.

DETAILS

> **QUICK TIP**
>
> Eudora is available in Paid mode (the user pays a fee to register it), Sponsored mode (the program is free and contains all the features of the Paid mode, but it displays advertisements targeted to the user), and Light mode (the program is free and does not display ads, but it does not contain all the features of the Paid mode).

- **Starting Eudora**

  To start Eudora, click **Start** on the taskbar, point to **All Programs**, point to **Eudora**, then click **Eudora**. If the Tip of the Day appears, click **Close**.

- **Examining the Mail Window**

  Figure 12 shows the Eudora mail window. To make your screen match the figure, double-click the **Eudora folder icon** in the pane on the left, if necessary, to display the list of folders, double-click **In**, then click the **Maximize button** in the In window, if necessary. In Eudora, folders can not hold messages. Instead, mailboxes hold messages; folders hold mailboxes. Eudora has the same components discussed in Lesson 2, "Starting Outlook Express and Exploring the Mail Window," in Unit C, *Using E-Mail*, and it has the following differences:

  - **Check Mail button**: Functions the same as the Send/Recv button in Outlook Express.
  - **Mailboxes window**: Is equivalent to the Folders list in Outlook Express; to open a mailbox or a folder, double-click it.
  - **In and Out mailboxes**: Are the same as the Inbox and Outbox folders in Outlook Express.
  - **Trash folder**: Holds deleted messages.
  - **Junk folder**: Holds junk e-mail, but the plug-ins for handling junk e-mail are disabled except in Paid mode.
  - **Window buttons**: Represents each open window.
  - There are no Sent Items or Drafts folders.

- **Saving an Attachment**

  To save an attachment, click the message in the message list, right-click the attachment filename link in the Preview pane, then click **Save Attachment As** on the shortcut menu.

> **QUICK TIP**
>
> There is no Sent Items folder in Eudora. To automatically save a copy of each sent message in the Out folder, click Tools on the menu bar, click Options, click Composing Mail in the Category list, then check the Keep copies check box.

- **Organizing Messages**

  To create a new mailbox, right-click the folder in which you want the new mailbox to appear, then click **New** on the shortcut menu. To file a message, drag it into the mailbox in which you want to store it.

- **Maintaining the Address Book**

  - To open the Address Book window, click the **Address Book button** on the toolbar, then click **Eudora Nicknames** in the list in the left pane of the Address Book window. See Figure 13.
  - To create a new contact card, click **New** at the bottom of the left pane in the Address Book window, type the nickname in the **Nickname text box**, type the contact's full name in the **Full Name text box** on the Personal tab, then type the contact's e-mail address in the **This nickname will expand to the following addresses text box**. See Figure 14.
  - To address a message using the Address Book, type the recipient's nickname in the To field or open the Address Book window, click the recipient's name in the list in the left pane, then click **To, Cc**, or **Bcc**; to continue adding names to the message header, click the **Address Book button** at the bottom of the window, click the next name, then click the appropriate button.

- **Creating a Group**

  To create a new group, create a new contact card, type the nickname for the group in the **Nickname text box**, type a descriptive name for the group in the **Full Name text box** on the Personal tab, then type the e-mail address of each recipient in the **This nickname will expand to the following addresses text box**, pressing **[Enter]** between each e-mail address.

FIGURE 12: Eudora mail window

New Message button

Check Mail button

Mailboxes window (you
might have additional
mailboxes and folders
in your list)

Window button for
In mailbox

Address Book button

Toolbar

In mailbox

Message list (you might
have messages listed)

Preview pane

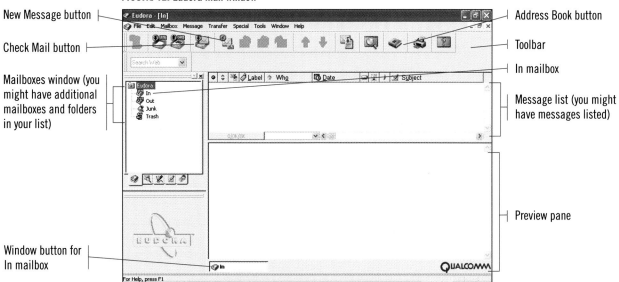

FIGURE 13: Eudora Address Book window

No contacts in
Address Book

Click to add
new contact

Advertisement in
Sponsored version

Address Book
window button

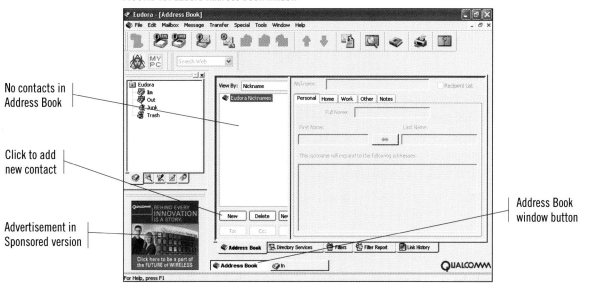

FIGURE 14: Eudora Address Book window with contact added

Nickname of
added contact

Type contact's
nickname here

Type contact's
full name here

Type contact's e-mail
address here

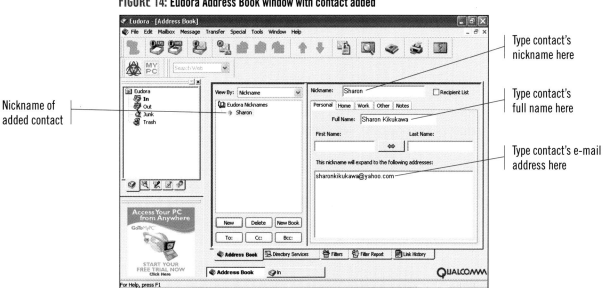

Internet

DETAILS

Using Thunderbird

Thunderbird is the e-mail client program from Mozilla. The steps for using Thunderbird are similar to those for Outlook Express. Start by reading the Outlook Express lessons and steps throughout the book, and then refer to this lesson in the appendix when you need additional information.

- **Starting Thunderbird**

  To start Thunderbird, click **Start** on the taskbar, point to **All Programs**, point to **Mozilla Thunderbird**, then click **Mozilla Thunderbird**.

- **Examining the Thunderbird Mail Window**

  Figure 15 shows the Thunderbird mail window. To make your screen match the figure, click **Inbox** in the folders list. Thunderbird has the same components discussed in Lesson 2, "Starting Outlook Express and Exploring the Mail Window" in Unit C, *Using E-Mail*, and it has the following differences:

  - **Unsent Messages**: Is equivalent to the Outbox folder.
  - **Trash folder**: Holds deleted messages.
  - **Get Mail button**: Functions the same as the Send/Recv button in Outlook Express.
  - **Write button**: Functions the same as the Create Mail button in Outlook Express.

- **Sending a Message**

  To add a Cc e-mail address, click in the box below the To box, click the **To arrow**, then click **Cc**. See Figure 16.

- **Saving an Attachment**

  To save an attachment, click the message in the message list, right-click the attachment filename in the Preview pane, then click **Save As** on the shortcut menu. See Figure 17.

- **Creating a Folder**

  To create a new folder, right-click the folder in the Folders list in which you want to store the new folder, then click **New Folder** on the shortcut menu.

- **Maintaining the Address Book**

  To open the Address Book window, click the **Address Book button** on the toolbar, then click **Personal Address Book** in the Address Books list on the left.

- **Creating Contacts and Groups**

  To create a new contact card, click **New Card** on the Address Book toolbar; to create a new group, click **New List** on the Address Book toolbar. To address a message using the Address Book, type the first few letters of a contact name or e-mail address in the To or Cc boxes in the Compose window, and then select the desired e-mail address from the list of choices that appears.

FIGURE 15: Thunderbird mail window

Get Mail button

Write button

Folders list (you might have additional folders in your list)

Address Book button

Toolbar

Inbox folder

Message list (you might have messages listed)

Preview pane

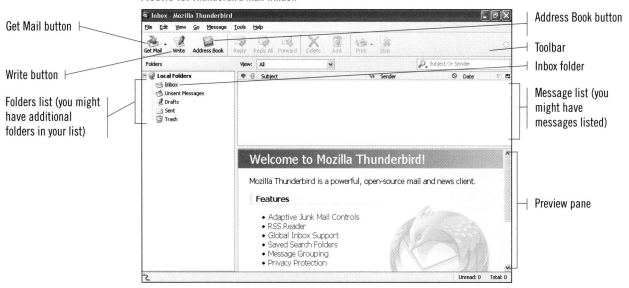

FIGURE 16: Compose window in Thunderbird

Send button

Click to change to Cc

Text entered in Subject text box also appears in title bar

Subject is hidden

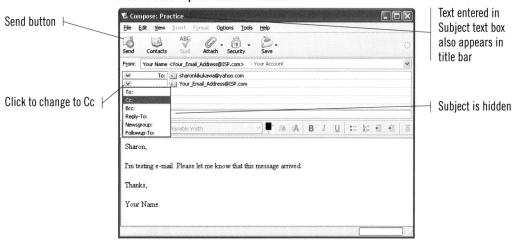

FIGURE 17: Saving an attachment in Thunderbird

Indicates an attachment

Right-click for commands to handle attachment

Messages received today show only the time

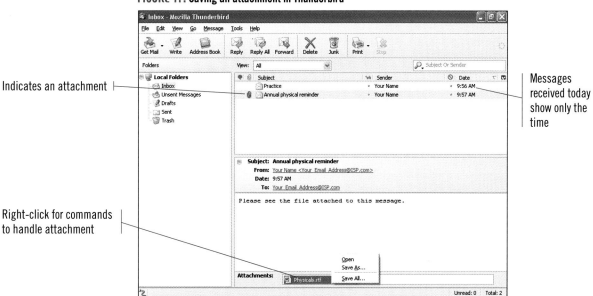

Using Gmail

Gmail is a Webmail service. As with Hotmail, you need to sign in with a user name and password to use the service. Start by reading the Hotmail lessons and steps throughout the book and then refer to this lesson in the appendix when you need additional information.

Additional Information

- **Connecting to Gmail**

  Start your browser, click in the **Address** or **Location Bar**, type **www.gmail.com**, type the username you received when you registered with Gmail in the Username text box, type your password in the Password text box, then click **Sign in**.

- **Examining the Gmail Mail Window**

  Figure 18 shows the Gmail mail window. Gmail has the same components discussed in Lesson 3, "Connecting to Your Hotmail Account and Exploring the Mail Window," in Unit C, *Using E-Mail*, and it has the following differences:

  - **Search text box**: Allows you to search your e-mail messages or the Web.
  - **Starred folder**: Stores messages you have flagged.
  - **All Mail folder**: Stores all messages, sent and received.
  - **Spam folder**: Functions the same as the Junk E-mail folder in Hotmail.
  - **Labels list**: Allows you to apply labels to messages to categorize them, and then filter your messages according to their labels.
  - **Archive button**: Allows you to archive your messages, which removes them from the Inbox, but keeps them available in the All Mail folder.
  - **Report Spam button**: Allows you to report a selected message to Gmail as spam.
  - **More Actions list**: Allows you to mark selected messages as read or unread, flag selected messages with a star, and move selected messages to the Trash folder.
  - **Refresh link**: Checks the Gmail server to see of you have any new messages.

- **Sending a Message**

  To create a new message, click the **Compose Mail link** above the Folders list; to add a Cc e-mail address, click the **Add Cc link** below the To box.

- **Checking Incoming Mail**

  To check to see if you have any new messages, click the **Refresh link** in the blue area above the message list.

- **Saving an Attachment**

  To save an attachment, open the message, then click the **Download link** below the attachment filename.

- **Viewing Replies and Forwarded Messages**

  A **conversation** is a message and all of the replies to that message. To read messages in a conversation, open a message that has a number in parentheses after the message header summary. The messages in the conversation open, layered one on top of another. See Figure 19. To read a message in the middle of the layers, click the visible portion of the message to expand it.

- **Organizing Messages**

  To organize messages, click a message check box to select it, click the **More Actions list arrow**, click **New label**, type a label name, then click **OK**. See Figure 20.

- **Maintaining a Contacts List**

  To add contacts to the Contacts list, click the **Contacts link** below the Folders list, click the **Add Contact link**, type the contact information, then click **Save**.

FIGURE 18: Gmail mail window

Compose Mail link

Click to archive messages

Inbox folder

Folders list (you might have additional folders in your list)

Contacts link

Labels list

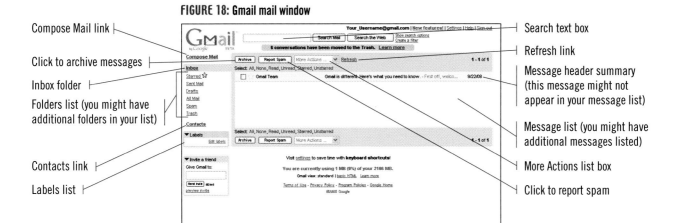

Search text box

Refresh link

Message header summary (this message might not appear in your message list)

Message list (you might have additional messages listed)

More Actions list box

Click to report spam

FIGURE 19: Messages in a conversation in Gmail

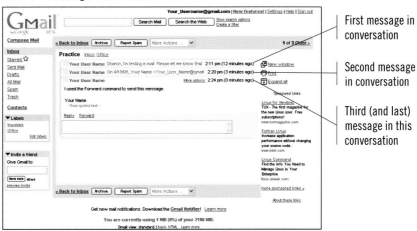

First message in conversation

Second message in conversation

Third (and last) message in this conversation

FIGURE 20: Labels applied to messages in Gmail

Indicates three messages in conversation

Labels list with new labels

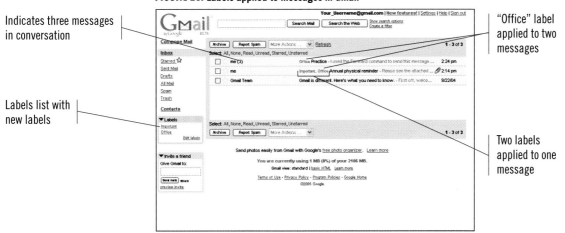

"Office" label applied to two messages

Two labels applied to one message

Clues to Use

Signing up for a Gmail account

Gmail, like most Webmail services, provides free e-mail service to anyone with an Internet connection. Before you can use it, you need to establish a user account. At the time that this book was published, the only way to do this was to respond to a Gmail invite sent to you by a current Gmail user. There are several sites on the Web to which current Gmail users donate their unused invites, which are then made available to anyone who wants one. To locate some of these sites, go to the Student Online Companion at **www.course.com/illustrated/internet4**, click the **Appendix link**, then click one of the links under Lesson 7.

Glossary

Acceptable use policy (AUP) A written policy at most schools and companies that specifies the conditions under which you can use their Internet connection.

ActiveX components Microsoft's technology for writing small applications that perform some action on Web pages.

Add-on A browser extension that enhances your browsing experience, such as a toolbar that lets you access a search engine without opening its Web site.

Address bar In Internet Explorer, a text box at the top of the browser window that indicates the URL of the current Web page and into which you can type a new URL and press [Enter] or click the Go button to go to another Web page; in Firefox, called *Location Bar*.

Address Book In Outlook Express, stores people's names and e-mail addresses, as well as other information, such as the person's postal address and telephone number; in Hotmail, called *Contacts list*.

Administrative address The e-mail address to which you send mailing list commands.

Advanced Research Projects Agency Network (ARPANET) An experimental WAN that consisted of four computers networked together by DARPA researchers in 1969.

Advanced Systems format (asf) A proprietary Windows Media Player file format that will play only in Windows Media Player.

Adware A general category of software that includes advertisements to help pay for the product in which they appear.

Aggregator Software that lets you receive newsfeed content.

Animated GIF A file that combines several images into a single GIF file so that the images can be displayed one after the other to simulate movement.

Annotations Summaries or reviews of Web pages in some subject guides.

Announcement list A mailing list that sends messages to subscribers, but does not allow subscribers to post to the list; similar to a newsletter.

Anonymous FTP The method of logging in to a publicly accessible FTP server without having a personal account.

Anti-virus software Software that protects your computer from viruses, worms, and Trojan horses.

AOL Instant Messenger (AIM) AOL's instant message software available to anyone (even those people without AOL accounts) for use on the Web.

Archive A compressed file in WinZip; or past messages stored in a file on a list server.

Archived file See *compressed file*.

ARPANET See *Advanced Research Projects Agency Network*.

Asf See *Advanced Systems format*.

Attachment A separate file sent with an e-mail message.

AU format The audio file format used by the UNIX operating system.

AUP See *acceptable use policy*.

Avatar An online character that a game player uses to represent him or herself.

AVI An uncompressed file format used for video on the Web that can be played using the same software that plays many other multimedia file types, including the player that comes with Windows.

Back button A button on a Web browser toolbar that allows you to go back to a previously viewed Web page.

Bandwidth A measure of the amount of data that can be transmitted simultaneously through a communications circuit.

Banner ad An advertisement that appears in a box on a Web page (usually at the top, but sometimes along the side or bottom of the page).

Bcc Short for blind carbon copy; in an e-mail program, the text box in which you type the e-mail address(es) of recipient(s) to whom you want to send a copy of an e-mail message without the knowledge of the other addressee(s).

Bits per second (bps) How bandwidth is measured; a bandwidth of 28,800 bps means that 28,800 bits of data are transferred each second.

Blog (Web log) An online journal in which the blogger posts entries for public viewing.

Blogger A blog owner.

Bookmark In Firefox, a shortcut on a menu to a Web site; in Internet Explorer called *favorite*.

Boolean operator Words that specify the logical relationship between the elements they join; the most common are AND, OR, and NOT; also called *logical operator*.

Bot See *web robot*.

Bps See *bits per second*.

Browse To use your computer and Internet connection to view Web pages.

Browser See *Web browser*.

Browser extension A program that enhances the capabilities of Web browsers by allowing a Web browser to perform a task that it was not originally designed to do; also called *extension*.

Brute force attack The act of using a program to enter character combinations until the attacked computer system accepts a user name and password, which allows the attacker access to the system.

Bug An error in software that could cause the program to halt, malfunction, or damage the user's computer.

Cable A method of connecting to the Internet used by individuals and businesses that uses the customer's television cable; connection speeds range from 300 Kbps to 10.0 Mbps.

Cable modem A special type of modem required to create a cable connection to the Internet through a cable television company.

Calendar page In Hotmail, the page that provides the user with an electronic calendar.

Category 1 cable A type of twisted-pair cable that transmits information more slowly than other cable types; used by telephone companies for years to wire residences and businesses.

Category 5 cable and **Category 5e cable** Newer types of twisted-pair cable that transmits data faster than coaxial cable.

Cc Short for carbon copy; in an e-mail program, the text box in which you type the e-mail address(es) of recipient(s) to whom you are sending a copy of an e-mail message.

Certificate authority (CA) A trusted third party that verifies a digital certificate holder's identity and issues the digital certificate.

Chat Real-time communication on the Internet or on the Web.

Chat room A public area in which anyone who is registered with the chat service can come and go.

Circuit switching A method for data transmission once commonly used by telephone companies in which all data transmitted from a sender to a receiver travels along a single path.

Clear GIF See *Web bug*.

Clearinghouse See *subject guide*.

Clip art A collection of individual icons, shapes, and other graphics.

Clickstream The sequence of links you click while visiting a Web site.

Client A computer connected to a server.

Client/server network A network consisting of one server that shares its resources with multiple clients.

Closed list A mailing list in which the list administrator must either reject or accept a request to become a list member.

Coaxial cable An insulated copper wire encased in a metal shield that is enclosed with plastic insulation.

Command A request to a list server to take a prescribed action.

Communications circuits The circuits through which data travels in network connections.

Complete Web page A Web page and all of its individual associated files saved to a disk; the Web page is saved as an htm file and the associated files are stored in a folder with the same name as the file you saved followed by an underscore and the word "files."

Compressed file A file created after using a file compression program to reduce a file to a fraction of its original size; also called an *archived file*.

Contact Each person that you add to an Address Book or Contacts list.

Contact card The information about a contact stored in an Address Book or Contacts list.

Contacts list In Hotmail, stores people's names and e-mail addresses, as well as other information, such as the person's postal address and telephone number; in Outlook Express, called *Address Book*.

Contacts page In Hotmail, the page on which the Contacts list is stored.

Contacts pane In Outlook Express, the pane in the mail window that lists the contacts stored in the Address Book.

Cookie A small text file that a Web site stores on your computer and that contains information that makes your Web-browsing experience simpler and more personalized by storing information about your clickstream.

Copyright A right granted by a government to the author or creator of a literary or artistic work.

DARPA See *Defense Advanced Research Projects Agency*.

Data packets Small chunks of data.

Defense Advanced Research Projects Agency (DARPA) An agency created by the U.S. Department of Defense in the early 1960s to examine ways to connect its computers to one another and to weapons installations distributed all over the world.

Deleted Items folder In Outlook Express, the folder that stores messages you delete until you permanently delete them; in Hotmail, called *Trash Can folder*.

Demo version See *trial version*.

Demodulation The process of converting an analog signal back into digital form.

Digital certificate An encrypted and password-protected file that contains information to authenticate and prove a person's or organization's identity.

Digital Subscriber Line (DSL) A method of connecting to the Internet used by individuals and businesses that creates a high-speed connection using the customer's telephone wiring; connection speeds range from 100 Kbps to 9.0 Mbps.

Distributed database A database stored in multiple physical locations with portions of the database replicated in the different locations.

Domain name The equivalent of an IP address that uses words and abbreviations.

Download To receive a file on your computer from another computer over a network.

Download Manager In Firefox, the window that opens when you download a file, and which lists files and programs you have downloaded.

Download site A Web site that contains freeware and shareware programs organized in categories.

Drafts folder In an e-mail program, the folder in which messages that you are not yet ready to send are saved.

Drop See *unsubscribe*.

DSL See *Digital Subscriber Line*.

DSL modem A special type of modem required to create a DSL connection to the Internet.

Electronic mail See *e-mail*.

E-mail (electronic mail) The method by which electronic messages are transferred between two or more computers.

E-mail address A unique identifier for an individual or organization that is connected to the Internet consisting of a user name, the at sign (@), and the host name.

E-mail list See *mailing list*.

Emoticon A form of electronic body language represented by a group of keyboard characters that represent a human expression when viewed together by tilting your head to the left.

Encryption The process of scrambling and encoding data transmissions using a mathematically based program.

Exploratory question A type of question for searching the Internet that starts with a general, open-ended question that leads to other, less general questions, which result in multiple answers.

Extensible 3D (X3D) The next generation for 3D on the Web.

Extensible Markup Language See *XML*.

Extension See *browser extension*.

Fair use The use of a copyrighted work that includes copying it for use in criticism, comment, news reporting, teaching, scholarship, or research.

FAQ See *frequently asked questions*.

Favorite In Internet Explorer, a shortcut on a menu to a Web site; in Firefox, called *bookmark*.

Federal Networking Council (FNC) An organization set up to meet the National Science and Technology Council's Committee on Computing, Information and Communications' research and education goals and to coordinate the use of its agencies' technologies by the commercial sector.

Fiber-optic cable A cable through which information is transmitted by pulsing beams of light through very thin strands of glass.

File compression program A program that reduces the size of a file, creating a compressed file.

File decompression The process of restoring a compressed file to its original form; also called *file extraction* or *file expansion*.

File expansion See *file decompression*.

File extraction See *file decompression*.

File Transfer Protocol (FTP) A set of rules established to enable users to transfer files between computers.

Firewall A software program or hardware device that controls access between two networks and controls port scans and other incoming traffic by rejecting it unless you have configured the firewall to accept the traffic.

Flame To use automated programs to send messages to multiple chat rooms simultaneously; also, to send profane and vulgar messages and threats to individuals.

Flash Player An animation plug-in from Macromedia that has become so popular that it is installed automatically with some browsers.

FNC See *Federal Networking Council*.

Folders list In an e-mail program, a list of folders in which e-mail messages are stored.

Forum A mailing list that is stored and read on a Web site, so you use the Web site's interface instead of your e-mail program to post and read messages; also called *Internet discussion group*.

Forward To send an e-mail message that you receive to someone else.

Freeware Software that is available fully-functional and available to users at no cost and with no restrictions.

Frequently Asked Questions (FAQ) A document that contains the answers to common questions that users ask about a mailing list and its subject.

From In an e-mail program, the text box that contains the sender's name, e-mail address, or both.

FTP See *File Transfer Protocol*.

FTP client program A program that resides on your computer and allows you to transfer files between your computer and another computer connected to it using the rules for FTP.

FTP server A server that uses FTP to transfer files rather than HTTP.

FTP server program A program that runs on an FTP server allowing file transfer to and from the server by FTP and managing FTP access to the server's files.

FTP session profile A collection of information about an FTP server.

Gbps See *Gigabits per second.*

GIF (Graphics Interchange Format) A compressed file format that uses lossless compression technology and can contain up to 256 colors.

Gigabits per second (Gbps) Approximately 1,073,741,824 bps.

Graphic An image or art incorporated into a document.

Graphical user interface (GUI) A method of interacting with a computer that uses text, pictures, icons, and other graphical elements to present information and allow users to perform a variety of tasks.

Group Two or more e-mail addresses combined in one contact card; also called *mailing list.*

Grouping operator See *precedence operator.*

GUI See *graphical user interface.*

Helper app See *helper application.*

Helper application A browser extensions that calls a separate program that is launched to display or play some files; also called *helper app.*

History feature A list of Web sites you've visited over the past days or weeks.

Hit A Web page indexed in a search engine's database that contains text that matches a search expression.

Home button A button on a Web browser toolbar that allows you to return to the home page (or start page) for your Web browser.

Home page The main Web page that all the Web pages in a Web site are organized around and link back to; also the first Web page that opens when you start your Web browser; also a Web page that a Web browser displays the first time you use it.

Host name The name of the computer that stores e-mail for a user.

Hot spot A wireless access point to a LAN that offers Internet access to the public.

HTML See *Hypertext Markup Language.*

HTML anchor tag An HTML tag that links multiple HTML documents together.

HTML document A text file that contains the Web page content and instructions in HTML tags for formatting that content.

Hybrid search engine An Internet tool that combines a search engine and a Web directory.

Hyperlink See *link.*

Hypertext link See *link.*

Hypertext Markup Language (HTML) A text markup language that marks text with a set of tags that define the structure and behavior of a Web page.

ICQ Pronounced "I seek you", one of the most popular instant messaging software programs available, with over 220 million worldwide users.

IETF See *Internet Engineering Task Force.*

IM See *instant message.*

Inbox folder In an e-mail program, the folder in which messages that the user receives are stored.

Inclusion operator See *precedence operator.*

Installation wizard A series of dialog boxes that help you complete the installation process of a program step-by-step.

Instant message (IM) A method of chatting with others in real time over the Internet.

Internet A collection of computers all over the world that are connected to one another.

Internet discussion group See *forum.*

Internet Engineering Task Force (IETF) A volunteer group that is the main body that develops new Internet standards and makes technical contributions to the engineering of the Internet and its technologies.

Internet hosts Computers that connect a LAN or a WAN to the Internet.

Internet Protocol (IP) A set of rules for routing individual data packets over the Internet.

Internet Protocol address (IP address) A unique number by which each computer connected to the Internet is identified.

Internet Relay Chat (IRC) A communications program that requires IRC client software to connect to an IRC server.

Internet service provider (ISP) A company that provides access to the Internet for individuals and businesses.

Intranets LANs or WANs that use the TCP/IP protocol but do not connect to sites outside the firm.

IP See *Internet Protocol.*

IP address See *Internet Protocol address.*

IRC See *Internet Relay Chat.*

ISP See *Internet service provider.*

Java applet A program written in the Java programming language that can execute and consume a computer's resources.

JavaScript program Instructions written in the JavaScript programming language that can send information to another computer over the Internet.

Join See *subscribe.*

JPEG (Joint Photographic Experts Group) A compressed file format that uses lossy compression technology and can store over 16 million colors.

Jump To open a new Web page in a browser by clicking a link.

Junk e-mail Unsolicited e-mail usually selling an item or service; also called *spam.*

Junk E-Mail folder In an some e-mail programs, the folder to where possible junk e-mail messages are automatically filed when they are copied from the server; also called *Spam folder.*

Kbps   See *kilobits per second*.

Key   The mathematical code used to decrypt encrypted data.

Keyword   A word in a search expression.

Kilobits per second (Kbps)   Approximately 1,024 bps.

LAN   See *local area network*.

License   To pay a fee for the full, unrestricted use of a program.

License agreement   A contract between the publisher of the software and the person who is installing the software that usually states that the software cannot be copied and resold and details restrictions for the software's use.

Limited edition (LE) software   A free, but restricted version of shareware that provides most of the functionality of the full version of the program, but omits one or more useful features of the full version.

Link   Text, a graphic, or another Web page element that connects to additional data on the Web when the user clicks it; also called *hypertext link* or *hyperlink*.

List address   The e-mail address mailing list members use to send a message to all members of the list; also called *list name*.

List administrator   A person assigned to oversee a mailing list.

List moderator   The person responsible for discarding any messages that are inappropriate for or irrelevant to the list's members and for accepting or rejecting membership requests to a closed lists.

List name   See *list address*.

List server   A server that runs mailing list software.

Load   The process of a Web page appearing in a Web browser window.

Local area network (LAN)   A group of computers no more than a few thousand feet apart connected through NICs.

Location Bar   In Firefox, a text box at the top of the browser window that indicates the URL of the current Web page and into which you can type a new URL and press [Enter] or click the Go button to go to another Web page; in Internet Explorer, called *Address bar*.

Location operator   A word (the most common is NEAR) that lets a user search for keywords that appear close to each other in the text of a Web page; also called *proximity operator*.

Logical operator   See *Boolean operator*.

Login   The combination of a user name and password that identifies a user to a computer.

Lossless compression   Technology that reduces the file size without any loss of data.

Lossy compression   Technology that eliminates redundant and unnecessary data in an image to reduce the file size.

Lurk   To observe messages on a mailing list or a newsgroup without posting any new messages.

Mail client software   A program that lets a user send and receive e-mail and store e-mail on the user's computer.

Mail page   In Hotmail, the page that contains the mail window.

Mail server   A server that runs special software for handling e-mail tasks.

Mail window   The interface in an e-mail program that allows a user to compose, send, receive, and manage e-mails.

Mailing list   A list of names and e-mail addresses for a group of people who subscribe to the list; also called *e-mail list*. See also *group*.

Mailing list software   Software that runs on a list server and maintains a database containing the e-mail addresses for all members, manages each user's request to join or leave a mailing list, receives e-mail messages posted to the list, and sends mailing list messages to list members.

Mbps   See *Megabits per second*.

Meetups   In-person meetings arranged over the Internet, usually via a political Web site.

Megabits per second (Mbps)   Approximately 1,048,576 bps.

Menu bar   In a Windows program, contains the File, Edit, View, and Help menus and other specialized menus that allow you to use the program.

Message body   The part of the e-mail that contains the actual message.

Message body pane   The part of the message window that contains the actual e-mail message.

Message digest   A message from a mailing list in which several postings are grouped into a single e-mail message.

Message header   All the information about an e-mail message, including the recipients' and sender's e-mail addresses, a subject line and, sometimes, the filename of an attachment.

Message list   In an e-mail program, the list containing the message headers of the messages in the selected folder.

Meta-search engine   A search tool that searches multiple search engines simultaneously.

MIDI (Musical Instrument Digital Interface) format   A file format used for creating small sound files that digitally records information about each element of the sound, including its pitch, length, and volume.

MMOG, MOO, and MUD   Short for massively multiuser online game, MUD object-oriented, and multiuser dungeon; three types of online adventure games that allow hundreds, and even thousands, of users to assume character roles and to play at the same time, interacting with each other.

Modem   Short for modulator-demodulator; a device that converts signals from digital to analog and back again between a computer and a transmission line.

Moderated mailing list   A mailing list in which all messages are read and evaluated for appropriate and relevant content by a list moderator before they are sent to members in the mailing list.

Modulation The process of converting a digital signal to an analog signal.

MP3 format See *MPEG Audio Layer 3 format*.

MPEG (Moving Picture Experts Group) format A common file format for video on the Web that uses lossy compression technology and can be played using the same software that plays many other multimedia file types, including the player that comes with Windows.

MPEG Audio Layer 3 (MP3) format The audio portion of a compressed video format that yields files slightly lower in quality than WAV files, but 90 percent smaller.

Multimedia The collective term for sound, animation, and video.

Musical Instrument Digital Interface format See *MIDI format*.

Named FTP The method of logging in to a computer on which you have an account (with a user name and password) and using that account to send and receive files.

NAP See *Network access point*.

Natural language query A type of search expression that allows users to enter a question exactly as they would ask a person that question.

NCP See *Network Control Protocol*.

Netiquette A term coined from the phrase "Internet etiquette" that refers to the set of commonly accepted rules that represent proper behavior on the Internet.

Network Two or more computers connected to each other that share resources, such as printers or programs.

Network access point (NAP) The physical locations where networks connect to the Internet.

Network backbone The long-distance lines and supporting technology that transport large amounts of data between the network access points.

Network card See *network interface card*.

Network Control Protocol (NCP) The first collection of rules for formatting, ordering, and error-checking data sent across a network.

Network interface card (NIC) A removable circuit board used to connect a computer to a network by running a cable from the NIC to a server or to another client.

Network operating system Software that runs on a server and coordinates how information flows among its various clients.

News search engine A search engine that searches only online news sites.

News server A server that stores a Usenet newsgroup.

Newsfeed A file that contains summaries of stories and news from a Web site.

Newsgroup An online discussion group that is part of the Usenet database and requires a newsreader to be able to read the messages, which are stored and sorted by topic on a server connected to the Internet.

Newsreader Software required by some newsgroups to access messages in the newsgroup.

NIC See *network interface card*.

Nickname In Outlook Express, a shortened name for a contact; in Hotmail, called *Quickname*.

Open architecture philosophy The philosophy that ensures that each network connected to the ARPANET could continue using its own protocols and data-transmission methods internally.

Open list A mailing list that automatically accepts all subscribers.

Outbox folder In an e-mail program, the folder in which messages waiting to be sent are stored.

Packet sniffer Software that can monitor and analyze the data packets and capture user names, passwords, and other personal information from unencrypted files as they travel on the Web; also called *sniffer program*.

Packet switching A method of sending information over a network in which files and messages are broken down into electronically labeled data packets.

Page tab In Firefox, a way of allowing the user to switch between multiple Web pages in the same Web browser window.

Page Tabs In Hotmail, tabs that provide access to the four different parts of the Hotmail service: Today page, Mail page, Calendar page, and Contacts page.

PDF format A file format that allows documents to maintain a consistent layout and format on different computers when viewed using Adobe Reader.

Peer-to-peer (PTP) The process of transferring files directly from one computer to another without using a server.

Petabyte Approximately 10^{15} (1,000,000,000,000,000) bytes.

Phish To try to obtain confidential information from people via e-mail by pretending to be a familiar organization or institution, such as a bank.

Plagiarism The failure to cite the source of material that you use in a published medium.

Plain old telephone service See *POTS*.

Plug-in A browser extension that a Web browser starts to display or play a specific file type.

Pop-under A pop-up that appears behind the current window.

Pop-up A small window that appears in front of the current window and that usually contains an advertisement.

Port Permits traffic to enter and leave a computer.

Port scan Using a computer to test all or some of the ports of another computer to determine whether its ports are open, closed, or stealth.

Post To send an e-mail message to a mailing list.

Postcardware Software that you can use freely for no charge but that the programmer requests you mail a postcard from your hometown in return for your use of it.

POTS (plain old telephone service) A method of connecting to the Internet used by individuals and small businesses using regular phone lines; connection speeds range from 28.8 Kbps to 56 Kbps.

Precedence operator A way of clarifying the grouping within a complex Boolean expression usually indicated by parentheses; also called *grouping operator* or *inclusion operator*.

Preview pane In Outlook Express, the pane that displays the contents of the selected message in the message list.

Printer friendly link A link that, when clicked, opens a Web page containing the same information as on the original Web page, but formatted like a printed page rather than a Web browser window.

Private chat A chat that occurs between individuals who know each other and are invited to participate in the chat.

Proximity operator See *location operator*.

Public chat A chat that occurs in a chat room in which anyone who is registered with the chat service can come and go.

Public domain Information that you can freely copy without requesting permission from the source.

Query See *search expression*.

Quickname In Hotmail, a shortened name for a contact; in Internet Explorer, called *nickname*.

QuickTime A proprietary video format developed by Apple Computer that works equally well on Windows and Macintosh computers and which requires the QuickTime player to play.

Real-time Occuring in the current instant.

RealAudio format A proprietary compressed audio format developed by RealNetworks, Inc.

Really Simple Syndication (RSS) A file format that makes it possible to share updates such as headlines, weather updates, and other Web site content via a newsfeed.

RealVideo format A proprietary compressed video format developed by RealNetworks, Inc.

Refresh button In Internet Explorer, a button that allows you to load again a Web page that currently appears in your Web browser so that you can view the latest information (such as news headlines); in Firefox, called *Reload button*.

Register To provide requested information, such as your e-mail address, name, birth date, and possibly your postal address, to subscribe to a mailing list using a form on a Web page.

Reload button In Firefox, a button that allows you to load again a Web page that currently appears in your Web browser so that you can view the latest information (such as news headlines); in Internet Explorer, called *Refresh button*.

Results page A page provided by a search engine that include links to Web pages that match the search expression.

Router A computer on a network that determines the best way to move the data packet forward to its destination while traveling through the network.

Routing algorithm A program that determines the best path for data packets being routed on a network.

RSS See *Really Simple Syndication*.

Satellite A method of connecting to the Internet that uses a satellite dish receiver; connection speeds range from 125 Kbps to 500 Kbps.

Script A program that Web pages can download to your computer and run.

Scroll bar A bar in a program window that allows the user to move the document page up, down, right, and left if the page is longer or wider than the window.

Search engine A Web site or part of a Web site that finds Web pages containing a search expression.

Search expression The words or phrases you enter when you conduct a search; also called *query*.

Search filter A search expression that eliminates Web pages from a search by specifying a language, date, domain, host, or page component (such as a URL, link, image tag, or title tag) or by specifying that the results pages will contain all or any of the keywords.

Secure Electronic Transaction (SET) protocol A new protocol that is more complex and more secure than the SSL protocol.

Secure Socket Layer (SSL) protocol A protocol for information traveling over the Internet that encrypts information in a secure channel on top of the TCP/IP Internet protocol; Web pages that use SSL are encrypted, the site has a server certificate that users can access to authenticate its validity, and the pages have URLs that begin with *https://*.

Security The protection of assets from unauthorized access, use, alteration, or destruction.

Self-replicate To create, and in some cases distribute, a copy.

Sent Items folder In Outlook Express, the folder that contains copies of messages you sent; in Hotmail, called *Sent Messages folder*.

Sent Messages folder In Hotmail the folder that contains copies of messages you sent; in Outlook Express, called *Sent Items folder*.

Server A computer that accepts requests from other computers that are connected to it and shares some or all of its resources, such as printers, files, or programs, with those connected computers.

Server certificate A file that authenticates a Web site for its users so the user can be confident that the Web site is genuine and not an imposter and to ensure that the transfer of data between a user's computer and the server with the certificate is encrypted.

SET See *Secure Electronic Transaction protocol*.

Shareware Software that is usually available for free during a short evaluation period, after which you must license it.

Shockwave Player An animation extension from Macromedia that is one of the most popular available.

Single-file Web page A Web page and all of its supporting elements, including text, graphics, and links, stored in a single file when the Web page is saved to a disk.

Smiley An emoticon that looks like a smile (:-)).

Sniffer program See *packet sniffer*.

Spam (n.) See *junk e-mail*.

Spam (v.) To send unsolicited and irrelevant messages to a chat room.

Spam folder See *junk e-mail folder*.

Specific question A type of question for searching the Internet that you can phrase easily and has only one answer.

Spider See *Web robot*.

Sponsored link A link connected to the search expression that a company pays to place near the top of the results page.

Spoof To design a Web site that looks like it belongs to one organization but actually belong to someone else.

Spyware A category of adware that tracks your use of the program and the Internet or collects data about you without the user having control over or knowledge of the ads and other monitoring features it contains.

SSL See *Secure Socket Layer protocol*.

Start page The first Web page that opens when you start your Web browser or the Web page that a Web browser displays the first time you use it.

Status bar The bar at the bottom of a program window that indicates the status of the document or provides important information for the user; in a browser, when you point to a link, its URL appears in the status bar.

Stop button A button on a Web browser toolbar that allows you to stop loading the contents of a Web page.

Streaming transmission When a Web server sends the first part of a file to a Web browser, and then, while the browser begins playing the file, sends the next segment of the file.

Subject In an e-mail program, the text box in which you summarize the main topic of an e-mail message.

Subject guide A Web site that organizes links in categories and subcategories; also called *clearninghouse*, *virtual library*, or *Web bibliography*.

Subscribe To send an e-mail message to the administrative address of a mailing list or submit information on a Web page form so that you can start receiving the mailing list; also called *join.*.

T1 and T3 lines Methods of connecting to the Internet used by large companies and organizations that offer a higher grade of service for connecting to Internet than telephone service does; connection speed is 1.544 Mbps.

Tag One of a set of codes used in HTML.

TCP See *Transmission Control Protocol*.

TCP/IP (Transmission Control Protocol and Internet Protocol) A suite of rules that includes a tool to facilitate file transfer and another to access computers that aren't part of a user's immediate network over the Internet.

Telnet A protocol that allows users to log on to a remote server.

Terabyte Approximately 10^{12} (1,000,000,000,000) bytes.

Thread Messages in a newsgroup arranged by discussion or topic.

Throughput The amount of data transmitted through any connector on a network.

Title bar In a program window, the top bar that shows the name of the open document and the name of the program; also contains the Minimize, Restore Down/Maximize, and Close buttons.

To In an e-mail program, the text box in which you enter the e-mail address(es) of the recipient(s).

Today page In Hotmail, the page that appears when you first log into your Hotmail account and displays the total number of messages in your mailbox and the percentage of your storage space on the Hotmail server that you have used.

Top-level domain The last part of a domain name.

Transmission Control Protocol (TCP) The set of rules that computers on a network use to establish and break connections.

Transmission Control Protocol and Internet Protocol See *TCP/IP*.

Transparent GIF See *Web bug*.

Trash Can folder In Hotmail, the folder in which you store messages you delete until you permanently delete them; in Outlook Express, called *Deleted Items folder*.

Trial version A version of software that you can use for a limited amount of time or without all of the features of the full versions so that you can try the software before purchasing it; also called *demo version*.

Trojan horse A program that hides inside other programs, and then causes problems when the other program is downloaded and run (similar to a virus).

Twisted-pair cable A type of cable that consists of two or more insulated copper wires twisted around each other and enclosed in a layer of plastic insulation.

Uniform Resource Locator (URL) The address that tells the Web browser the transfer protocol to use when transporting the file, the domain name of the computer on which the file resides, the path name of the folder or directory on the computer on which the file resides, and the filename.

Unsubscribe To send an e-mail message to the administrative address of a mailing list or submit information on a Web page form so that you will stop receiving the mailing list; also called *drop*.

Upload To send a file from your computer to another computer over a network.

URL See *Uniform Resource Locator*.

Usenet An acronym for User's News Network, the first newsgroups started in 1979 by a group of students and programmers at Duke University and the University of North Carolina.

User authentication The process of associating a person and his identification on a Web page with a very high level of assurance.

User identification The process of identifying a user to a computer, usually with a login.

User name The part of an e-mail address that the ISP uses to identify you.

Virtual library See *subject guide*.

Virtual Reality Modeling Language (VRML) A programming language used to create three-dimensional environ-ments in which users can navigate and interact with a three dimensional scene.

Virus A program that runs without your permission and performs undesired tasks, such as deleting the contents of your hard disk.

VRML See *Virtual Reality Modeling Language*.

WAN See *wide area network*.

WAV format See *Wave format*.

Wave (WAV) format An uncompressed file format that digitizes audio waveform information at a user specified sampling rate and can be played on any Windows computer that supports sound.

Web See *World Wide Web*.

Web bibliography See *subject guide*.

Web browser Software that lets users browse HTML documents and move from one HTML document to another; also called *browser*.

Web bug A small, hidden graphic—usually a GIF file with a size of one pixel—on a Web page or in an e-mail message designed to work in conjunction with a cookie to obtain information about the person viewing the page or e-mail message and to send that information to a third party; also called *clear GIF* or *transparent GIF*.

Web directory A list of links to Web pages compiled by human editors or computers organized into hierarchical categories.

Web log See *blog*.

Web pages Documents that are formatted in HTML to be viewed using a Web browser.

Web robot A program that automatically searches the Web to find new Web sites, updates information about old Web sites that are already in the database, and deletes information in the database when a Web site no longer exists; also called *bot* or *spider*.

Web server A computer that stores files written in HTML and lets other computers connect to it and read those files.

Web site A collection of related Web pages.

Web-based e-mail service See *Webmail*.

Webmail (Web-based e-mail service) A service that allows you to send and receive e- mail by using a Web browser and the service's Web site.

Welcome message A message from a mailing list that informs you that you have been subscribed to the list and often tells you how to unsubscribe from the list, how to request a list of commands from the list server, how to temporarily suspend your subscription, and how to access older messages.

White page directory A search engine based on the printed telephone directory that enables a user to search for addresses and telephone numbers for individuals as you would in a white pages phone book.

Wide area network (WAN) Several LANs connected together.

Wi-Fi See *wireless fidelity*.

Wimax Short for Worldwide Interoperability for Microwave Access, a new wireless fidelity technology being developed for use in metropolitan areas that will have a range of up to 31 miles.

Windows Media Audio (wma) format A proprietary Windows Media Player file format that will play only in Windows Media Player.

Windows Media Video (wmv) format A proprietary Windows Media Player file format that will play only in Windows Media Player.

Windows Messenger Microsoft's instant messaging program that is installed with Windows.

Wireless A method for connecting to the Internet that uses high frequency radio waves; connection speeds range from 722 Kbps to point 2 Mbps.

Wireless fidelity (Wi-Fi) A short-range wireless network that connects a wireless access point to wireless devices located within a distance of approximately 200 feet.

Wireless network A network that uses technologies such as radio frequency (RF) and infrared (IR) to link computers.

Wireless network interface card (WLAN card) A circuit board in a computer that allows a user to connect to the Internet without cables as long as the user's computer is within range of a wireless access point that is connected to the Internet.

WLAN Short for wireless LAN.

WLAN card See *wireless network interface card*.

WMA format See *Windows Media Audio format*.

WMV format See *Windows Media Video format*.

World Wide Web (Web) A subset of the computers on the Internet in which resources on the Internet are organized in a way to make them easily accessible to all users.

Worm A self-replicating program that causes problems by reproducing so many times that it uses all available computer resources or it sends itself as an attachment to e-mail messages to everyone in the address book on the infected computer.

X3D See *extensible 3D*.

XML (Extensible Markup Language) A markup language that uses customized tags to describe data and its structure.

Yellow page directory A search engine that specializes in finding businesses, which are grouped by type and location as in the yellow pages phone book.

.Zip files Another name for a compressed file because .zip is the most common file extension for compressed files; also called *zipped file*.

Zipped file See *.zip file*.

Index

downloading programs with, 170–171

errors and, 30

finding Web site with, 30

lack of tabbed windows in, 28

opening Web pages with, 38

popularity of, 12–13

saving graphics with, 43

saving Web pages with, 38–39

security and, 213–217, 224–225

URLs and, 27

user interface, 13

Internet Public Library Web site, 124

Internet Relay Chat. *See* IRC (Internet Relay Chat)

intranets, 10

IP (Internet Protocol)

addresses, 26

described, 8

TCP/IP and, 11

iPIX, 196, 197

IR (infrared) connections, 6

IRC (Internet Relay Chat), 148

iRider, 242–243

ISO (International Standards Organization), 194

ISPs (Internet Service Providers)

attachments and, 62

described, 14

mailing lists and, 137

NAPs and, 15

service options, evaluating, 16–17

Web sites of, 17

iTunes, 167

▶ J

Janet (Joint Academic Network), 9

Java applets, 212, 216–219

JavaScript programs, 216–219

Joint Academic Network. *See* Janet (Joint Academic Network)

JPEG (Joint Photographic Experts Group) images, 192, 196–197

junk mail

described, 52

folders, 53, 56, 246, 250

Junk E-Mail folder, 53, 56

Junk folder, 246

▶ K

Kazaa, 195

Kbps (kilobits per second), 7

keys, 214

keywords

advanced techniques and, 104–105

described, 92

narrowing search results and, 92

search filters and, 104

subject guides and, 102–103

kilobits per second. *See* Kbps (kilobits per second)

▶ L

LANs (local area networks)

described, 4

file sharing and, 166

hosts and, 10–11

hot spots and, 16

intranets as, 10

LE (limited edition) software, 164

Library of Congress (United States), 124, 125

LibrarySpot, 124

license agreements, 164, 174, 175, 178

link(s). *See also* URLs (Uniform Resource Locators)

described, 12

printer-friendly, 40

selecting, 32

sponsored, 93

subject guides and, 102–103

LinkedIn, 154, 155

Links bar, 242

Linux, 23

list boxes, 33

list moderators, 136

Listserv, 138–139. *See also* mailing lists

local area networks. *See* LANs (local area networks)

location bar

described, 28–29

entering URLs in, 30–31, 32

location (proximity) operators, 104–105

login, defined, 214. *See also* passwords; security

LookSmart search engine, 98–99

L-Soft list server, 140

Lycos search engine, 100–101, 108–109

▶ M

Macintosh, 23, 194

mail client software, 52

Mail page, 56

mail servers, 52

Mail tab, 57

mail window, 54, 56–57

mailing list(s). *See also* groups

addresses, 136

administrators, 136

closed, 136

commands, 136, 139

described, 2, 136–145

forums and, 147

locating, 137–139

lurking in, 142

monitoring, 142–143

newsgroups and, 147

objectionable posts to, dealing with, 143

open, 136

registering with, 136

servers, 136

software, 136

subscribing to/joining, 136, 140–141

unsubscribing to/dropping, 136, 144–145

warnings about, 137

mainframe computers, 23

Manage Folder window, 73

MapQuest, 121

maps, obtaining, 120–121

Maximize button, 28, 58

Mbps (megabits per second), 7

MCI Mail, 10

Media Player (Windows), 194

meetups, 154

megabits per second. *See* Mbps (megabits per second)

menu bars, 28–29

message(s). *See also* e-mail

auto-replies, 137

body, 52

checking for, 60–61

content, correcting, 58

copying, 75

deleting, 74–75

digests, 140

forwarding, 70–71

headers, 52, 53, 55

organizing, 72–73

replying to, 68–69

saving drafts/copies of, 60

sending, 58–59

subjects, 53

Message list, 54, 56

meta-search engines. *See also* search engines

advanced techniques for, 104–105

described, 100–101

MIDI (Musical Instrument Digital Interface) format, 194, 195

Midland Pet Adoption Agency Web site, 30–43, 227, 242

military research, 8–9

MILNET (Military Network), 9

MLA (Modern Language Association), 128

MMOGs (massively multiuser online games), 2

modems
    compressed files and, 166
    described, 14
    downloading and, 166

moderating mailing lists, 136. *See also* mailing lists

Modern Language Association. *See* MLA (Modern Language Association)

modulation, 14. *See also* modems

modulator-demodulator. *See* modems

MOOs (MUD object-oriented games), 2

Mozilla Update Web site, 203

MP3 (MPEG Audio Layer 3) files, 195

MPEG (Moving Picture Experts Group), 194

MSN (Microsoft Network)
    Chat, 149
    Maps, 120–121
    Messenger, 148
    Search, 97, 100–101

MUDs (multiuser dugeons), 2

multimedia
    animation, 196–197
    browser extensions and, 196–197
    described, 194
    streaming, 194
    understanding, 194–195

music. *See also* multimedia
    browser extensions and, 196–197
    copyrights and, 167, 195
    downloading, 167

Musical Instrument Digital Interface) format. *See* MIDI (Musical Instrument Digital Interface) format

MusicMatch, 167

MySpace, 154

▶ N

named (full-privilege) FTP, 176, 177. *See also* FTP (File Transfer Protocol)

NAPs (network access points)
    described, 8
    ISPs and, 14, 15

Napster, 167, 195

NASA (National Aeronautics and Space Administration), 116, 126–127

National Biotechnology Information Facility Web site, 103–104

National Resources Defense Council. *See* NRDC (National Resources Defense Council)

National Science and Technology Council, 10

National Science Foundation. *See* NSF (National Science Foundation)

natural language queries, 100

NCP (Network Control Protocol), 8

.NET Passport (Microsoft), 152

Netcraft Web survey, 13

netiquette, 68, 148

Netscape browser
    described, 238–239
    Mail, 244–245
    search engine, 99
    Toolbar, 238

network(s). *See also* Internet; LANs (local area networks); WANs (wide area networks)
    backbone, 8
    connectors, 6–7
    described, 4–5
    operating systems, 4
    wireless, 6–7, 14–17

network access points. *See* NAPs (network access points)

Network Control Protocol. *See* NCP (Network Control Protocol)

New Archive dialog box, 182

New button, 58, 78, 82

New Group option, 80

Newmark, Craig, 154

newreaders, 2

news. *See also* newsgroups
    archives, searching, 117
    -feeds, 116
    readers, 146–147
    search engines, 116–116
    servers, 146

newsgroup(s)
    closed, 146
    described, 2
    finding, 146–147
    forums and, 147
    moderated, 146
    Netscape Mail and, 244
    open, 146
    unmoderated, 146

nicknames, 76

NICs (network interface cards), 4

NRDC (National Resources Defense Council), 126–127

NSF (National Science Foundation), 9, 10

NSFnet (National Science Foundation Network), 9

▶ O

Office (Microsoft), 193

Ofoto, 167

Oikarinen, Jarkko, 148

online reference tools, 124–125

open architecture philosophy, 8

Open dialog box, 38

Opera browser
    aggregators and, 116
    described, 240–241

options (listed by name)
    Add Sender to Address Book option, 77
    Clean Up option, 172
    Extract option, 180–181
    New Group option, 80
    Rename option, 73
    Save to Disk option, 172
    Show Folder option, 66

OR operator, 104–105

Organize Favorites dialog box, 34, 35

Outbox folder, 54

Outlook Express (Microsoft). *See also* e-mail
    Address Book, 75–76
    attachments and, 62–66
    checking incoming e-mail with, 60–61
    copying messages with, 75
    creating groups with, 80–81
    deleting messages with, 74–75
    forwarding e-mail with, 70–71
    mail window, 54–55
    newsgroups and, 146
    organizing messages with, 72–73
    replying to messages with, 68–69
    saving drafts/copies of e-mail with, 60
    security options, 64
    sending e-mail with, 58–59
    spell-checking e-mail with, 58
    starting, 53, 54–55

▶ P

packet switching, 8

padlock icon, 240

"Page cannot be displayed" error, 30

Page Setup dialog box, 40

Page tab, 28, 56–57

Pages list, 242

Panel bar, 240

paperclip icon, 64

parsing, 100

services, 14, 16–17

SET (Secure Electronic Transaction) protocol, 214

shareware
    described, 164–165
    downloading trial versions of, 170–171

Shockwave MX (Macromedia), 197–205, 212

Show Folder option, 66

Shutterfly, 167

single-file Web pages, 39

smiley characters, 70

Snapfish, 167

sniffer programs, 212

sound players, 196

spam. See junk mail

Spam folder, 53, 250

spamming, 148, 150

speakers, 194

Spelling button, 58

spiders (Web robots), 92, 98

sponsored links, 93

spoofing, 212

spyware, 222

SRI International, 8

SSL (Secure Sockets Layer) protocol, 214

start pages, 22

status bar, 28, 240

status codes, 129

Stop button, 28–29, 240

streaming multimedia, 194

subject guides, 102–103

SuperPages Web site, 123

▶ T

T1 connections, 14–15

T3 connections, 14–15

Tagged Image File Format. See TIFF (Tagged Image
    File Format)

tags, 12

TCP/IP (Transmission Control Protocol/Internet
    Protocol)
    described, 8
    intranets and, 10

Telnet, 8, 9

Templates folder, 244

Teoma, 100–101, 105

terabytes, 125

text
    copying, 42–43
    saving, 42–43

Thomas Legislative Information Web site, 124

3D Groove, 196–197

throughput, 7

Thunderbird, 116, 248–249

TIFF (Tagged Image File Format), 192

Timex.com Web site, 205

title bar, 28–29

Today page, 56

top-level domains (TLDs), 26, 27

translation Web sites, 124–125

Trash Can folder, 56, 74–75

Trash folder, 244, 246, 248

trial software, 2

Tribe.net, 154

Trillian, 152

Trojan horses, 65, 67, 212

Turbo 10 meta-search engine, 101

twisted-pair cable, 6–7

▶ U

United Kingdom, 26

University of California, 8

University of Chicago, 26

University of North Carolina, 2

University of Utah, 8

UNIX, 23, 194

uploading, use of the term, 163

URLs (Uniform Resource Locators). See also links
    citations and, 128–129
    described, 26
    entering, 30–31, 32
    FTP and, 177
    moving/disappearing, 129
    saving Web pages and, 38–39
    security and, 214
    selecting, 30–31, 32
    Wayback Machine and, 125

Usenet (User's News Network), 2, 147. See also
    newsgroups

user
    identification, 214
    names, 52

▶ V

Van Gogh, Vincent, 192–193

video
    browser extensions, 196
    file formats, 194–195

virtual communities, 154–155

virtual library. See subject guides

viruse(s). See also anti-virus software; security
    attachments and, 64–65, 67
    checking downloaded programs for, 175
    described, 212
    Outlook Express and, 64–65
    protection from, 228–229
    self-replicating, 65, 67

Vivisimo search engine, 106

VRML (Virtual Reality Modeling Language), 196

▶ W

WANs (wide area networks), 4, 10–11, 166

warning dialog boxes, 74, 170, 174

WAV (Wave) format, 194

Wayback Machine, 125

weather reports, 118–119

Web. See World Wide Web

Web bibliography. See subject guides

Web browser(s). See also browser extensions (plug-
    ins); specific browsers
    aggregators and, 116
    alternative, 231–251
    capabilities, extending, 191–209
    chat and, 150–151
    described, 12, 21–50
    downloading programs with, 170–172
    errors, 30, 129
    finding Web sites with, 30–31
    FTP and, 177
    opening Web pages in, 38–39
    saving Web pages in, 38–39
    search engines and, 96–97
    starting, 28–29
    terminology used with, 22–23

Web bugs, 222, 223. See also bugs

Web directories, 98–99

Web logs. See blogs (Web logs)

Web pages. See also Web sites
    described, 2
    home pages, 22
    jumping to, 32
    printing, 12, 13, 40–41

Web robots (bots), 92, 98

Web servers, 12, 23. *See also* servers

Web sites. *See also* Web pages; World Wide Web
  copying text/graphics from, 42–43
  described, 2
  evaluation guidelines, 127
  finding, 30–31
  navigating, 32–33
  security features on, 220–221

Webmail (Web-based e-mail service), 52, 146

WebMuseum Web site, 192–193

welcome messages, 140

white page directories, 122–123

WhitePages.com Web site, 123

Wi-Fi (wireless fidelity), 6, 14

wide area networks. *See* WANs (wide area networks)

WiMAX (Worldwide Interoperability for Microwave Access), 6

Windows (Microsoft)
  Web browsers and, 23
  file name extensions and, 62

Windows Messenger, 152

WinZip, 176–183

WinZip Setup dialog box, 178–179

wireless networks, 6–7, 14–17

WiseNut, 101

WLANs (wireless LANs)
  described, 6–7
  interface cards for, 14

WMA (Windows Media Audio) file format, 194

WMV (Windows Media Video) format, 194

Word Pad (Microsoft), 42

World Wide Web. *See also* Web browsers; Web pages; Web sites
  described, 2
  getting information from, 116–134
  how it works, 12–13
  resources, evaluating, 126–127
  searching, 92–114

worms, 65, 67, 212

WS_FTP Home, 164–167

► X

X3D (Extensible 3D), 196

XML (Extensible Markup Language), 13

► Y

Yahoo! search engine, 98, 108–109
  Chat, 150–151
  IDs, 150
  mailing lists and, 137, 139
  Messenger, 148
  toolbar for Internet Explorer, 200, 202

yellow page directories, 122–123

► Z

ZDNet Web site, 168, 169

ZeroDegrees, 154

zipped files, 166, 180–181. *See also* compression

Zoom field, 240

gsherman@gprc.ab.ca
bwing turn left inside CRI
dstandish@gprcstudent.net